FACING IT

THE SEVENTH GENERATION
Survival, Sustainability, Sustenance in a New Nature
M. Jimmie Killingsworth, Series Editor

A WARDLAW BOOK

FACING IT
Epiphany & Apocalypse in the New Nature

M. JIMMIE KILLINGSWORTH

Photographs by Mary Ann Jacob

TEXAS A&M UNIVERSITY PRESS • COLLEGE STATION, TEXAS

Copyright © 2014
by M. Jimmie Killingsworth
All rights reserved
First edition

Manufactured in the United States of America
This paper meets the requirements of
ANSI/NISO, Z39.48–1992
(Permanence of Paper).
Binding materials have been
chosen for durability.

Library of Congress Cataloging-in-Publication Data

Killingsworth, M. Jimmie.
  Facing it : epiphany and apocalypse in the new nature / M. Jimmie Killingsworth. — First edition.
     pages cm — (The seventh generation: survival, sustainability, sustenance in a new nature)
  Includes bibliographical references and index.
  ISBN 978-1-62349-145-1 (pbk. (with flaps) : alk. paper)—
  ISBN 978-1-62349-177-2 (e-book)
  1. Killingsworth, M. Jimmie. 2. Environmentalists—United States—Biography.   3. College teachers—United States—Biography.   4. Environmentalism—United States—History—20th century.   5. Environmentalism—United States—History—21st century.   I. Title. II. Series: Seventh generation.
  GE56.K55A3 2014
  363.70092—dc23
  [B]
  2014015254

Contents

Series Preface. The Seventh Generation: Survival,
Sustainability, Sustenance in a New Nature   viii

    Overture. End of a World   1
1. Influence and Confluence: Family, Nature, War   11
2. Ecology Then: The Lake of Tears   35
3. Dispelling Déjà Vu, Part One   65
4. Dispelling Déjà Vu, Part Two   101
5. Defying Apocalypse   133
6. Apocalypse Redux and the Fate of Sustainability   157
7. No Illusions, No Fantasy, No Melodrama:
    The Legacy of Rachel Carson   191
8. Epiphany Matters   209
9. Imagination Wild and Tame: The Smell of Money   235
10. The Presence of Roadkill   263
    Reprise. World's End: Seeing and Sustenance   285

Acknowledgments   295
Bibliography   297
Index   309

Preface
The Seventh Generation:
Survival, Sustainability, Sustenance in a
New Nature

⁂   Global warming, species decimation, habitat loss, pollution of the rivers and oceans, runaway urbanization, worldwide terrorism, displacement of whole populations by war and wild weather, environmental engineering projects that touch the very composition of the atmosphere—this is not your grandmother's world. The old books on environmental pollution and protection, written in the 1960s and 1970s—Rachel Carson's *Silent Spring*, Paul Ehrlich's *The Population Bomb*, the Club of Rome's *Limits to Growth*—became famous for prophesying doom in the wake of postwar growth and development. We need to change the course of human history, they said, or suffer the consequences. The latest books on the environmental crises have gone further. The new books—Bill McKibben's *Eaarth: Making a Life on a Tough New Planet*, Timothy Morton's *The Ecological Thought*, Frances Moore Lappé's *Eco-Mind: Changing the Way We Think, to Create the World We Want*, Ian Angus and Simon Butler's *Too Many People?: Population, Immigration, and the Environmental Crisis*, Clive Hamilton's *Requiem for a Species*, and Mark Lynas's *The God Species: Saving the Planet in the Age of Humans*, all published within a single year (2010–11)—differ widely in their views of the nature and causes of the problems we face. The solutions they propose range from downsizing and living close to the earth in small, decentralized communities to urbanizing and reengineering the earth on a grand scale. But they all agree that, far from being set off in the far future like a scary science-fiction story, Armageddon has come and gone. We live in a postapocalyptic world with a new nature. The question is, what are we going to do about it?

This book series invites authors from a variety of fields and professions to reflect on the new nature and to address the questions of survival, sustainability, and sustenance from their own special perspective. The authors are professors, researchers, novelists, nature writers, ecologists, and activists from many regions and walks of life. Setting aside their narrow professional and specialized affinities, they speak to a wide audience in their own voices from personal experience informed by years of study and reflection. They share the aim of providing an illuminating perspective on what it means to be alive today and to make a lasting and positive contribution to the new nature.

The title of the series comes from the concept of sustainability that prevails in many Native American cultures. The Native scholar Daniel Wildcat explains it this way: Everyone alive at this moment in history is the seventh generation. All decisions should respect the memory of the previous three generations (at least) and account for the well-being of the next three generations. From our great-grandparents to our great-grandchildren stretches a long communal story. We stand in the middle, thinking of the ways our actions and attitudes reflect the ancestral values that we bring to the moment and will shape the future to which we devote our legacy.

This series is the voice of the seventh generation.

M. Jimmie Killingsworth
Series Editor

FACING IT

Overture. End of a World

Whatever man does on this planet has to be done in the lived truth of creation, of the grotesque, or the rumble of panic underneath everything. Otherwise it is false. Whatever is achieved must be achieved from within the subjective energies of creatures, without deadening, with the full exercise of passion, of vision, of fear, and of sorrow. . . . The most that any of us can seem to do is to fashion something—an object or ourselves—and drop it into the confusion, make an offering of it, so to speak, to the life force.

Ernest Becker, *The Denial of Death*

Summer evening a long time ago. My grandfather and Uncle George are sitting quietly in the yard chairs under the tall pines of the old family home in Ware Shoals, South Carolina. Dressed in shirtsleeves and necktie after work, Granddaddy is wearing his fedora hat as usual and smoking a filterless cigarette. Every so often, he spits a little piece of tobacco off the tip of his tongue.

Granny and Aunt Hazel are poking around in the flower garden. Their musical voices mix with the sound of a little breeze rustling the needles at the top of the old pines.

As I see Granny coming toward me, I stop my running around. The jelly jar with holes in the lid rests warm in my hand, its glass sides slippery with sweat. Inside, the lightning bugs I've caught flicker on and off, on and off.

Granny holds out something in her hand, a grasslike branch of tiny bell-shaped blossoms. "Smell this," she tells me. I put my nose to the little flowers and then pull back suddenly. The strength of the scent, fine as fancy perfume, has startled me.

"It's lily-of-the-valley," she tells me. "I just love that smell."

The years spin by. I go to summer camp with the Boy Scouts. The scoutmaster yanks a little seedling from the wet ground of the mountain trail. He shows us the rounded lobes of the leaves, then opens his pocketknife and with a whittling motion exposes the white wood of the root. He holds it out to me and says, "Smell this."

"Smells like root beer," I say.

He smiles and explains that root beer used to be made out of these roots, but now they use chemical flavors to imitate the smell and taste.

"It's called sassafras," he says.

The two generations before my own—the grandmothers and scoutmasters—passed the world to me via the senses and passions. Look, they said. Listen. Have a taste. Run your hand over this texture. Smell this. Don't you just love it?

I never mourned completely for my mother until I went out on my morning walk one day in late winter—which amounts to early spring in my part of Texas—and smelled the dirt of the yard wet with dew. At the time, I didn't recall the way she gave her love of the earth to me: how she told me stories of growing up on the farm and how she put the place behind her when she took up life in the suburban middle class—shook the dirt off her heels, as she used to say, alluding to the verse in the Gospels when Jesus says, "And whosoever shall not receive you, nor hear your words, when you depart out of that house or city, shake off the dust of your feet" (Matthew 10:14 KJV)—yet how the dirt clung to her, the old ways modified into a love of gardening, in the service of which, as an overgrown adolescent, I became her pack animal, dreading the sight on a fine summer day of a massive pile of topsoil left by a dump truck on our driveway, dirt that we would form into beds for irises, purple and yellow and white, whose bulbs came from the gardens of two grandmothers, the same plants that bloom now in my Texas yard every spring, removed (like me) from their home grounds in the Carolinas and Georgia, maybe as old as the families themselves, bearing molecules of European soils that have migrated steadily westward and continued to bloom after their human cultivators pass from this earth.

No, I didn't think of her long history with the soil when I smelled the earth that morning in the spring that comes early in Texas, the ground warming and giving up its scent even in February, little more than a month after she had died in the deep winter of 1999. I only thought how she would never smell the ground again. And at that moment, the end of a world was complete.

The moment was for me at once an epiphany and an apocalypse. It was an *epiphany,* a flooding of insight in a single moment, a bright crystallization of inner and outer life, normal perception overwhelmed by a sense of *presence* other than my own. It was also an *apocalypse*—similar to epiphany in its literal meaning: a revelation or unveiling—but apocalyptic in the popular definition as well: an episode in the end of the world, my mother's world.

Since that moment, I have increasingly devoted myself—in both study and practice—to the literature known as *nature writing,* which thrives on epiphany and apocalypse. I am driven to give an account of the world that departed with my mother and the new nature that I have gone looking for with accumulating intensity since that moment of mourning, a version of nature revealed not in its completeness but in flashes and glimpses, recollected over time and put together in tentative form as stories and essays. I'd studied the language and literature of environmental consciousness on and off for a couple of decades by the time my mother died, but I realize in retrospect that my personal investment in the work had never been so urgent or extreme as it then became. Urgency and extremity find an outlet in epiphany and apocalypse, terms based in religious tradition but refurbished and redefined in the modern literature of nature. My commitment to nature writing is tied to the life I received from my mother. I owe my love of the land and my love of the written word mostly to her, whose world ended in January 1999.

It's more than a coincidence that many of the most celebrated nature writers of my generation take the death of the mother as a starting point:

- Rick Bass's short memoir, "On Willow Creek," with its poignant image of discovering mint growing by the creek where his mother used to throw out the dregs of her minted iced tea in the last years of her life, can be paired with his moving novella *The Sky, the Stars, the Wilderness*, the story of a young ecologist who tries to remain connected to her lost mother through an obsessive preservationism, enacted on the Texas Hill Country ranch she has inherited, the land that her mother loved and seems still to haunt.
- Terry Tempest Williams in her masterpiece *Refuge* uses her mother's life and death as a meditation on her place in the Great Basin of Utah and her membership in "a clan of one-breasted women," downwinders and cancer victims who live in a land invested with the twin history of Mormon patriarchal culture and nuclear war. She returns to

these themes in the recent book *When Women Were Birds* to consider her life as a writer in light of a strange heirloom left by her mother—a neat shelf of personal journals, without a single word on any page.

- Cheryl Strayed's recent memoir, *Wild: From Lost to Found on the Pacific Crest Trail,* tells of the total collapse of her world following her mother's death—a failed marriage accompanied by a descent into purposeless promiscuity, drug addiction, and fatal loneliness—then a recovery that begins with a strangely underinformed decision to hike the Pacific Crest Trail alone.

These authors, narrators, and characters are driven to nature by the death of a mother. They are like foundlings who wake up in the bosom of the wilderness, lost and uncertain. Beyond tempting clichés about the retreat to Mother Nature, what is going on here?

The key elements are mother, death, nature, writing. The passing of the mother brings the grown children face to face with their own impending deaths. And herein lies a big issue with nature writing, or literary environmentalism: how to face it. It's no simple matter. Consider the complaint of one David Owen, author of a recent book about urban sustainability called *Green Metropolis*. He, like so many others, is put out with the negativity of "the environmentalists": "On a shelf in my office," he writes, "is a pile of recent books about the environment, which I plan to read obsessively if I'm found to have a terminal illness, because they're so disturbing that they make me less upset about being snatched from life in my prime" (60–61). It's a good joke, but it demands more than an amused chuckle. Owen wants to make the treatment of environmental problems into a *rhetorical* issue, a matter of literary taste: can't we be more upbeat and proactive? Why all the negativity?

But I find it *psychologically* telling that he compares the reading of environmentalist literature with the experience of facing his own death. The problem goes deeper than an affinity for a positive or negative slant in our preferred styles of writing; it touches our deepest fears. Facing environmental degradation becomes aligned with confronting the loss of comfort, the defeat of joy, the passing of generations and whole worlds, and ultimately death itself. The view is more than merely negative; it is fraught with uncertainty and often tragic.

In the case of the nature writers, the fear of one's own death or annihilation is displaced onto the death of the mother. The parent's death, and particularly the mother's, especially for children whose parents die before they grow old themselves, is always an apocalyptic event—a glimpse of a world undone. The mother is practically a world in herself, from whose body we emerge and to whom we cling as we first make our way. Facing the death of the mother, even grown children often find themselves questioning their relationship to the fragments of the world bequeathed to them. The parent, now lost, was likely the child's hero, the very prototype of other heroes in life, the champion over death. The parent (ideally) shields the child not only from actual death and harm but also from a full realization or awareness of death and its power to annihilate. The life-giver in the matter of birthing and nursing, in many cultures (including the one I share with Bass, Williams, Strayed, and probably Owen) the mother is also the primary teacher of the young child in matters of religion and other cultural means by which death is deflected and seemingly defeated.

An educated woman, my mother never gave up on the notion of heaven. To the end of her life, she spoke of meeting together in that better place after we died. She was a Sunday school teacher for seven-year-olds and worked every summer in vacation Bible school, which I loved to attend and to which I partly attribute my early affinity for the written word (all those verses memorized and lessons studied). She gave me Bibles, not just one, but repeated the gift to celebrate propitious occasions—my joining the church, my graduation from high school. My earliest memories find me sitting in church between her and my paternal grandmother, thumbing through their Bibles before I could even read—white leather ladies' Bibles, made soft from much use, the pages edged with gold like the streets of heaven. (My grandfather dressed up and went to church every Sunday but spent the whole time outside, smoking cigarettes with other men dressed in suits and ties and fedora hats. My uncle, the high school principal, deigned to sit with my aunt in church but slept through the sermon every Sunday.) My mother and grandmother and aunts read me bedtime stories from the Bible—heroic tales of Moses, Joseph, Samson, David, Jesus—death defeated every night before I closed my eyes to sleep and dream. (The prayer I was taught to say was "Now I lay me down to sleep. I pray the Lord my soul to keep. And if I die before I wake, I pray the Lord my soul to take.") My mother's life was struck by tragedy—a difficult childhood in a poor farming and mill-working family, the death of her first husband—and just when life was getting easy after she remarried and built her family, becoming by early middle age the wife of a successful doctor and the mother of four thriving children, she was overtaken by a debilitating illness that sapped her energy, limited her activity for the rest of her life, and finally killed her. Her name was Dolores, lady of sorrows. But through it all, she remained a believer, or perhaps because of it all. The reality would have been too much to bear without the cushion of belief.

The death of such a mother can only mean an influx of death's full weight. That's how I felt in my grief—heavy. Every step, I had to bear my own weight. I lost twenty pounds in the months after she died just as, some years earlier, I'd lost thirty when my first marriage ended in divorce. On both occasions, my world was suddenly my own to bear, and it was heavy with death.

After my mother died, I suppose the study and practice of nature writing became a way of lightening the load by sharing it. Telling my own story was like distributing the weight. I hoped others could help to carry it the way I took on memorable images from the stories I read when I recognized versions or hints of my experience in other writers' work: the way Rick Bass's protagonist Anne in *The Sky, the Stars, the Wilderness* clings to the land and fights off the ranchers and developers on all sides to protect the endangered life that lingers from her time with her mother; the way Bass himself moved north and west to make a new home in the Yaak Valley of Montana, where to this day he crusades to preserve the integrity of the land, the wildness he had seen forfeited in his homeland of Texas; the way Terry Tempest Williams, also an activist in the cause of land protection, stayed rooted in the place sanctified by family tradition even as it was sacrificed to the gods of war and energy production; the way Cheryl Strayed learned, by traversing the wild land on her hiking excursion, that she could walk alone—without any more than the memory of her mother and without the crutch of drugs and codependency—settling finally in the Northwest, near the place of her redemption.

These writers are all very different from each other and from me, but one thing we hold in common is that we received from the last generation a love of the land and an affinity for the written word. The two gifts are somehow related. Our mothers bestowed the gifts (again in different ways), and after they departed, we remembered and went to work writing and storytelling as a way of tending the land.

Nature writing has a reputation, perhaps deserved, for being boring and out of touch on a good day, negative and depressing on a bad one. It's dismissed as the province of nerdy birdwatchers (or "twitchers," as they're called in England), nostalgia addicts, eco-nut-jobs, and misanthropes ranging from Henry David Thoreau to the Unabomber. "Eco-terrorist" is the favored term in the mass media today for environmental activist, *terrorist* being in our times the term of choice for *enemy* and *evil.* Even Adolf Hitler was a nature lover and vegetarian, the historians tell us. Communion with the other-than-human world seems to require separation from people with a kind of antisocial thrust that pushes sociable folks away.

I don't see it that way. I associate my experiences in nature with my closest friends and family, beginning with my mother. On top of that, the *writing* of nature writing, to me, represents a reaching out, an appeal to an audience to join the sometimes solitary author in an act of communion with life as a whole. The eco-ethicist Kathleen Dean Moore suggests that the act of saying "*Look!*" to a fellow human opens a door on the moral as well as the natural world. She makes me think of my grandmother and scoutmaster, who said, "Smell this," and opened a portal to a place where the senses were enhanced and caring augmented.

According to this view, nature writing amounts to an invitation to come out of your hiding places (in language, in habit, in lifestyle, in climate-controlled homes and offices) to see what else life has to offer. At the risk of overstatement, I'll say that the continuation of life on earth may depend on just such a coming out and communal recovery of the senses.

1 Influence and Confluence
Family, Nature, War

> Were you thinking that those were the words, those upright lines? those curves, angles, dots?
> No, those are not the words, the substantial words are in the ground and sea,
> They are in the air, they are in you.
>
> Walt Whitman, "Song of the Rolling Earth"

My mother was the first source of my literary life, the first *influence*, which literally means to *flow in*. But it took the confluence of two parents to instill the values I now associate with writing and nature. And it also took the context of war, a childhood bookended by the conflicts in Korea and Vietnam, living always under the threat of global nuclear disaster. The world seemed always about to end. It needed writing down.

I was late learning to read. The fault may have been my own developmental tardiness or the result of starting school in the underfunded educational system of South Carolina in the late 1950s. By the time I began my education, Mom and I had been through a lot together. My father was killed in Korea on the day before I was born. Because he died on the other side of the International Date Line, the date of his death and my birth date happened to coincide—October 14, 1952—a fact that I have never quite fully absorbed, having been unable honestly to read it as a sign or portent. Still, it somehow made a difference in the way I saw my life.

I was the only son of my mother and this soldier who died (himself the only son of an only son). For three years, my widowed mother and I lived in the small mill village of Ware Shoals, South Carolina, across the street from the Killingsworths, my doting paternal grandparents. Then my mother remarried, accepting the proposal of another young man of our town, Lewis Jones, with the blessing of the Killingsworths. My mother changed her name to Jones but, out of respect for my grandparents and my father's memory, left mine as Killingsworth. When three other children came along from her second marriage, I was the only Killingsworth in a family of five Joneses. I also grew taller and darker and heavier than everybody else, so in family photos and outings, I appeared as an aberration that was always in need of explanation.

My new dad moved us to Charleston, where he was studying medicine, then a few years later to Greenville, where I went to kindergarten and part of first grade. When he finished his internship year at the General Hospital, he took us for a two-year stint to Oregon, where he satisfied the requirement for compulsory service in the armed forces as an Air Force doctor at Kingsley Field in Klamath Falls.

That's where I found out I couldn't read. When I arrived, I was halfway through the first grade, and the other kids in the class were way ahead of me. I faked it for a while, but the teacher found me out and called my mother to school for a conference. And thus began my own compulsory service in the leagues of literacy—hours spent at the kitchen table every day. I can still see its vintage 1950s yellow linoleum top supported by shiny galvanized steel sides and legs. I sat there, imprisoned, laboriously slogging through the inane tales of Dick and Jane, Puff and Spot, the contemptible Baby Sally. *The Cat in the Hat*—a new book in those days—yielded to *The Cat in the Hat Comes Back*. By then there were two little sisters for Mom to contend with and a baby brother on the way. But she made me her project. She had been valedictorian of her high school class and spent a year in college at Winthrop (all she could afford), and no son of hers was going to be labeled an illiterate cracker from the benighted South.

I guess I became an English professor to compensate for those early days. At any rate, something clicked, and at some point I went from hating reading to loving it. When it came time to learn to write—I mean really write, not just move the pencil in the elegant curves of cursive script—my mother was there again. We were back in South Carolina, where Dad had started his medical practice in Greenville. It was 1962, and I was a ten-year-old fourth grader. My teacher, the gentle old Mrs. Bell, had assigned us to write an autobiography, and I asked Mom for help. We sat on the sofa in the downstairs den of our new split-level house, and she told me of the times before there was memory. Then I just started to write, and it all flowed out, following like a swollen stream from that first sentence with its partial truth: "My father was killed on the day I was born."

So it was that the first story I remember writing was a survivor's memoir, composed in the heart of the Cold War with tales of military service and global conflict on all sides—at home, on television (*Combat* and *Hogan's Heroes*), in the movies (John Wayne and Lee Marvin), and in the daily news (Kennedy and Khrushchev). The day my teacher handed back the papers, she took me aside as the other kids hurried off to recess. She told me that my autobiography was very good, that I should always remember these things, and that I should keep practicing to be a good writer.

From that moment, I was a storyteller. Years later, when my friend Nick Melehes and I were both college students, he told me that he wasn't surprised when he heard I'd changed my major from chemistry to English. Back in Mrs. Bell's class, he said, I was always the first called on to read my papers aloud. I'd forgotten, but Nicky remembered that my stories were funny and entertaining. I read them with different voices, mimicking accents I'd heard on TV, German soldiers and British spies.

It took the passage of even more years for me to realize that before I was a war memoirist and Cold War storyteller, I was a nature writer—and that the two roles were intimately related. By then, I was a middle-aged man going through some old papers that had turned up at my parents' house. At the time, I was focused on writing stories about my encounters with the natural history of Texas, so I guess I was open to the possibility that my personal history with nature writing was longer than I had previously suspected. What I found was a folder of work from my third-grade year, the time just after my family had left Oregon and returned to South Carolina. There were two reports, both illustrated and composed on heavy construction paper, with pictures and cut-out sections of wide-lined writing paper pasted onto the colored background. The first was a report on the state of Oregon, a kind of travelogue illustrated with old roadmaps, postcards, and snapshots of places like Crater Lake. The information appeared to have come straight from the *World Book Encyclopedia*, a set of which my parents had purchased for our new home in Greenville, circa 1961—pretty white volumes with forest green trim and gilded edges on every page. The second project was a bird guide, a paragraph on each of a dozen common birds—blue jay, cardinal, robin, Carolina wren—with a badly colored page torn from a coloring book to illustrate each entry.

The two reports were companion pieces, the escapist work of a displaced lad. I was trying to recover and reinforce a happier recent past or retreat into the freedom of a former wildness. At school a would-be bully had called me a "Yankee" on the playground because of the way I'd learned to talk in Oregon. I tried to explain that I was a South Carolinian, born and bred, but he just started pushing me. I punched him in the gut and left him gasping for air as the teacher marched me off to the principal's office. Mom came to school, exasperated, to take me home. With four growing kids to mind now, she didn't have time for a behavior project. As for Dad, he was busy setting up his private practice and dealing with the patients who flocked to see him. He worked long hours and came home tired.

I see myself writing these reports down in the den. I can remember sitting there for hours with the *World Book*. If I wasn't writing a report, I would just choose a letter of the alphabet and pore through the whole volume in an afternoon. (P and S were long; G and H so short, they shared a volume.) I read the articles, studied the colored maps and photographs, and looked up places I remembered from my trip out West—the Grand Canyon, the bullring in Juarez, the Painted Desert, the Hoover Dam, the Redwood Forest—and then Oregon, and the birds.

❧ Dad had been a presence for me in our western days. He was the one who freed me from what I later learned to call (after the poet Shelley) the prison-house of language—which for me meant the kitchen table, the forced march through Dr. Seuss, the reading out loud to prove I could do it, the memorization and faking it till I learned to decode the letters, the little girl at school who showed me how to read silently, without whispering or moving my lips.

After a day of work at the dispensary, Dad would sometimes sit with me in the backyard on the officers' hill of base housing and point out the birds. "Those are Canadian honkers. Those are probably mallards." He also schooled me on the different fighter planes that flew over all the time and shook the house with their sonic booms. "That's an F-104. That one's a 102—see the sweep of the wings?" He had flown all the way to New Mexico himself in a two-man jet to attend a course at Sandia National Labs on medical first response to nuclear attack. From the fence by the runway, I waved good-bye as he taxied down the blacktop, tucked into the second seat behind the pilot, looking like a spaceman with his flight helmet and oxygen mask. Nature craft and war craft were the warrior's lore he taught me, the edge of adventure in an otherwise boring middle-class life. (In his later years, I would sit with my widowed dad on the patio swing in his backyard in Greenville. He was still watching the skies. "Is that a bird or a bat?" "I think that's a chimney swift, Dad." "Do you reckon that plane way up high is heading to England?" "Could be. It's going east.")

I'll always remember the day in Oregon that Dad came home, still dressed in his captain's uniform, and said he wanted to show me something. He brought a big package in from the car and unwrapped a gigantic shotgun, a Remington 12-gauge pump action. I was struck dumb. I'd never been so close to the object of my many fantasies—all formed, in those days, by war movies, westerns, and adventure stories. I looked up and said, "What are you going to do with that?" He explained that the man down the street, one of his fellow officers, had invited him to go duck hunting.

"You know," he said as I stared at the big gun, "I haven't done any shooting in a long time. Maybe I ought to go out to the marsh and see if I can't get a duck or two on my own before I go with the major, what do you think?"

"Good idea," I said, still marveling at the long barrel and polished wooden stock.

Then he floored me: "Do you want to go with me?"

Mom bought me some grown-up-looking boots for walking on the cold, wet ground, and I had them on my feet before anyone else got up the next morning. Dad met me in the hall. We went to the all-night truck stop for a quick breakfast and then headed out to a marshy area close to the irrigated fields nearby. He told me always to walk a little behind him and to be quiet so we wouldn't scare off the ducks. For once, I did everything I was told.

We stepped up slowly to a small pond, crunching the partially frozen ground. Every sound seemed magnified by the surrounding quiet. Dad held his gun carefully, pointing the barrel toward the ground in front of him. While we were still in the brush, just before we got a clear view of the pond, he stopped and loaded some shells into the gun. He had already showed me all about the shotgun and helped me get over the disappointment that it used these ugly shells made of brass and heavy paper rather than silver bullets.

As soon as we stepped into the open, a group of mallards burst off the water. Dad raised the gun quickly and fired once, then pumped and fired again. My heart nearly beat out of my chest. I looked everywhere but couldn't see any ducks, alive or dead, only smoke in the frosty air, with clear blue sky behind. "Got one," he said and gave me a big grin.

We worked our way slowly around to the side of the pond where he thought the bird had fallen. We heard something in the brush and crept up to find the brown-striped female mallard flapping around on the ground. I held on to Dad's pants leg, terrified, but he said calmly, "Must have only winged her."

"Shoot her again!" I said.

"No need for that," he said and walked right over and with his doctor's hands picked up the bird by the head and wrung its neck quickly and smoothly with a swing of the body. Then it was still.

"That's called wringing its neck," he explained. "It kills it quickly so it won't suffer." He handed me the limp bird to hold and let me carry it all the way back to the car, the smooth feathers soothing my electric hands.

We were home by noon. I found my sister Belle in the backyard and brought the bird out for her to see. She backed up cautiously but then let me put her hand on the soft feathers. She looked up at me in wonder. I showed her the pretty blue feathers on the wings, then the mysterious wound in the wing pit that had brought the bird to the ground, pink blood staining the white feathers. I showed her how Dad had finished the bird off, holding it by the head and swinging it round and round—a few too many times, for the neck broke open a little. I laid the carcass on the ground and we stared at the little slit that had opened in the neck. The bird's exposed craw was full of good Oregon grain. "That's what the duck eats," I told Belle, who scrunched up her nose in disgust. Then Dad came out and said he needed to take the duck and prepare it for cooking. I sat down with Belle and told her the whole story again—about five times, actually—until she lost interest and wandered off.

❧ We ate the duck, as we did the other birds that Dad shot over those two years. I went out hunting with him many times, and Belle even got to go once. The time I remember best was the trip we made with the major just after our first trial hunt (which I realized later was as much a trial for me as it was for Dad's shooting eye). The major had a beautiful dog, a jet-black Labrador retriever. I'd never had a dog and was a little wary at first, but after a few licks in the face, he won me right over. I still remember his name—Rocky.

We found our way down to the edge of a game refuge at the California border. We were hunting smart ducks, according to what the men were saying. They said the birds knew exactly where the game refuge began and would turn upward to fly higher when they reached the dangerous air space. Living close to the Air Force must have taught them good flight tactics.

The major managed to shoot one anyhow—a green-headed male mallard—as we walked out along the embankment of an irrigation ditch. The bird fell right into the ditch, which was running full with water. As the carcass began to float away, the major gave a little waving hand signal to Rocky. I jumped with surprise as the dog leaped into action. He splashed into the water and went swimming after the duck. He caught it in his mouth, swam to shore, ran right back to us, and dropped the bird at our feet.

I was nearly overwhelmed with admiration. I picked the duck up and ran my fingers through its feathers but found not a single tooth mark. "Why didn't he eat it?" I asked in amazement.

"He's bred and trained to have a 'soft mouth,'" Dad explained. "That's why they call him a retriever. He retrieves birds, brings them back to you." I rubbed Rocky's neck with respect. He looked up at me with a big panting smile.

Within an hour, Dad had shot a duck himself, and the major had shot another one. Each time, Rocky retrieved them, to my great delight.

We separated and walked back to the car along different paths, the major and Rocky going along the irrigation ditch while Dad and I worked our way through a field of grain, wheat maybe. We were nearly to our destination when the grain exploded about ten yards in front of us. Dad responded with a hunter's instinct and shot a large bird out of the air just as it was rising. I ran forward to retrieve it myself.

What I found was a heavenly sight: a ring-necked pheasant, its exotic green head and golden feathers shining in the bright sun and crystalline air. I was still staring in amazement when Dad came up and told me what it was.

I would never become a hunter myself. Dad gave it up, too, once he left the Air Force. Private medical practice left no time for hunting. But I would always seek the surprise of a bird bursting out of ground cover or winging into sight. Nor did I ever take up the life-listing and amateur science of the true birder. Birdwatching would always be casual and personal for me, rooted in family life, a sacred trust I received from my dad.

When we moved back to South Carolina from Oregon, I was on my own more of the time. Almost in proportion to my solitude, my interest in birdwatching grew deeper over the years. The evidence of the rudimentary bird guide from third grade shows that I sustained the interest during my time of adjustment, but, as I recall, things really took off as I entered junior high school. I was propelled by boredom. About the time that social life began to mean more than anything else—my preteen years, with puberty setting in—Mom and Dad began to insist that we leave our friends every summer for a family vacation on a deserted beach.

That's what Hilton Head Island was before the developers took over. Back in the sixties, you got to Hilton Head by crossing a rusty old bridge. The island had long stretches of beach and marshland where you could spend a whole day walking or sunning or fishing and not see another person. Mom and Dad heard about Hilton Head from our neighbors, who had a summer home there. They helped us find a rental house big enough to hold our family comfortably. We went every summer for years.

It was a retreat for Mom and Dad from the pressures of work and householding.

At first, it seemed there was nothing much for me to do. Without friends, I grew lonely and bored and was pretty surly to my family, I suppose. At any rate, they never complained when I drifted off by myself along the broad hard beaches of golden sand, or took my bicycle out to the marshland paths, or walked the trails in the woods of live oak and sea pine.

Gradually the birds appeared. I began to trace the flights and staggers of the marsh and shore and woodland birds—the pelicans cruising in squadrons low across the surf, the little plovers skittering along the beach in numbers I would never see in later years, the gray-brown osprey sweeping into the water with its eagle's talons and bringing out a fish so big it could barely fly back to feed its nested young, and the pileated woodpecker breaking the still air of the pine woods with a wild cry before taking my breath away by cruising across a clearing with its big black-and-white wings and bright red crest.

Watched over by the gulls and terns, we would fish in the surf or off the bridge that connected the island to the mainland. Because Dad never had time to fish at home, he had no tackle to use, so he'd just buy a couple of balls of twine and tie on a sinker and hook and bait the thing with headless shrimp. You never knew what you'd pull up. Belle amazed us all one day by catching a spiny blowfish off the bridge. We got the hook out with a pair of pliers and sent the monster back to the deep. We dragged a couple of small sharks out of the surf one year. That made swimming and wading seem more like an adventure (or, according to my sisters' way of seeing, more of a decision).

After several years at the old rental house, Dad bought some property at Hilton Head, and work began on a house of our own.

From a realtor's point of view, his investment timing was excellent. Development was just beginning to sweep over the island. The old bridge was replaced by a new one; the Mercedes-Benzes and Jaguars poured across.

But, as the house was nearing completion, Mom almost died before being diagnosed with systemic lupus. The disease could not be cured, we learned, but doctors were getting better at helping people live with it. With Dad's close attention and home care, Mom came back from the edge of death, adjusted her life to the disease, and became something of a record case, surviving twenty-six years with the disease, long enough to see her children finish college and get good jobs, then to see most of her grandchildren born.

After she recovered and went into remission, though, she could never again bake for hours in the sun or take morning-long walks on the beach because the lupus made her sick from the least exposure to sunlight and heat. But even if she could have behaved in the old ways, she would have missed the privacy of a nearly deserted beach, for now the beach was teeming with people. And as the number of people increased, the birds began to decline. DDT sprayed for mosquitoes threatened the brown pelican and the osprey. The waving sea oats on the sand dunes and the turtles we saw coming out of the ocean to lay eggs in the moonlight were included on the earliest versions of the Endangered Species List when the protective law was passed in 1973.

The new house was never the same as the old rental place. The old house, without air-conditioning and set up tall to catch the sea breeze, was open to the elements and vulnerable to critters—palmetto bugs in my sisters' beds (the youngest one, Kathy, had a mortal fear of insects, which they seemed to detect and crowd toward her), raccoons in the garbage, tree frogs, and once even a water snake in the outdoor shower. The new house had central air and was set back from the beach. It had the insulated feel of any suburban single-story brick dwelling. The cedar-shake roof and custom showers that opened both to the outside deck and an indoor hall were the only features that made it really different from any house you might see in an upland middle-class neighborhood. It did have the old-fashioned screened porch in the back, looking onto a piney lot that gave a good view of the woodland birds. I saw downy woodpeckers, yellow-billed cuckoos, solitary vireos, and the hermit thrush as I sat on that porch—until the woods gave way to first one new house, then another; the woods thinned and all but disappeared.

The new house was completed after I went off to school in Tennessee. I took my college friends there a few times, and once, on a spring break during graduate school, I sat on the screened porch with a portable Smith-Corona typewriter and drafted a chapter of my dissertation on Walt Whitman. My snippet of life by the Atlantic on the southern coastal island seemed to resonate with Whitman's poems that venerated the memory of his childhood on Long Island and his young adulthood on all the sea islands that made up New York City—"Out of the Cradle Endlessly Rocking," "As I Ebbed with the Ocean of Life," "Crossing Brooklyn Ferry."

Eventually the house on Hilton Head became a burden. Mom was too sick to travel much. She worried over the upkeep, the rental agents, the furniture, the hurricanes. When Hilton Head became an issue of private property for my family, it ceased to be an escape from the pressures of life—a vacation in the truest sense, vacating the scene of work to occupy a scene of resort and retreat—and became instead an occupation in its own right, full of demands and responsibilities. Mom was too sick and Dad too busy for that. They sold the house at a tidy profit and released themselves from the stress it induced.

Once my sisters and brother and I were grown up and had families of our own, Mom and Dad began to rent a big house at Pawley's Island and invite us all to join them there every summer. For many years, we made the trip a priority. My wife Jackie was the one who said the time was "sacred." Although the northern coast of South Carolina was crowded and overdeveloped, we stayed close to the shore and ate our meals at the house on this family beach (no restaurants or hotels on the entirety of the little island). We taught our daughter Myrth and our nephews and nieces to fish off the pier, swim in the surf, collect shells, and watch the birds.

Mom made the trip the last summer she was alive, though with some difficulty. She was tethered to an oxygen tank and very weak. The lupus had attacked her lungs. As we sat in the ocean breeze one night, she told me, "It can't go on this way." We more or less said our good-byes in that hallowed place. She died at home in the old Upstate split-level the next winter.

❧ I would have told you at that point that my adventures with Dad were long since over. He wasn't in the best health himself and had retired from medical practice the year before. But then, after Mom's death, in the year 2000, an interesting opportunity arose. I was invited to participate in a conference on Walt Whitman in China and decided to make a side trip to Korea to see the place where my blood father had died. I was able to schedule some lectures through friends and former students in Korea, so we managed to make the trip affordable for Jackie and Myrth (a teenager by then) to go, too. Thinking of Dad alone in his house without much to do, Jackie suggested that I invite him to go along. And so I did. He wavered, but with Belle's urging, he agreed to go.

One cloudy and cool October day we found ourselves standing

on Tiananmen Square in Beijing. With the great portrait of Mao looming in the distance over the entryway to the home of emperors, the Forbidden City, we stood in a long line to the south across the square, waiting with hundreds of Chinese tourists and patriots for our chance to view the august remains of the architect of the Chinese Revolution in the Chairman Mao Memorial Hall. Inside the big stone mausoleum was the body of the man who sent the Chinese troops across the Yalu River into Korea, where their bullets would kill a young lieutenant from South Carolina and set the course for my life story.

The great sea of Chinese tourists closed around us and swept us forward past the stalls selling commemorative flowers and the uniformed guards selling pamphlets, and finally into the big hall, where more guards kept us moving toward the main display. And then, there he was, Mao in a glass-covered case, laid out on a thick wooden slab and surrounded by fresh flowers, the eyes closed, the mouth set in a kind of steely determination, the body clothed in the notorious blue cotton uniform with the "Mao jacket." We were urged quickly through the room. And then we were outside again in the cloudy day, with peddlers offering us souvenirs—miniature Chinese flags, the little red books preserving the sayings of Mao in Chinese and English, postcards of various scenes on Tiananmen Square.

As we walked along, Dad said, "I don't think it was really him. I think it was a wax figure."

"Really?" I asked. I had not doubted that the waxen-faced body was the real thing.

"No, they wouldn't just put him out there. It didn't look right."

After four decades of medical practice, he'd certainly seen enough dead bodies to know, but I doubted his view this time. "No, I think it was real," I said.

"Well, maybe," he conceded in his agreeable way. "We did go by pretty fast."

But he wasn't buying it, I could tell, and in a minute or two, he came back to his point: "I bet they keep the real body in a safe place and just put the wax one out for people to see."

"You could be right," I admitted. It was so hard to know what was real in China. After all, we had seen Starbucks Coffee in the Forbidden City. (I had a tall latté.)

I finally decided that, whether wax or flesh, Chairman Mao's body could only have appeared unreal to us. Mao lived for us not as a figure in eternal repose but as a huge, moving presence on the world scene, a hulking historical reality. The serene figure lying in the mausoleum could only have seemed absent to us, a mere sign of a former presence and of a power strong enough to order the building of great tombs in a country where most folks (like people everywhere) can only hope that the memories dear to their hearts will immortalize their loved ones.

In the months before we arrived in China, the US Congress voted to give China favored-nation status as a trading partner. American relations with the great power had not been better since the communist revolution. Just one week before our trip, South Korean president Kim Dae Jung won the Nobel Peace Prize for his efforts to reconcile the differences between North and South. The United States established newly hopeful diplomatic relationships with North Korea. President Bill Clinton dispatched Secretary of State Madeleine Albright to meet in Pyongyang with the North Korean leader, Kim Jong Il, the son of the notorious Kim Il Sung, who had ordered the invasion of South Korea fifty years earlier and opened the way for a half century of internecine struggle on the Korean peninsula.

On the very day that Secretary Albright met with Kim in

Pyongyang, October 23, 2000, a short distance to the southeast, in Panmunjom, a village reduced to a military outpost in the Demilitarized Zone, Dad and I stepped across the border into North Korea. (At the suggestion of our Korean hosts, Jackie and Myrth had stayed behind in Seoul. The DMZ is not to be taken lightly, people said. Jackie said it seemed fitting anyway for Dad and me to make the trip on our own, a kind of father-son pilgrimage.) On a cue from a military guide, we walked across a dramatic yellow line painted on the floor in the room where the cease-fire was negotiated, where the diplomatic efforts had stalled one October forty-eight years before and prompted the American and South Korean generals to make a point about their resolve in a campaign called Operation Showdown, the name invoking the cowboy stories that fueled my childhood fantasy life. My father had been killed in that campaign, leading a rifle platoon up Triangle Hill against impossible odds.

Dad and I had taken a bus from Seoul. In English, an articulate Korean guide gave us a brief history of the war along the way. She pointed out key sites, the Han and the Imjin Rivers, the beautiful rice fields along their banks, the barbed wire and guard posts that made infiltration by water a difficult matter for North Korean spies. Finally, we could see North Korea itself across the river. Along both sides of the border, great neon billboards on the hills shouted propaganda in Korean characters.

Once we passed through the checkpoint on the bridge leading into the DMZ, the tour guide committed our little group—visitors from countries all around the globe, Americans, Germans, Dutch, Japanese, Indonesians, Indians—to the care of the US Army. We had lunch at Camp Boniface, named for the American officer who, in 1976, during a tree-trimming operation designed to improve surveillance, had been killed by ax-wielding North Korean troops.

We were told to stay within the confines of three buildings—the command post, the mess hall, and a kind of crude museum and gift shop that doubled as a bar—and not to wander away, for all these areas, we were told, were within sight of the other side. I thought of Uncle Tunk's story about how, one day during the war, "full of vinegar and school spirit," he walked the trench line along the Main Line of Resistance and offered a "one-finger salute" (the middle one) to any sniper who might be watching from across the way.

It became clear to me that the MLR was now the DMZ when Dad and I strolled around the corner of the gift shop and suddenly caught sight of the old trenches. Long green grass had replaced the rat-tracked mud of the war days, and the trench had become a feature of a peaceful landscape that looked almost natural, like the cut of a narrow creek. It ran for several hundred yards along the line, with the ruins of old bunkers set into it every ten or twenty yards. This place, the sort of place where my father spent his last months on earth, looked exactly the way I had pictured it.

That was my dominant impression of the entire scene. It was exactly as I had pictured it—uncannily so. I felt as if I were revisiting a scene from my childhood, the kind of place that was different when you were there before—in the old days when it was bigger, starker, more ominous—but for all the changes, still recognizable.

I turned this impression over and over in my mind. I decided that the feeling of familiarity was partly the effect of reading and listening to so many stories about the war and partly the result of noticing that the hilly countryside of central Korea—natural features like woods and knolls mingling with small cleared and long-cultivated fields—was much like my homeland in the Piedmont of the Carolinas. But none of these rational explanations quite sufficed. I knew this place in my blood, in my heart.

Our army tour guide, a young captain from Indiana, gathered the group up, scolding those of us who had wandered a bit beyond the area he had outlined and reminding us that taking pictures in unauthorized areas could represent a threat to South Korean security. He led us all into an old-fashioned briefing room in the command post and gave us the history of the DMZ. Then we boarded a bus and rode a few miles up to the site of the old negotiations. We were herded carefully up a tower to look across at the armed guards to the north and then ushered into the Quonset hut where the negotiators met to set the terms of the cease-fire. An armed South Korean trooper was dramatically ordered to stand ready by the door that opened onto North Korea, and then the tour leader allowed us to step over the yellow line that divided the room in half. And there we were: on enemy ground snapping pictures of each other.

Before long, we were back on the bus. We rode by the Bridge of No Return, where prisoners were exchanged during the war and again in the 1960s after the *Pueblo* incident in 1968, when North Korean vessels fired on and captured a US Navy intelligence-gathering ship, one of the tensest (but least remembered) moments in the Cold War. The guide told us that the farms in the DMZ were worked by people whose families had been displaced from the land during the worst parts of the conflict. The South Korean government offered military protection and subsidized the farming operations to make their work profitable and to compensate them for the danger of working and living in the DMZ. It was a propaganda issue, we were told, a way of showing the communists that life went on as usual in spite of their continual threats. We saw the darkened greenhouses where the farmers grew their world-famous ginseng root (an herb that grows in the Appalachians as well and used to bring a good price on the Japanese and Korean markets).

And we saw a farmer in a wide-brimmed hat fishing in a canal, watched over by a soldier on the bank with an automatic rifle slung on his shoulder.

I had read in the tour book that although it remains one of the most dangerous places in the world for human traffic, the DMZ had ironically become a safe haven for endangered species, including the legendary Asian crane. Even bears had been spotted. Like the farmers, the animals enjoyed the protection of the government.

I told Dad to help me watch for the cranes, and as soon as we entered the DMZ we saw a variety of herons and egrets in the marshy canals surrounding the fields and at the margins of the wood lots. Later, at a stop for legal photos, a good-sized bird stirred in the grass close to us. We watched quietly as, about ten yards away, a male ring-necked pheasant waddled boldly into sight, his green head shining and golden wings gleaming in the mellow autumn sunlight. Again the uncanny recognition rose within me.

I said, "It's just like the one you shot in Oregon, Dad," and he replied dreamily, "It sure is," a big smile forming on his face.

Finally, just before the bus left the DMZ, Dad shook my arm and said "Look!" with the hushed voice of an old hunter. Standing by the canal, near the close edge of a rice field, was a group of four Asian cranes. They were huge, nearly six feet tall. How strange it was to see them. It was as if the cranes I had known during my adult years in New Mexico and Texas, the pheasant of the Oregon farm canals where I had gone hunting with Dad during his years in the Air Force, and the egrets of the Atlantic coast all came home to roost in this oddly familiar land on the other side of the world.

The next day, as I admired a handsome image of a crane inset in a wooden panel of an ancient palace in Seoul, I asked the tour guide if she knew of any myths associated with the crane in Korean lore and legend. She considered the question for a moment, and then said, "Oh yes, I have heard that the crane is the bird that carries souls between heaven and earth. It flies so high and so strong, and cries with a voice that you can hear high and low."

꽃 Thoughts of heaven were with me again two days later when, guided by graduate students from the university where I was a guest lecturer, we visited the ancient Korean city of Kyung Ju. We were going to a place loosely translated as Buddha Land, a holy village conceived by its founders as an image of something like heaven on earth. The group of old painted temples in an ancient forest was a still-active Buddhist monastery in what had become the most Christianized nation in the world.

The westernization that characterized Seoul had barely touched this place. In the asphalt parking lot, where the vendors hawked their wares, I saw one old lady cooking biscuits in a kind of dutch oven and stirring a wok filled with what looked to me like some kind of beetle or cockroach mixture. I asked one of the graduate students with us, "What is she selling?"

"Uh . . . bread," he said evasively, with a shy smile.

"No, I mean, what is that in the wok?"

"Uh . . . what would you call it?" he said with a quizzical expression, pleading loss of language.

"I'd call it bugs," I said.

"That's right!" he agreed, with a big smile. "Bugs it is."

It was a gorgeous autumn day, full of blue sky and sunlight, a cool breeze blowing. Busloads of schoolchildren had arrived to tour Buddha Land. They grinned and stared at us, the only foreigners in sight that day, more than two hundred miles from Seoul. (The Chinese tourists in Beijing had been equally curious about the family of Americans traveling Chinese-style—in three generations. We posed frequently for photo ops.) The braver of the Korean kids at Kyung Ju walked right up and said their favorite English word, "Hello!" Then others would try and a chorus of hellos would come at us once we answered. They seemed delighted that their English really worked. The star students—or class clowns (the difference was hard to tell)—would then try other bits of dialogue, like "What's your name?" When we answered and asked back, "What's yours?" more often than not they'd revert to "Hello" and then "Good-bye" and go off giggling. The scene was repeated dozens of times throughout the day and never failed to charm us.

For all the experience of foreignness, though, the sense of familiarity would not leave me alone. This time what seemed to say "home" to me was the hills covered with the hardwood trees in their autumn colors, so much like Appalachia that it almost hurt—the maple reds and sugar gum yellows, the old leaf shapes close to the same, the ground moist from recent rains, the moisture held tight by newly fallen leaves, the pleasant smell of last year's leaves rotting into black soil, the trails from temple to temple curving and rising upward, then opening on lovely vistas of the modern town of Kyung Ju or the farms in the valleys.

The last site we visited required that we walk some distance and then finish with a short, steep climb up to a small hillside temple. Inside the temple was a huge Buddha carved from gray granite and seated permanently there on the hillside, looking outward. The hellos quieted as we entered the little enclosure that protected the Buddha from the elements. As we stood admiring the Great One, one of our guides showed me a window positioned directly in front of the stone image. He explained with a warm smile, "That's so Buddha can see the sun rise over the ocean." We looked and sure enough, several miles to the east, we could glimpse the sea, a dark gray misty blank on the horizon. For a moment, I was entranced, the oxygen of the mountain air filling my blood, gazing with the Buddha's view eastward, toward America.

We left the Buddha on his hillside and followed the path back down toward the van. Now and then a group of Korean children with their teachers swelled around us.

"Hello."

"Hello."

"What's your name?"

"What's yours?"

The peals of laughter from the well-fed Asian faces brought to mind something Mom told me a few years before about Father's pity for the children of the Korean refugee families. Then I remembered another thing she told me on the phone long-distance one day. I was in Texas and had just managed to make contact with a survivor of Operation Showdown who verified for me how most of Father's outfit had been wiped out along with many others in three days of hard fighting. They had perished while charging up Triangle Hill into the gunfire of the Chinese in their trenches. My father's military records had been lost in a fire at the National Archives, so I was pleased to get this eyewitness account.

After hearing of my finding, Mom said, "You know, in some ways it was a blessing that he died there. He was so tenderhearted. He could never have lived with the thought of all his men dying like that."

I suppose that Dad and I were doing what Father could not do, coming down the big hill full of life and swarming with children, coming down from a place the Koreans called heaven, following the Buddha's gaze homeward, eastward, the world turning, the birds flying, the old stories buzzing in our minds.

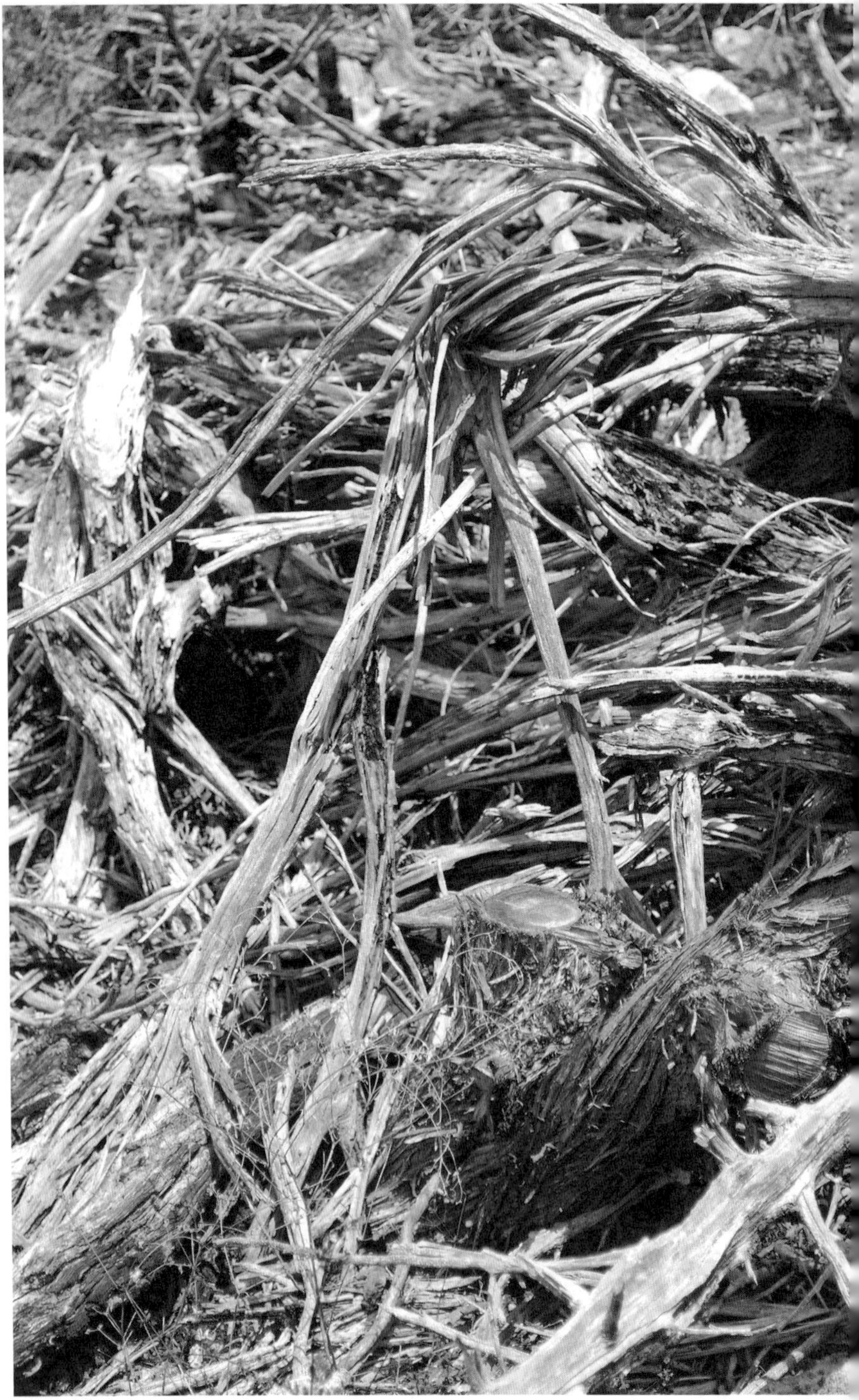

2 Ecology Then
The Lake of Tears

> In a damaged habitat, all problems merge.
> Ted Majors, echoing César Chávez, quoted by
> Terry Tempest Williams in *When Women Were Birds*

🙞   Fall 1970, my freshman year at Tennessee, my high school friend Rita McKinney came up for a visit from South Carolina. I took her to see the Great Smoky Mountains. Stuck in a traffic jam in the middle of the lush woods—contemplating what it means to get back to nature in America's most frequently visited national park—we found ourselves pondering a bumper sticker on the car in front of us. In large green letters, it said, "ECOLOGY NOW!" Next to the slogan was what looked like the Greek letter theta, also in green, or a kind of yellow-green chartreuse. Taken as a whole, the message was a parody of the antiwar bumper sticker, common in those days, that had the words "PEACE NOW!" next to the then-ubiquitous peace symbol. So we knew, with the war in Vietnam still plowing its controversial course through history, that some kind of protest was afoot. But what exactly?

"What does that even mean?" she said.

I was the one who was a chemistry major, but I was still a little shaky on the definition of *ecology* and really unclear on what it could mean to have it *now*. I gave it my best shot. "Isn't ecology the study of nature?"

"So it means STUDY NATURE NOW?" she said. "I'm sorry, but that doesn't make sense."

"I guess not."

Any effort to make sense of ECOLOGY NOW! would have required a big stretch of logic, which over the succeeding months I was finally able to work out:

> Define *ecology* in the usual way as the *study of the relationship of organisms to their environment and to each other.*
>
> Drop the *study* part and focus on the *relationship* part. Now we have the attractive concept (at least for those of us growing up in the Age of Aquarius) that *everything is connected.*
>
> Then, if the connections that are everywhere and involve everything have come undone—especially the connection between the human organism and all the rest—then ECOLOGY NOW! would mean that people need to reconnect with the environment and their fellow organisms.

It was a stretch all right—the bumper sticker never caught on—but the elasticated definition did. Before long, we found ourselves able to speak of Deep Ecology, Social Ecology, and the Ecology Movement as alternate names or different versions of environmentalism.

The theta-looking symbol also has an interesting history that took me years to uncover. Now it's available to anyone with access to Google and Wikipedia. The image was not a theta in fact but a new symbol for ecology created by the cartoonist Ron Cobb and first published in the Los Angeles *Free Press* on November 7, 1969. It combines the letters *e* (for environment) and *o* (for organism). Cobb used the symbol in a flag he created, based on the design of the US flag, and placed it as an image in the public domain.

It was adopted as the first official flag for the original Earth Day, which took place in the spring of 1970, a few months before my bumper sticker episode. But Cobb's creation didn't last long in this capacity. The organizers of Earth Day eventually replaced it with the so-called "Blue Earth flag" that featured the more easily recognized and soon-to-be-iconic photograph of the planet taken by Apollo astronauts from space.

It was a time when new imagery and new terms were emerging, morphing, and shifting meanings in a burst of creativity that reflected the social and political turmoil of the nation. The year I started college, 1970, was the birth year of the Environmental Protection Agency and also the year that the word *environmentalism* (or *environmentalist*), used to signify devotion to the cause of environmental protection, joined the regular vocabulary of the English-speaking people, according to the *Oxford English Dictionary*. Before that, people with an interest in environmental protection were called *conservationists,* a term that first appeared almost a century earlier, in the time of John Muir, Gifford Pinchot, and Theodore Roosevelt. *Conservationism* didn't quite cover what had happened in the decade of the 1960s, when scientific activists like Rachel Carson, Barry Commoner, Garrett Hardin, Donella Meadows, and Paul Ehrlich were revealing a deep, systemic problem in the relationship of people to nature, an *ecological* problem, which was a whole lot more complicated than the overuse of natural resources. Ecology taught that the problems were deeper, wider, more thoroughly linked together, more troubling, and more fraught with political implications. Words like *ecology* and *environment* began to be heard on the evening news and in the halls of Congress. The National Environmental Policy Act had been signed into law by President Nixon in 1969. Among other things, it required government agencies to produce environmental impact statements and hold hearings for all projects involving public lands. As the ECOLOGY NOW! bumper sticker suggested—along with another campaign button of the day that said "Give Earth a Chance," substituting *earth* for *peace* in the slogan that John Lennon and Yoko Ono's song made popular (Rome, *Genius* 97)—the protests against the draft and the war in Vietnam were merging with protests against the poisoning of the planet. The celebration of Earth Day, the brainchild of Wisconsin senator Gaylord Nelson, took off with unexpected success in every region of the nation.

I missed the first Earth Day. And maybe that's why I was slow to catch on to ECOLOGY NOW! Considering my long-standing interest in nature—the hunts with my dad, the birdwatching, the scouting and camping, the hiking and beach-combing, my interest in science and nature writing that was emerging at the time, and my later environmental activism and studies in the field—it seems absurd that I could have missed what should have been an identity-congealing moment for me. But I missed it all right.

Earth Day happened during my last semester of high school, the April before I graduated in June 1970, the end of a year in which the tumult of the nation had left me, like many other young people, deeply unsettled. In that one short year, I had gone from being a (mostly) obedient son of Southern Republican parents, a devout Baptist, a starting tackle on the football team, and a loyal patriot to becoming a budding intellectual with politics that trended toward the radical edge. Formerly a supporter of the war in Vietnam, I became a protestor. In my junior year of high school, 1969, I had written a letter to the school newspaper objecting to pronouncements against the war by an intellectual coterie that included a few of my good friends. I cited my father's death in Korea as the kind of sacrifice Americans were required to make in the war on communism. Within a year, partly under the influence of the same friends whom I had criticized in my letter and with the support of other friends in school government, the drama club, and my advanced classes (all of which I gave more time to after an injury ended my football career in the fall of '69), I began to have my doubts. In the meantime, my home church hired a new minister. He seemed considerably dimmer than our previous pastor, a scholar and gentleman who, though sometimes stern on matters of sin and biblical interpretation, had encouraged my interest in books and learning during my formative years. The second Sunday of the new guy's term, he preached an anti-evolution sermon. Here I was embarking on a career in science, and the pastor of my own church was raising the specter of the Scopes Monkey Trial in a congregation populated by the educated middle class—professional people like my dad and literacy freaks like my mom, schoolteachers, factory managers, business owners, and skilled laborers—folks with strong educational values and high hopes for the kids whom they were, almost without exception, sending to college. It was the first indication I had of the growing anti-intellectualism and rebirth of fundamentalism in the Southern Baptist churches of the era. I was headed in a different direction. I never attended church during my ten years in Knoxville except on visits back home, and then only to appease my parents.

By the spring of 1970, as I prepared to leave for college in the fall, I was avidly following the newspaper accounts and television reports on the campus protests throughout the nation, including one at my prospective university, where campus and city police broke out the riot gear to quell an enormous gathering of protesters during a campus-wide general strike that threatened to spill over into the city streets. Reports came from our friends about students hospitalized with broken heads and bruised bodies. The confidence in American unity was already shaken by a decade of controversy over civil rights (especially in the South) and the regular occurrence of political assassinations—John and Robert Kennedy, Martin Luther King Jr., Malcolm X—and now the generations seemed to have become divided as never before. Riots erupted at the Democratic National Convention in Chicago in 1968. I read Norman Mailer's account in his instant book *Miami and the Siege of Chicago* on summer vacation in 1969, the same summer that I watched the Apollo team's landing on the moon as a guest of a family in Houston, Texas (while I was on tour, playing guitar, with the church youth choir).

Then, on May 4, 1970, the Ohio National Guard opened fire on a demonstration at Kent State University, killing four and wounding nine students. The nation was shocked; our fellow citizens, officially militarized, were shooting down unarmed middle-class youngsters. I remember a friend telling me about the shootings during a class break in the halls of my high school, much as I remember getting the news about President Kennedy's assassination from another student at our elementary school before the announcement came over the intercom. (I have no idea how he got the news early, but I didn't really believe it until the principal's voice on the intercom made it official. The boy had said, "They shot President Kennedy in the head.") The pictures of the young people dead on the ground of the Kent State campus were in all the magazines. Crosby, Stills, Nash, and Young brought out the rock anthem that chanted the news over the strains of grinding electric guitars: "Four Dead in Ohio." But in my hometown of Greenville, South Carolina, Dr. Bob Jones Jr., president of the fundamentalist Bob Jones University founded by his father, said that the students deserved to be shot and that any students subverting the military mission of the nation deserved the same. In my mind, protest against the war came to seem an act of bravery on a par with the bravery of the soldier, which in my childhood had seemed the very touchstone of courage.

I began to see my father's death in Korea as the beginning of an injustice whose most recent iteration was the Vietnam War. I know now that I was performing the kind of mental somersault that simply exchanged one simplistic view of my life story for its opposite number, equally simplistic. As I learned later, my father was no passive victim; his college buddy, whom I called Uncle Tunk, told me that Father cheated on his eye exam so that he would be eligible to go to war in Korea. But in 1970, the times had come to seem desperate to me, requiring sharp lines of demarcation and black-and-white contrasts in moral discernment. I guess that's the way it is in times of high social stress. You simplify to survive, take sides, draw lines, make enemies, name your allies, and go to war—with words if not with bullets. My mother eventually banned political discussions at the dinner table to maintain peace in the family. Angry talk or uncomfortable silence seemed the only options. Just as I might have become an English professor partly in compensation for my early problems in learning to read, I likely took up the study of rhetoric as a way of transcending the war of words that disrupted my family and made me so intolerably self-righteous in those days—both in my first role as jingoistic patriot and later in the radical politics I adopted. The fall of 1970 would find me joining throngs of students, chanting "ONE-TWO-THREE-FOUR-WE-WON'T-FIGHT-YOUR-FUCKING-WAR," marching from the university to a rally on Marketplace Square in downtown Knoxville, under the watchful eyes of nervous university administrators and police in riot gear. Never mind that I, for one, would not have had to go to war anyway because of my draft status as Sole Surviving Son, which my father had bought with his life. I don't remember anything about the speeches I heard that day except a witticism that a Brazilian exchange student crafted at the expense of the local newspaper. He referred to the *Knoxville Journal* as the *Knoxville Urinal*. With his accent, it cracked me up.

As for missing Earth Day, my first thought in retrospect was that, though it was a great success all across the country, even in places like Alabama, maybe it bypassed South Carolina, always a special site for reactionary politics and always slow to come around to national trends. We used to say, when speaking later of the upheavals during the Vietnam era, that by the time the revolution arrived in South Carolina, it was over.

To test the hypothesis, I emailed the environmental historian Adam Rome at the University of Delaware. I knew that he had just finished a book on the first Earth Day, though it had not yet come out. He wrote back to tell me that, in fact, there were Earth Day celebrations all over my home state, including one at Furman University, the local Baptist college and my dad's alma mater. "Even conservative places had Earth Days!" he said.

Rome's parting comment sealed it for me. I had missed Earth Day not because it was too politically charged to make it to South Carolina but because, at the time, it seemed politically tame enough to pass under the radar even in ultraconservative places. Maybe it was that way by design, as the change of official flags suggests—the potentially controversial redesign of the American flag in Ron Cobb's version (in a day when flag burnings were not uncommon) yielding to the patriotic pride associated with the Apollo mission photograph on the Blue Earth flag.

Whatever the cause, Earth Day had surely passed under *my* radar. My attention was riveted by the war in Vietnam and the campus protest movement that would eventually be documented in films like *Hearts and Minds* and *War at Home*. Nature must have seemed innocuous by comparison; it had not yet become political for me—and I suspect it had not for many Americans of my generation. After nearly a decade of gestation since the publication of Carson's *Silent Spring* in 1962, environmentalism, or political ecology, was only then coming to life for most young people. The first Earth Day seems to have heralded the birth of something radically new, but at the time, many of us still did not recognize the infant movement as somehow different from the kind of conservation we'd read about in the old *Weekly Reader* during elementary school. Barry Commoner had said, around the same time, that it was hard to mobilize political action on environmental issues because it was seen as a "motherhood issue," something that everybody favored and to which nobody paid much mind. But the time when that view prevailed was coming to an end, and the attitudes with which we contend today—best seen perhaps in the listing of eco-activists as a major threat to national security by agencies like the FBI and the Department of Homeland Security—were beginning to come into focus.

But my own activism remained focused on the war. I responded with a radicalism that now seems rather pale and cerebral, though you could not have convinced me at the time that I was not fully committed to changing the world. I grew my hair long and wore the uniform of jeans, blue cotton work shirt, boots in the winter, sandals in the summer. I attended the protests and spent a short time in a group on campus called the Student Committee for a Radical Union, the SCRU Party. The crudely witty acronym reflected the group's whimsical approach to campus politics—more folk art than political action, the kind of thing that resulted in happenings with rock music and ironic parodies rather than winning elections or instigating concrete changes in university policy. In a typical move, a group of SCRU partiers attended a debate during student government elections while dressed as Nazi soldiers. Every time the name of the university president or the US president (Richard Nixon) was mentioned, the parodists leapt to their feet and gave the "Heil Hitler" salute.

The revolution became a mental process for me, an intellectual transformation more than anything else. For one thing, my interest in science could not hold me in my major. Few of my friends were science students. Science and engineering were, to many minds, too deeply implicated in the military establishment to be trusted as guides to life and learning. My closest friends leaned toward literature, philosophy, psychology, and political theory. More and more, I was drawn in that direction myself, though my own objections to science were not ideological. I liked the ideas of science but was bored and frustrated by the endless homework problems and long, pointless-seeming labs. Finally, one dark afternoon in the winter quarter, after watching a titration drip for three hours, I walked out of the stinking chemistry lab and never looked back. With the tolerant blessing of my parents, I switched majors to English the next term and focused my coursework on literature, philosophy, and religious studies.

At the beginning of my senior undergraduate year, by which time the war in Vietnam was lurching toward its sad completion—"Peace with Honor" was the slogan that Nixon used to win the election—I was making plans to stay on for graduate school. I was granted an assistantship that put me at the front of the class as a teacher with new and, to my mind, grave responsibilities. My politics drifted toward theory and away from practice, opening a space that would eventually be filled by a politicized understanding of environmental issues.

❧ The episode of the bumper sticker was maybe the first time that the politics of nature dawned on me. My revised outlook became part of the general dawning of a new perception of nature in 1970. The impulse gained more of a foothold during my time in undergraduate and graduate school, partly through my reading—

which, as an English major, included the whole gamut of nature literature from British Romanticism on down, from Wordsworth's lament over "what man has made of man" and Thoreau's critique of the "quiet desperation" of modern humanity to the meditations of modern nature writers like Joseph Wood Krutch and Edward Abbey, the essays of science writers like Loren Eiseley and Isaac Asimov, and the rebellious strains of the Beat poets Jack Kerouac and Gary Snyder.

I also spent a great deal of time outdoors. I finished most days with a run through the moist air and green spaces of Knoxville, I played tennis with my professors and fellow students, I biked or walked to class every day, and on weekends I frequently fished the lakes and streams of the region or visited the Smokies for picnics, camping trips, and hikes. In graduate school, the man who directed first my master's thesis and then my doctoral dissertation, Professor F. DeWolfe Miller, a native of east Tennessee, served as my guide to the mountain trails and the many flowers, trees, and birds of the place, every one of which DeWolfe could name (trillium, orchid, wild iris, bee balm, tulip poplar, hickory, sassafras, nuthatch, hermit thrush, pileated woodpecker). Many spots on those trails attained a kind of sacredness in my memory—the always flowing spring from the moss-covered rocks on the trail to Spence Field that DeWolfe had first pointed out to me, the taste of water there "like ambrosia," he would say; Cades Cove, with its old cabins of wormy chestnut and fields where even a casual glance could show you a groundhog, wild turkey, white-tailed deer, or mother black bear with her cubs; the passage into the calm lushness of virgin hemlock forest on the trail to Mount Guyot from out of the lower trail's poplars and oaks, now heavenly tall but nonetheless second growth that appeared after decades of logging ended with the opening of the national park in the 1920s;

the quiet havens that determined hikers could find on those turning trails after getting past the overused and paved walkways that led to places like Laurel Falls. In the background of my thinking during all this time, the fuzzy sentimentalism of MAN VERSUS NATURE sounded as a faint but steady motif.

As I was completing work on my PhD and preparing for my first professorial job, I began to realize the deeper implications of political ecology when I found myself in the middle of a crucial historical moment in the environmental movement, which produced not only a political controversy in my adopted home of east Tennessee but also a considerable literary response. Like so many environmental crises before and after, it was all about a dam.

The controversy is remembered today, if at all, because of a little fish known as the snail darter, which became the first major test case of the Endangered Species Act of 1973. The Tellico Dam, a project of the powerful Tennessee Valley Authority, was several decades in the planning and nearing completion—despite the long-term protests of farmers, who stood to lose land that had been in some families for generations, as well as local sport anglers who favored the Little T, as the Little Tennessee River was called, as the best trout stream in the region—when University of Tennessee scientists found that the snail darter thrived exclusively in that river and was thus listed as endangered. The project ground to a halt, and what was locally called "the million-dollar minnow"—actually not a minnow but a perch—became a media sensation and caught the interest of the big environmentalist organizations.

It got my attention, too. My friends and I eagerly followed the news reports on the project, especially after the story started to get national coverage. A friend of mine said that people he knew were growing the best marijuana on earth—Tellico Green, he called it—in an old cornfield near the proposed dam. "What a shame!"

he said, contemplating the new lake that would cover the field. (The same guy had a bumper sticker on his truck that offered a weird parody on a popular sticker of the day. Instead of "I BRAKE FOR ANIMALS," it said, "I BRAKE FOR GNOMES.") Some wanted to see TVA brought down a notch as an agency whose power had outgrown its contribution to the region, while others worried about the effect on the local economy that would result from a national chastening of TVA. But most of my friends focused on the snail darter issue. By then, I had read not only Emerson's *Nature* and Thoreau's *Walden* but also Carson's *Silent Spring* and Abbey's *The Monkey Wrench Gang*. I knew the history of protests against dams from John Muir's failed campaign against the Hetch-Hetchy reservoir project in late nineteenth-century California and Abbey's indignation over the damming of Utah's Glen Canyon to produce Lake Powell. The intellectual fervor and passion of the literary environmentalists resonated with my experience at Hilton Head, where my family had vacationed every summer. There, the widespread use of DDT had decimated the brown pelican population, and the destruction of habitat through the development of golf courses and luxury housing threatened not only wildlife but also the lifestyles of local fisher folk and the Gullah people who'd held property on the island since Emancipation, weaving their intricate fishing nets and sweetgrass baskets, singing the songs that became famous as "Negro spirituals," and working the tomato fields and truck farms. Whole microcultures as well as whole ecosystems hung in the balance. The experience of Hilton Head made me suspicious of the claims by TVA and local politicians that the economic lot of the poor Appalachian folks in the Tellico region would be greatly improved by the jobs and tourism that the new dam and lake would bring. Ultimately I was dead set against the dam and terribly disappointed by the defeat of the opposition in the fall of 1979, the very semester that I defended my dissertation, went on the job market to look for a professorial position, and set the wheels in motion to leave east Tennessee for good.

❧ For me and for many others at the time, the endangerment of the snail darter and the problem of overdevelopment overshadowed another key element in the controversy—the preservation of the place known as Chota to the Cherokee Indians, a locale of deep ceremonial significance, the burial ground of ancestors, and the birthplace of Sequoyah, famous for creating the syllabary that allowed Cherokee to become one of the first written languages among Native Americans. By the time the Eastern Band of the Cherokees filed suit in October 1979, the offending project had achieved the status of the proverbial "done deal." Even earlier in the decade, when the university scientists had invoked the Endangered Species Act (ESA), they were engaging in a rear-guard action that merely delayed the closing of the gates in the already-constructed dam. The plan had been on the books since the building of Fort Loudoun Dam in the forties. The concrete was already poured. TVA was poised to close the gates and fill the new lake. The delay proceeded from injunction to injunction until TVA scientists declared that specimens of the snail darter were thriving in the Hiwassee and other streams. By then, the local congressional delegation, led by the powerful Sen. Howard Baker, had been able to find a way around the new law by manipulating legislative proceedings, establishing a precedent that may have permanently damaged the ESA's effectiveness. When Pres. Jimmy Carter signed the legislation that closed the dam (and the deal), he tried to deny the possibility of a precedent by expressing his regret even as he caved in to spurious arguments based on economics and energy needs. The story eventually produced a large technical literature among historians and legal scholars, including a book coauthored by my favorite history professor at Tennessee, Bruce Wheeler.

Despite my efforts to follow the controversy through the news, I didn't find out about the Cherokees' interest in the project until the gates of the dam were closed and the new lake covered the sacred grounds. I had a subscription at the time to the *New York Review of Books,* and, in the spring of 1980, my last term at Tennessee, I was surprised to find an article in those pages about Tellico and even more surprised to find out that its author was Peter Matthiessen, the famous nature writer, novelist, and former editor of the *Paris Review.* In the course I was teaching on English composition at the time, one of the readings on the syllabus was his latest book, *The Snow Leopard,* which appealed to my interests in Eastern mysticism and scientifically savvy nature adventure stories. And here he was, writing about *my* issue in *my* home region.

But as I dove into the article, my delight and pride of place melted into dismay when I realized that somehow, just as I'd missed Earth Day, I'd also missed a big part of the Tellico controversy. It took an article in a New York journal by an internationally known essayist to open my eyes to the side of the question involving indigenous rights.

I must certainly take my share of responsibility for knowing so little; I was a young and underinformed activist, more devoted to research about nineteenth-century literature (I needed to finish my dissertation on Whitman) than to gathering dependable information about the causes that I took up. But some of the blame must also rest on the inadequate coverage by the mass media, which I still believed at the time (naively, it seems in hindsight) to be a reliable source of information rather than (as I came to believe in more cynical moments) primarily an avenue of popular entertainment and a vehicle to reinforce dominant values.

Matthiessen's essay, "How to Kill a Valley," was later collected as a chapter in his 1984 book *Indian Country* under the title of "Lost Eloheh Land." It leads with testimony taken by the Cherokees' attorney, Ben Bridgers of Silva, North Carolina, copies of which I was able to read many years later in the Matthiessen papers collected at the University of Texas Humanities Research Center. One of the affidavits, taken from an elder named Goliath George, recounts a prophecy from the early days of the twentieth century, a warning that if the Cherokees continued to follow the ways of the whites in disturbing the earth, including the natural flow of rivers, the homeland of Chota would be covered with water and the spiritual knowledge of the ancestors contained in the land washed away forever. Here's the way Matthiessen dramatizes the prophecy in the opening of "Lost Eloheh Land":

> In the late nineteenth century, a remnant band of Cherokee—descendants of those who had hidden in the Great Smokies in the 1830's when the rest of the tribe was "removed" on the Trail of Tears to Oklahoma—came down from the North Carolina mountains to a ceremonial place overlooking the valley of the Cherokee River. There an old prophet, climbing onto a high stump and gazing out over the traditional heartland of his people, received a vision of a dreadful day still several generations in the future when this valley would be flooded over, and the faces of countless buried ancestors would glimmer upward through the unnatural waters as through a floor of glass. Tearful and frightened, the old man told his people that they must resist the projects of the white men, "who didn't know what they were

doing"; when the river no longer ran free through the sacred valley, the Ani Yunwiyah—"the Principal People"—would be destroyed forever as a tribe. The recent damming of the Cherokee River, now known as the Little Tennessee, fulfills this prophecy and affirms an older one that anticipated the white man's disturbance of the earth's natural balance, with calamitous consequences for mankind. (*Indian Country* 105)

The prophecy is verified by other elders speaking through the affidavits. Lloyd Sequoyah says, "If the homeland of our fathers is covered with this water, it will cover the medicine and spiritual strength of our people. . . . When this is destroyed, the Cherokee people cease to exist. . . . Then all of the peoples of the earth cease to exist" (qtd. in Matthiessen, *Indian Country* 116).

"How To Kill a Valley," one version still in print in *Indian Country* and the original also available on the Internet (with an amusing caricature of Senator Baker, who now has a beautiful building named for him on the campus of my alma mater), stands as a key work in late twentieth-century literary environmentalism. It is a watershed moment captured in prose with the eloquence at full blast, all stops opened, and subtlety be damned. It draws on the romantic tradition that runs from Wordsworth to Rachel Carson, with its attentive invocation of the east Tennessee flora and fauna and the sense of a forsaken time: "I had not expected that the place would be so lovely. In the sad, soft light of early November, the muted fire colors of the fall, the moss-green faces of the rock walls of the river bends were reflected like memories of other centuries in the clear, swift water rolling down from the blue ridges of the Great Smoky Mountains" (*Indian Country* 110). Against the background of this pastoral landscape, haunted by "the wistful resonance that echoed in the autumn calls of birds" (110), Matthiessen unleashes his indignation over the militarization of the place, the armed guards and barbed wire at every turn, the convoys of military vehicles, the "large herds of yellow earth-moving machines" (122). Though the war in Vietnam was five years past, the culture of war continued to permeate the life and the land of the rural South, much as the culture of World War II persisted into the Cold War decades. The very title of *Indian Country* resonates with the term that the fighting men in Vietnam used for enemy territory.

To the literary tradition that mourns the peoples and the lands lost to modernity, Matthiessen adds a layer of rhetoric from the tradition of the jeremiad, a public display of outrage that hearkens back to the style of the biblical prophet Jeremiah. It is a hallmark of American social criticism—the most famous study of which, *The American Jeremiad* by Sacvan Bercovitch, was published at the height of the Tellico controversy, in 1978. All of us literary types read the book in grad school. I recognized almost immediately that the jeremiad finds a strong outlet in literary environmentalism, from John Muir to Edward Abbey, and here it was in Matthiessen's essay. Angrily anticipating the objection that the Tellico Dam has already been completed by the time he writes so it's too late to waste the investment, Matthiessen answers with a flourish of Abbey-esque rhetoric: "Let them dynamite the dam and drain the valley. Let the concrete ruin stand as a monument, not to short-sightedness and greed but to the wise redress of a national calamity; as a symbol and deterrent, the ruin would more than justify the wasted money" (124–25). "If the Cherokee River is not restored," Matthiessen concludes, "the 'strong water' will be transformed into *ama huli wotshi*, or 'dead water,' the floor of glass of the old prophecy through which the faces of the ancestors will appear, like pale dead leaves seen dimly through black ice" (125).

In the epilogue appended to the essay when it was published in *Indian Country,* he reveals that the elders Ammoneta and Lloyd Sequoyah, "the last Cherokee medicine men to be born into their ancient tradition," both died in 1981, and he hints that their passing fulfills Ammoneta's own prophecy, preserved in the affidavits, that "his own world would come to an end" with the destruction of the Tellico valley by water (126).

❧ Another decade and a half would pass before Linda Ely, a graduate student of mine, also a native of Appalachia, would direct my attention to another essay about Tellico, this one entitled "Arrow of Warning and Hope," by the Cherokee poet and storyteller Marilou Awiakta. Awiakta based the essay on articles she wrote for Southern newspapers and finally published it as a retrospective chapter in her 1993 book, *Selu: Seeking the Corn-Mother's Wisdom.* Awiakta's words had a soothing effect on my guilt for overlooking the Cherokee issue back in the late seventies. She begins with the story of how she nearly missed it herself. She was living in Memphis at the time and did not realize that the ancient region of Chota was threatened by the TVA project until the spring of 1978, when a friend from east Tennessee alerted her, only a year and half before the project was forced to its grim completion. "I thought the controversy was about the snail darter," she writes. "I was stunned. Angry. How could such a momentous issue go unnoticed by the national media? And even the Memphis media?" (43). What she ultimately learned was that it was not the Eastern Cherokees who were remiss or late in their legal actions, as the opposition suggested, but rather the news coverage of their claims. They had been ignored by the national press since the 1960s, as surely as they were dismissed by the courts and bulldozed by the politicians in the 1970s.

Awiakta connects the Tellico project with the infamous Trail of Tears, the "removal" of the Southeastern tribes to reservations in the West. I see the removal as the very model for federal land grabs in the Appalachian South (and elsewhere, as in the Southwest, where history would witness the "Long Walk" of the Navajos and the nationalizing of the old Spanish land grants in the nineteenth century, then the twentieth-century impoundment of land for military reservations like the White Sands Missile Range, a story told with epic drama by Ed Abbey in his novel *Fire on the Mountain*). Awiakta writes that, for the Eastern Band, "the Trail of Tears was not only a vivid memory" but "an old pattern repeating in the Tellico Dam controversy." As one young Cherokee told her, "Tellico is the Removal all over again. First our ancestors. Then our history. Then us" (*Selu* 44). As Awiakta puts it, "Tellico had become a Lake of Tears" (61); "I felt America heading West, the direction of death and destruction: the Darkening Land" (54). She might have added that the string of broken treaties that figures into the history of nearly all the Indian nations in America also prefigures the undercutting of the Endangered Species Act in the name of economic progress.

Published in the early nineties, the book version of Awiakta's essay closes on a positive note. No doubt, the dam was completed over the protests of many voices. No doubt, the Cherokee story was slow in coming forth and never got a full hearing. But the protest and the literature that came of it had an effect. "The seven-state bureaucracy of TVA, like a giant ocean liner, slowly altered its course of the previous two decades," she writes. "Instead of being negligent of the environment, the agency became its bellwether.... [A] nuclear project was scrapped, with a loss of sunk costs many times greater than what it would have cost to drop the Tellico project. The power of the agency scaled down to a size more compatible with the land and its people" (*Selu* 61–62).

While the nuclear record of TVA is more extensive and more conflicted than this statement suggests, my own experience at the time bears out the general claim about the growing environmental conscience of the agency. When my coauthor (and wife) Jackie Palmer and I were completing work on our book *Ecospeak: Rhetoric and Environmental Politics in America* in 1988–89, she was codirecting an environmental education center in Memphis, funded by TVA. Even before the Tellico Dam was completed, the new TVA administration, headed by David Freeman, had admitted that the project was a mistake. It was the last dam built by TVA.

In this light, the writings of Awiakta and Matthiessen, like the Cherokee lawsuits, appear not as throwbacks to a lost way of life but as harbingers of the new that speak for the future—for the burgeoning movements of sustainability and environmental justice. Even so, Awiakta and Matthiessen certainly cannot have been happy with the short-term results of their resistance—the destruction of the valley of the Little T and the drowning of the impounded land and history of Chota beneath the dead water of Tellico, the Lake of Tears. And even after the passing of what the legal activist Zygmunt Plater called "the old TVA," the "new TVA" had what seems in retrospect the insensitivity to name a new nuclear facility the Sequoyah Plant. It was built in 1981, the same year the old Sequoyah brothers of the Eastern Band passed from this earth. Then, after the somewhat surprising recommitment of Pres. George W. Bush's administration to nuclear power, projects that had been mothballed were revitalized, often at tremendous costs.

The process continues. In the summer of 2011, I watched a "Zombie Walk" near the TVA Plaza in Knoxville, protesting the reactivation of a nuclear project in Alabama, one that had been deemed a bad investment a decade earlier. The zombie costumes were a new thing for me, but the political theatrics reminded me of my days in the SCRU Party, and the speeches sounded many of the old themes and brought the prophecies and protests of Tellico to life again. I was amused by the appropriateness of the new style of street theatre (small and poorly attended though it was). What, after all, could be a better image for an issue that won't die than a parade of the Living Dead?

⁂ I guess I've become something of a zombie myself. I've spent half a lifetime pondering my attitude toward the Tellico controversy. Unlike my professor, Bruce Wheeler, who wrote his book and let it go and never, he told me recently, attended the reunions of the old radicals and other folks connected to the Tellico protests, for me, the issue won't die, though my interpretation of it has shifted over the years. I've seen it as a culminating point for the disaffection of young people and poor farmers and Native Americans confronting the military-industrialization of their land—the People of the Snail Darter, I once called the unlikely collective—people endangered by the power plays, the draft, the overwhelming obsession of postwar America with giant technologies, the dominance of urban economies over rural life and of one race over the others, the loss of the opportunity to live close to the land. I've read Tellico into the history of environmental protection that runs from John Muir—"REMEMBER HETCH-HETCHY," said a bumper sticker I saw as late as 2011, commemorating the Alamo of environmental lost causes—down to Wallace Stegner at Dinosaur National Monument, John Graves contemplating the loss of wild stretches of the Brazos River in Texas, Edward Abbey and Earth First! at Glen Canyon, and then, at the turn of the twenty-first century, the campaigns of tribal peoples and peasants in India, southeast Asia, and Latin America against megadams built with foreign financial aid and according to foreign ideals of technological development—the movement known these days in the Global South as "the environmentalism of the poor." I've measured Tellico by the standard of sustainability after learning how the great dams, for all their power production and flood-control prowess (the city of Chattanooga used to disappear under the waters of the Tennessee River every generation or so before TVA solved the problem), are ultimately *unsustainable,* how first the turbines and then the lakes themselves fill with silt and polluted runoff and become useless baths of dead water and ruined land (as the Cherokee prophets foresaw), how the two or three generations of productivity they gave us will be offset by the two or three generations it will take (at least) for the changes in the ecosystem wrought by these giant technologies to be undone and the land restored. As I've been drafting this chapter, the secretary of the interior has been considering a controversial proposal to remove a series of dams on the Klamath River in California and Oregon—in and around the irrigated fields where I went hunting with my dad in his Air Force days—thus restoring the salmon runs and bringing back elements of a seemingly lost way of life for the indigenous peoples in the area.

But, after all these revelations and realizations over the last three decades, I've decided that the deep truth for me comes down to personal history. I feel moved to confess it here, because I worry that nature is in danger of losing its meaning—so that ECOLOGY NOW! will become ECOLOGY THEN—not just because words like *nature* and *environment* are so easy to deconstruct with our sophisticated criticism (and it's true that they are) or because ecological ideology has somehow failed (which it possibly has) but also because as surely as we might fail to bequeath a clean, beautiful, enjoyable, and useful environment to our grandchildren, we may also fail to pass on a sense of place and a passion for nature that has driven some of us to seek refuge and deep meaning in the outdoors. I want my descendants to remember and reclaim the emotions I've felt as I stepped up to the rim of a great canyon or simply smelled the wet dirt of the front yard in early spring. I don't necessarily want everyone to *love* nature. I just want to see some passion, some curiosity, some kind of care.

So here's the real truth of the matter: *I hate the lake.*

The invitation "Let's go to the lake!" used to fill me with dread, disgust, and foreboding. I was late learning to swim (just as I was late learning to read), and I never learned to water ski. My Uncle Charles used to boast that his boat could pull anyone up on skis, but not me. The scene was repeated again and again—with Uncle Charles at Lake Greenwood, with others at Lake Hartwell, Lake Loudoun, Center Hill Lake, Watts Bar Lake. The tension of my less-than-buoyant body would be focused in my hands feverishly gripping a wooden handle on a long rope connected to the fiberglass hull of an open boat with a loud and stinking outboard motor straining to haul my always imperfectly balanced bulk onto the surface of the water atop two thin wooden planks with stirrups pinching my outsized feet (skating never worked with my flat-footed, top-heavy body either, and even cross-country skiing usually involved the unintended hugging of trees). There would be a moment of rising from the water, somebody yelling "bend your knees" or "straighten your back," before I'd find myself plowing face-first through the green water of some bass-scaly, cottonmouth-infested, algae-growth-and-duckweed-clogged, silt-laden former river valley whose pastures had been flooded by TVA or the Army Corps of Engineers or some other agency determined to perpetuate its own budget by convincing fools like me that this sort of thing was fun. I'd finally remember to let go of the rope, float free of the motor's pull, unlatch the recreational shackles, climb into the boat, and watch my friends do tricks and skim over the surface of the lake like water striders on two skis, one ski, bare feet. One guy I knew would ski barefoot, then let go of the rope and bounce along on his butt, like a rock skipping over a wide river in a game of ducks and drakes. Me, I sat in the boat and tried to be inconspicuous as I stared at the bodies of my companions in their swimsuits.

As a kid, I loved a creek. You could see the pebbly bottom, stay connected to the earth as you walked along with the water lapping at your ankles, search for crawfish and snakes and bream in the shallows of living, moving water. *Living water*—the symbol of spiritual life in the story that occurs to the old Baptist layer of my Bible-haunted mind, Jesus with the Samaritan woman at the well of Jacob, their mutual ancestor—"I will give you *living* water," he says, the literal meaning of which is simply water that moves, as from a river or spring, water more likely to be drinkable and fresh; it makes a fine symbol for sustenance, both material and spiritual, in a thirsty desert land like Palestine. But for me, the metaphor favors the creek over the lake. Dams take the life from the water and leave a dead stagnation in the place of a moving stream.

Instead of nervous rides in power boats, as a kid I loved rowing a johnboat or paddling a canoe in a shallow river, like the one at Camp Socareda—the name sounding vaguely Indian but actually a compression of South Carolina Education Association—the "science camp" where I cultivated my affection for the study of insects, frogs, newts, salamanders, and snakes in their natural habitat, only to learn in my college years that this was natural history, not really modern science, which is conducted in stuffy classrooms and fluorescently illuminated labs infused with the indelible stench of formaldehyde or sulfuric compounds. When my parents came to retrieve me at the end of my first session, I begged them to let me stay at science camp an extra week. Surprised but pleased, they readily agreed (my mother maybe glad to have one fewer offspring under foot during summer vacation). The counselors made a pet of me, letting me help with the snake cages and read their personal collections of books and field guides. I kept a notebook on dragonflies that one counselor, a pretty young woman from the local college, asked to keep in the library as a model for future campers. I adored her and gladly said yes. One of the guy counselors schooled me on what counted as the coolest music—certainly not Sonny and Cher (who had the number-one hit "I Got You, Babe"), not even the Beatles, but the Rolling Stones. It was the summer of 1965, and their big hit was "I Can't Get No Satisfaction." We would sing the guitar part as we walked in the woods—*DIRT DIR, dir-dir-dir dir dir dir.*

There was a lake at Socareda. But it was small, its waters gathered behind a low earthen dam and feeding gently back into the stream where we took the boat to gather samples, some of which literally fell into our laps, like the queen snake that dropped out of an overhanging tree into the boat between the legs of one of the counselors, who had the aplomb to get it into a collection bag without capsizing the craft. In the warm afternoons, we would swim out to a small floating dock in the middle of the lake and sun ourselves like turtles on a log, talking about music and school and the parties and sports that awaited us in the fall. That was the only lake I remember fondly from those days. It was an old one, and the forest grew right down to the edge.

Not so the big lakes that supported the play of motorboats and sun-scorched beer drinking and water skiing under the power lines running every which way, carrying hydroelectricity from the turbines to the power grids of the nation—the very symbol of Power, the Machine, the System, the Man. The water looked like nothing more than a perpetually flooded pasture, the edge like a bathtub ring, the rise and fall of the water under the control of the agency operating the spillways at the dam.

There was much to fear from the lake in the imagination of a fast-growing lad. In one story I heard—first at science camp in the darkness of the cabin after lights-out but repeated so often it achieved the status of a rural myth (one variation of which found a literary home in Larry McMurtry's *Lonesome Dove*)—a hapless water skier on a big lake is dragged through a nest of cottonmouth moccasins. The legend—like the murdered body that surfaces from the lake in the dream of the protagonist at the end of James Dickey's novel *Deliverance* (played by Jon Voight in the movie version)—signifies the repressed fear of the unnatural lake and the likely revenge of nature's creatures that lurk just beneath the surface of all the power and superficial fun. (I guess I wasn't alone in hating The Lake.) When the body of the fated skier killed by the cottonmouths is retrieved, the story goes, the poisonous serpents are still hanging desperately and suicidally from the bluish corpse lifted from murky water.

The water was always murky. More serious than the myth of the angry snakes was the real danger posed by the lakes' floors. We were warned never to swim alone or dive deep. It's not like they cleared out a nice smooth bed for the water before they closed the dams. They just flooded the impounded farms and fields, with no regard for the hedgerows, wood lots, rotted barns, and barbed-wire fences. The seriousness of the matter came home to me and my family when a friend from down the street in Greenville, a boy only a year older than me, while taking scuba lessons in a local lake, failed to appear at the surface on schedule. He was apparently caught in the snags and drowned. The Navy divers brought in to search for him never found the body. They said you couldn't see two feet in front of your face down there. It happened when I was fourteen years old.

So I hated the lake. I avoided it; I made excuses. But then I got married right out of undergraduate school and found myself in the company of a new father-in-law who owned a distributorship for freshwater recreational equipment and kept a cabin cruiser on Old Hickory Lake near Nashville (where Johnny and June Carter Cash owned a nice house on a high bluff overlooking the waters, a house memorialized later, after Johnny's death, in a fine song by his daughter, Roseanne Cash). We spent whole weekends out there. I read all of *Walden* on the front deck of the boat. I read Justin Kaplan's then-new biography of Walt Whitman (and felt my spirits lift when I found a citation of my first published article in the endnotes). I watched birds with the good binoculars I found onboard. I got my first clear look at black-crowned night herons, once saw a young bald eagle, and from regular sightings learned to recognize the eastern kingbird, prothonotary warbler, indigo bunting, and other winged jewels of the lakeshore. I went out some days in a small boat and fished for bass with my father-in-law—hooked a northern pike and a couple of hard-fighting smallmouths once in the cold water of a newly dammed lake upriver on the Cumberland from Old Hickory. I saw cottonmouth moccasins coiled in the shade on the muddy banks. But mostly I sat morosely on deck, popping one can of cold beer after another and waiting impatiently to reclaim control of my life.

Ed Abbey's disgust over what Lake Powell did to Glen Canyon rang true though I'd never been to Utah when I first read his rants against the dam, the lake, the project. It wasn't only because of his appeals to the man-versus-nature theme, or the loss of pristine wilderness and the human capacity to feel the wildness within, or his contempt for giant technology and the Great Machine of the state, which he describes so well in his book *Down the River*—"the technological superstate, densely populated, centrally controlled, nuclear-powered, computer-directed, firmly and thoroughly policed" (117). None of the nature I'd ever seen was pristine at all, but I got his point just fine because I hated the lake. The experience of Tellico and my subsequent study made me hate it all the more.

I offer my confession in hopes that readers who are inclined to see environmental activism as the history of a political ideology or some other abstraction will be more inclined to see the human face on that history. It is not only a face red with political anger, placid with the love of nature, or saddened by the loss of the old ones and their worlds. It possesses and expresses a whole palette of emotional colors and moods. The loss of nature-inspired passion in all its variety is the kind of loss I fear the most.

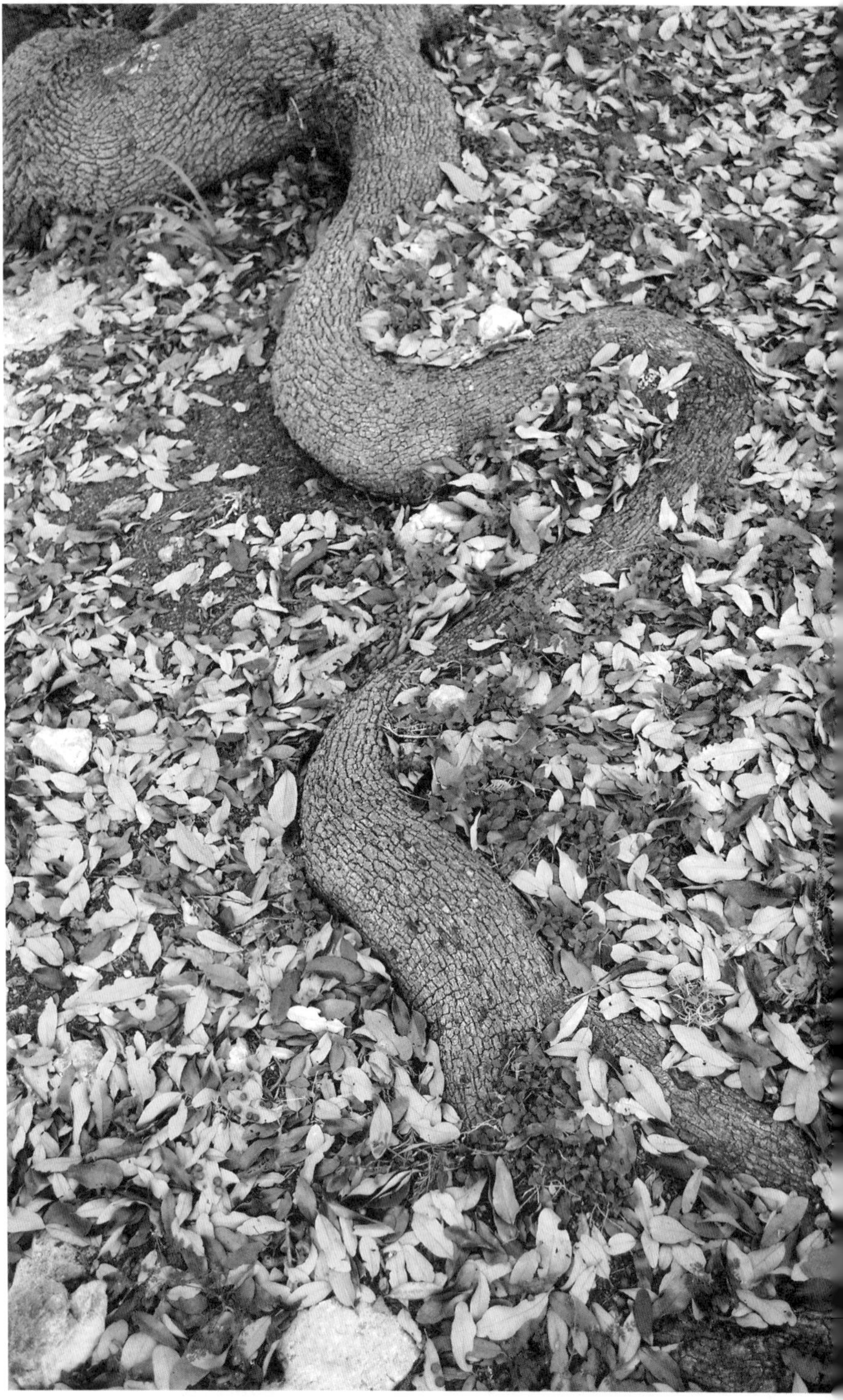

3 Dispelling Déjà Vu, Part One

I felt America heading West, the direction of death and destruction: the Darkening Land.

Marilou Awiakta, *Selu*

In May 2011, I was going through the boxes of Peter Matthiessen's papers collected at the University of Texas, reading material related to the Tellico controversy, when I came upon some yellowed pages of old newsprint that stopped me short. The pages came from a newspaper called *Americans before Columbus,* identified as the monthly publication of the National Indian Youth Council—a group, I figured out later, associated with the Indian Unity Movement and the radical American Indian Movement, or AIM (Matthiessen, *Indian Country* 82). The issue was dated December 1, 1979. The front-page banner headline—"Bury My Heart in the Tellico Valley"—alluded to Dee Brown's famous book, *Bury My Heart at Wounded Knee.* The reference connected the Tellico case to the general history of place-based injustice to Native Americans, in particular the Wounded Knee Massacre of 1890. In this way, it resonated with Marilou Awiakta's image of the "Lake of Tears" that tied Tellico to the historical Trail of Tears. Two columns on page 1 give a history of the project, and the story continues on page 8 with an account of the site's cultural significance for the Cherokees and the failed resistance efforts. Apparently written before the gates of the dam were closed, though published a month afterward, the story ends this way:

> On November 9, the area is scheduled to be flooded. The pierced heart of the Cherokee Nation will be drowned. The dam and the reservoir will be a memorial to greed and folly. All the pleas of the living Cherokees for their rights have gone unheard.
>
> It is popular today for people to go around speaking of the rights of the living and the rights of the unborn, but it should be remembered that the dead have their rights too. ("Bury" 2)

With its claim for the rights of the dead—a traditional domain of reverence in almost every culture and the topic of pending legislation to protect Indian burial sites (resulting finally in the Native American Graves Protection and Repatriation Act of 1990)—the article shows clearly that the Native press had picked up the story of the Cherokees almost completely shunned by the national media up to that point. The preservation of the faded newsprint at the University of Texas indicates that Peter Matthiessen was in close contact with indigenous journalists and activists across the country as he continued the work that would become *Indian Country* and the more controversial book *In the Spirit of Crazy Horse,* the publication of which was delayed for nearly a decade by the threat of lawsuits.

But what stopped me cold was a story that began on the third column, sharing the front page with the Tellico story and fitted underneath the same banner headline—obviously intended as a companion article. The headline was "Churchrock, the Tragedy of Another Three Mile Island." The information contained in the story ultimately found a place in the "Four Corners" chapter of Matthiessen's *Indian Country.* Placed in parentheses, the material on Church Rock interrupts Matthiessen's more general narrative about uranium mining on Indian land and may have been a late addition to the chapter. He must have received the news story from *Americans before Columbus* when the book was nearing completion and decided to include it as a recent example of the trouble with uranium mining on Navajo land. The story is contained in a single paragraph:

> (In addition to the mines and tailings piles, the Church Rock Navajo are also threatened by what the Nuclear Regulatory Commission has called the worst contamination in the history of the nuclear industry: not long after the antinuclear demonstration at Mount Taylor, on July 16, 1979, the dam at a United Nuclear Corporation tailings mill pond gave way near Church Rock, releasing ninety-five million gallons of radioactive water into the Rio Puerco, that once-great, now dead tributary of the Rio Grande. Although the pond had been overfilled, and the dam itself was known to be cracked and fissured, this event got almost no publicity, unlike the spectacular episode at Three Mile Island, Pennsylvania, which reminded the world that a nuclear disaster was "inevitable." In northwestern New Mexico, events have been unspectacular, insidious, and slow, and so far, most of its victims have been Indians—conditions which apparently permit the authorities to ignore a nuclear tragedy that has already occurred.) (302)

A footnote to Matthiessen's chapter connects Church Rock to Tellico as effectively as the front-page banner headline from *Americans before Columbus:* "a federal district court ruling in 1981 (UNC Resources v. Benally) forbids the Indians from suing United Nuclear in Navajo Court for damages or injuries, declaring that the Navajo tribe's exercise of jurisdiction on its own territory conflicted with 'the overriding sovereignty of the United States'" (302–303n). This time, the courts defended not a government agency (TVA) but an allegedly private corporation (United Nuclear) whose primary customer was the US government. If you ever doubted the viability of Pres. Dwight Eisenhower's old term "military-industrial complex," I would recommend a closer look at episodes like the Church Rock incident in the waning years of the Cold War.

Pawing over the old papers in May 2011, then reading the section from *Indian Country* that folded in the information, I recalled a conversation from a month before, when I gave a talk at the University of New Mexico for a symposium on Earth Day. My friend Professor Gary Harrison had said to me, "The story of the Church Rock uranium spill has never really been told." He assumed that I knew what he was talking about because I had been living in New Mexico around the time of the incident, the worst nuclear accident in US history to date. That's where I took my first academic job straight out of graduate school—at New Mexico Tech in Socorro.

But he was wrong. Like most Americans then and now, I'd never heard of the Church Rock disaster. But in the space of a month, as I pursued a relatively casual course of research, mostly related to other matters, it had twice come to my attention.

Déjà vu is what I felt. The sensation that accompanied my reading of Matthiessen's "How to Kill a Valley" back in 1980, when the realization struck that I'd missed the Cherokee involvement in Tellico, rushed back over me thirty years later when I sat reading *Americans before Columbus* and realized that the Navajo plight at Church Rock had also eluded me in the same year, despite my growing awareness in those days of the relationship between social and environmental issues.

Déjà vu suggests more than a mere repetition of experience—the literal translation of "already seen." The phrase hints at the uncanniness of the repeated experience, a creepiness emanating from the edges of consciousness, a glimpse into an alternate reality or a folding of time back on itself. The way déjà vu figures into the 1999 science fiction film *The Matrix* captures it perfectly. The film offers a vision of a future world in which the seeming reality of offices and restaurants and urban life is in fact an illusion projected into the minds of human beings by intelligent machines that have taken over the earth. In truth, humans continue to exist merely as organic sources of energy for the perpetuation of the machine world. The people are kept barely alive in vats that draw off their metabolic energy as the machines pump dreamlike images of an ordinary world into the people's brains. The collective set of images, the mass hallucination, is called *the matrix*. A renegade group of humans has escaped from this perpetual slavery and lives underground, planning a revolt that will free the people and defeat the machines. As this group introduces the nature of the matrix to the hero of the story, the character Neo (played by Keanu Reeves), the experience of déjà vu is said to have a special status. When it happens, Neo is told, it signals something like a glitch in the programming of the matrix, a moment of malfunction that deserves special attention in Neo's ongoing quest to see the code of the matrix for what it is and break the spell of the illusion for all humanity.

I can think of no better allegory for my experience in the Land of Enchantment. I struggled in my first job to hold together the pieces of my life—the new place, the new responsibilities, my relationship with my young wife whom I had taken away from the support of family and old friends. Looking back, I began to wonder if my old habit of seeking refuge in nature from the pressures of life indoors had not contributed to an unwitting illusion that all was well despite hints to the contrary. Had natural beauty become my matrix? Was my fascination with my new home place and the sense that I was living out a fated purpose in a land of promise part of a matrix of denial and disbelief that caused me not only to miss the widening cracks in my personal relationships but also the troubles brewing all around me in the political arena? We nature lovers are fond of belittling our fellow citizens for jamming their awareness and sensitivity to the outer world by plugging into the matrix of indoor electronic stimulation—TV, Internet, video gaming. But are we not also vulnerable, under very different conditions, to the psychology of denial, distraction, and defensiveness?

In summer 2012, beginning a year of research leave from my professorial duties at Texas A&M, I decided to take a hard look at these questions. Jackie and I had bought a little place in Taos, in northern New Mexico, a second home devoted to retreat and reflection for now and for full retirement a few years down the road. Facing déjà vu almost daily—every whiff of sage-scented air, every glimpse of the local birds and animals, every taste of green chili and corn tortillas opening avenues of remembrance—I made a plan to confront the memories, and the lack of memories, head on. I would start by visiting the natural sites that stuck hardest in my recollection of those years at New Mexico Tech, 1980–86, and then test out my impressions with more readings and research into the history of Church Rock and Tellico. My aim was to dispel the discomfort of the déjà vu by weaving the experiences at the haunted edge of consciousness into a coherent narrative, to try out storytelling as an antidote to the three Ds of modern psycho-social life—denial, distraction, and defensiveness—at least in retrospect.

❧ I arrived in Socorro at 11:30 a.m. on August 5, 2012. It wasn't the first time I'd returned in the years since I lived there, but it was the first time I'd purposely tried to reenact my earliest, deepest, and most personal connections to the Southwestern earth. In the next twenty-four hours, I planned to visit three sites—Water Canyon Park in the Cibola National Forest, the Bosque del Apache National Wildlife Preserve, and the ditch bank just west of town—all on public land.

I filled the car with gas and headed straight for Water Canyon, west on Highway 60, in the nearby Magdalena Mountains. Within thirty minutes I was out of the car and searching for the trailhead to the path that leads up and over the mesa south of the canyon from the picnic area. The picnic area had shrunk to a couple of tables, a basic outhouse for restrooms, and a group shelter. The campground that used to be there had moved a little ways to the north.

The trail was nowhere in sight. The reconfiguration of the campground/picnic area and the roads leading in and out had me confused. But, convinced that the trail was somewhere nearby, I put on my daypack, grabbed my stick, and started walking up the new road toward Langmuir Lab, where physics professors from New Mexico Tech study thunderstorms in the thin air at 10,000 feet on the ridge near the summit of South Baldy Mountain. My former student, the science writer Joe Chew, now working at the Lawrence Berkeley National Laboratory, wrote a history of Langmuir years ago.

Not far up the road I met a young man standing by a truck, drinking from a water bottle. A mountain bike rested on the ground beside him. I said hello and asked directions. "There used to be a trail up Water Canyon Mesa and over to South Canyon. It started around here somewhere. Do you know it?"

He told me that he did know it, that the forest service had closed the trail for a while to protect falcon-nesting on the cliffs and made a new trail up the road about a half mile. "But you can still find your way along the old trail, turn right at the top, and make a loop with the new trail if you want. Works great." He pointed to the east. "The old trail starts right over there, just past that wash."

"Can I do it?"

He cut the Gordian knot of my two implied questions—"Can I actually make it up the old trail?" and "Is it legal?"—by glancing over at his bike. "I'm going to do it."

"Okay, then, thanks."

I headed the way he pointed, found what appeared to be the trail, and soon came to an old-fashioned gate in a barbed-wire fence, the cedar shaft on one end hooked under a loop of wire on a fixed post. I remembered these from my uncle's dairy farm. I opened the gate and closed it behind me, like a good cowhand.

Now I was on the old mesa trail for sure, ascending quickly from the canyon floor, the desert landscape opening out to the east before my eyes. The Sierra Ladrones—a single high peak in a compressed range of mountains—rose craggy and impressive on the horizon. As I climbed in the ninety-degree heat on the sunny mesa side, I was quickly drenched with sweat—and memories.

Water Canyon was the place my new colleagues directed my wife and me to begin our hiking adventures when we moved from Tennessee to New Mexico in 1980. We'd been married five and a half years by then, all the time I'd been in graduate school. I'd given her a pair of hiking boots on our first anniversary so she could join DeWolfe Miller and me on our rambles in the Smokies. It wasn't the most romantic gift—she let me know—but it got her started on what became a passion. By the time we discovered the trail at Water Canyon, she was a seasoned hiker and had expanded her work as a university press editor to include freelance editing of hiking guides and outdoor books. (She was much needed in this field. An author of a popular book on back-country cooking once told her, "I'm just a writer. I don't know nothing about grammar.") The mesa trail became our go-to hike, the place we'd bring visitors from back East who only had a few days in town. With the deep canyons and impressive peaks of the Magdalenas in sight, it offered quick relief from the somewhat "squalid" townscape (her word) and the "quaint" college campus (her mother's word).

I almost literally stumbled over the slag heaps of the abandoned mine, which used to offer something authentically "Western" to show our visitors. I'd forgotten about it. Barbed wire and old timbers stretched across the opening into the canyon wall. A rusty sign said "Danger!" and "¡Peligro!" Looking at the mine, which is on a little side trail, I realized that I'd wandered off the main track. I fumbled around on the faint game trails in the intermittent shade of stunted ponderosa pines and juniper-oak scrub on the rocky hillside until I found my way back to the old trail. The higher I got, the rockier it became. It wasn't this way before, I was thinking, but then it occurred to me that, since it'd been closed, the cliffs had crumbled and small rockslides had worked to reclaim the path, obscuring it in places and making the walking harder than it used to be. Sharp red chunks of sandstone tormented my feet (shod only in running shoes, since I didn't bring my boots with me). The trail was still there for the most part, though—like an old friend you haven't seen for twenty-five years, the lines of the face worn with age, not as clearly defined, but still recognizable and fully capable of stirring the heart.

The guy with the mountain bike came up behind me, and I stepped aside to let him pass, thanking him again for the directions. I watched him get on and off his bike to negotiate the rocky path and the intrusions of scrub oak until he disappeared in low gear around a turn. He was the last person I saw the rest of the day at Water Canyon.

It's always been a remote place that accommodates silent and solitary retreat. Once I lost a white water bottle in the snow on a winter hike and found it after the spring thaw in the middle of the trail, so few feet and hands had passed the spot. On some of my visits, the silence was broken only by the call of the acorn woodpecker or the cry of a soaring hawk by day, the hoot of an owl at dusk, the singing of the coyotes or the scream of a big cat in the deep dark of night, the whisper of an intimate companion. The place is still remote and relatively deserted, quieter than anything I know in my suburban life back in Texas, where constant traffic and power tools craze the air of the micro-industrial neighborhood. Water Canyon welcomes the ear-sore pilgrim.

In the bright sun, I watched the cliffs of the canyon wall for falcons, but none appeared, only ravens and vultures playing on the thermals and one small hawk calling "*kee kee kee.*" I checked the app with the birdcalls on my smart phone (one of my favorite concessions to high technology) and decided it might be a sharp-shinned hawk. It was certainly not a peregrine.

I pressed on through a virtual forest of waist-high gray and gambel oaks. I recalled that not everyone we brought on this hike appreciated the stark beauty of the crumbly sheer cliffs and the trees fighting for a foothold. A forester friend of mine from Tennessee said, "It's nice, but I would miss the woods." We were standing on the mesa top in the parklike shade of the tall ponderosa pines.

I said, "What do you call this?"

"Nice, but not my kind of woods," he said.

He preferred the wet density of the Smokies and the swampy pinewoods of the Eastern lowlands—places where, in my profession, I had failed to gain a foothold, though I tried. I applied for more than fifty jobs in my search for work, ranging as far away as Alaska, but mostly concentrated in my Southeastern homeland. At the end of the search, I found myself out here, like the scrub oaks and drought-resistant pines, looking for livelihood in the desert hills of the high plains.

As I reached the ridgeline, I was breathing hard but felt the grin form on my face when I saw the old trail marker at the top—the words "Mesa Trail 13" barely legible on the weathered-gray wooden sign, cracked and ragged with time, but holding firm in its old place and, unlike a number of trail markers I'd seen recently on the lands of the understaffed national forests, still standing upright.

I looked once more at the view behind me to the northeast, the expansive desert with the jagged mountains lifting their heads into blue air, then struck out onto the soothingly soft footing of the trail cushioned by pine needles. The place was the same as ever, but then not. The lightning-blasted alligator junipers were there, but fire and drought seemed to have diminished the size and number of the ponderosas. I saw no sign of bark beetles, but the forest was definitely thinner. Even so, the shade was nice enough, and memory flourished. Once on this part of the trail, I found a little pile of rabbit jawbones at the foot of a tall pine and took one back for my colleague in biology to identify. He told me they were probably spit out or coughed up by a great horned owl, the one part of the prey it could not swallow. Another time, I saw the abandoned kill of a mountain lion—the dismembered leg of a mule deer fawn, long scratch marks down each side, quite fresh—lying directly in my path. I felt the eyes of the predator on me though I never saw or heard the beast. It was the first of many times in the silent woods of the Southwest that I felt the presence of the thing that sees you that you cannot see.

On this day's hike, I saw nothing more threatening than bear scat—back down in the oak thickets—relatively fresh but not pressingly so. I didn't feel the slight chill of fear I've known before in deserted places like this or the itch of the hair standing up on the back of my neck. Maybe I don't scare as easily at my age, or maybe a quarter of a century and many wildlife encounters have left me a little numb.

I sat on a log and ate an apple. The first time I brought Jackie up here with me, probably in the fall of 1985 or spring of '86, we ate apples and fed the cores to my spitz Sissy, short-haired for her breed and white as snow, the best running and hiking dog I ever knew. I still had the occasional care of her after my divorce while my first wife was getting her new life sorted out. Jackie was amused that Sissy would eat apple cores. She would eat anything I ate. Once I was munching on chips, a favorite snack of hers, at the kitchen table, and she was sitting at my feet, making the case for sharing with her deep brown eyes. I decided I would break her of begging once and for all and dipped the chip in some hot salsa before I gave it to her. The plan failed. She loved it so well that she learned to recognize the jar whenever I got it out of the refrigerator.

Now I was walking alone except for the company of my memories. It was probably only the second or third time I'd walked this trail by myself. The first was sometime in 1984 when my marriage was coming undone. That's the time I saw the lion sign.

I strolled over to South Canyon, enjoying the quiet that's like none I've ever known. I never found the new trail to make the loop. But it seemed oddly appropriate that I was bound to the old trail. After a couple of hours out (about twice as long as it used to take me to walk that far), I turned back and retraced my way. I skidded a few times in the loose rock of the old trail but, with the help of my stick, managed to stay upright.

When I got back to the car, I drove up the "primitive road" toward Langmuir Lab ("not suitable for passenger vehicles," the sign said, but the road, at least at the lower end, was better than many of the neighborhood avenues I'd been driving in Taos all summer). A little less than half a mile up, I found the new trailhead, just as the mountain biker had promised. A nice new sign bestowed the venerable name: "Mesa Trail 13." I said to myself that I'd come back later and go that way, perhaps with Myrth. Or maybe she'd have to walk it on her own in memory of the stories I've told her. Only time would tell.

⁂ I got back to Socorro around 4:00 p.m. It was ninety-five degrees, and the searing heat of the high desert hit me full force when I got out of the car. I always liked that feeling. It's like the driest sauna. When I lived in Socorro, the average rainfall was seven inches a year. It's up to ten these days, but you would never have known it on the afternoon of my return.

I checked in at the motel, showered, went for a quick meal at a café I remembered called El Sombrero, and headed down to the Bosque for the last two hours of the day, the best time for the birds and animals to be out except for early morning—and I had other plans for the morning. On the twenty-mile drive south, through the villages of Luis Lopez and San Antonio, I considered my history with the Bosque. The story actually begins in the mid-1970s, the time I almost abandoned my casual birdwatching and became a full-tilt birder with the life list, research profile, good equipment, and obsessive hunt for the rare and collectible view of that bird-I've-never-seen.

It happened on hallowed ground. That's the way I had come to feel about Hilton Head at the time, after the place had become infused with a decade of family memories. In December 1974, I was hoping to add to that heritage by honeymooning with my young wife in the house that Mom and Dad had built in the development called Port Royal Plantation. Also an English major, she'd graduated from Tennessee one semester after me. I had begun my graduate work in the fall while she had taken a part-time job at the university press, which she was able to expand into full-time work beginning in January after her graduation and our December wedding and honeymoon. The staff there loved her. Not only did she have a keen wit, charming demeanor, and clear devotion to hard work, she had an eye for detail, knew the English language inside and out, and was exacting in her work—the perfect editor—and a born birder.

I shouldn't have been surprised when what had been a hobby and cherished pastime for me became for her a study and an area of expertise. Everything I introduced her to went that way. I bought her a pair of hiking boots, and she took up the writing and editing of outdoor guides. I got her to jog with me and she ended up a race-runner. I was the one pursuing the PhD, but she was the one with the natural hunger for deep knowledge and the drive of a true expert. When I began to show her the sandpipers and shorebirds, the egrets and herons, the winter warblers and sparrows, she started marking the dates of sightings in the index of the bird book we bought together on a shopping spree in Savannah, the same time we bought a big book of Audubon prints on sale, which I keep to this day. We made our first entries in the bird book at Hilton Head. To tell the truth, I had no idea there were so many different kinds of gulls and terns over the water and sandpipers and plovers on the beach. I began to look with different eyes.

Back in Knoxville, we rented a little house out in the country in what turned out to be a despicable neighborhood. But the birding was good. We put a crude feeder on the fence behind the house that separated us from a wood lot—just a flat board nailed to the fence post outside our bedroom window—and spent hours learning the birds of the mixed woods and hills of east Tennessee. The triplets of the Carolina wren and somber whistling of the white-throated sparrow woke us in the mornings. The purple finches and cardinals added a splash of color to the drab winter woods. And occasionally we got a fine surprise. A quick check of the feeder could show us an evening grosbeak or some other new bird for the life list. Once we saw a yellow-billed cuckoo using our feeder plank for a launching pad to feed on tent caterpillars. We learned to recognize its strange croaky call that was supposed to be a harbinger of summer rain. A friend told us that the local people called the cuckoo the rain crow.

When we moved to New Mexico in 1980, we bought a book on Western birds and started marking a new index. The western tanager with its striking red-orange face and canary yellow body, the flickers with shafts of red instead of yellow in their wing feathers, the burrowing owls, prairie and peregrine falcons, the whimsical roadrunner—we marked them all down.

The birding and the hiking were probably the best parts of our new life. Otherwise we were struggling. She never liked our house; it lacked character, being brick and not adobe; it was small and felt cramped at times. I had trouble settling down at the little college where I worked; my research interests were hard to maintain with the heavy course load and meager library; most of my colleagues were geologists and physicists, not humanities scholars like me. She couldn't get enough work in her freelance business and began to cultivate an old interest in mathematics, taking a course here and there at the school until she finally earned a second bachelor's degree and began to think about graduate school, which of course would take her away from our little town. In short, the marriage was on the skids. You've heard it all before. I was one of some 60 percent of married Americans in my age group in those times—unhappy and heading for divorce.

As with the old days in Oregon when I was having trouble learning to read and adjusting to a new place, things were easier outdoors. At least once a week, sometimes twice, sometimes with my wife, more and more frequently alone, I drove the twenty miles south to the Bosque. Then as now, it was a big wildlife preserve on the Rio Grande, a broad marshland with an extensive cottonwood grove. The place was called the Bosque del Apache because legend says it was a favorite camping ground for hunting parties of Indians from the mountains in the south. It was perfect for birding year round but glorious in the winter when snow geese and sandhill cranes flocked there, filling the air with their honking chatter and covering the fields and marshes like a living snowfall. *Audubon* magazine featured the Bosque in the first issue published after we moved to New Mexico in 1980. The magazine's cover showed a gray sky swirling with snow geese. The feature article explained the experiments that the naturalists at the preserve were carrying out on one endangered species, the whooping crane.

During that lonely time, the Bosque was a place where my memories of Oregon and the Carolina coast could live again among slow-moving shorebirds—the avocets, ducks, herons, and stilts, and the predators who rivaled them in beauty and exceeded their power—the bald eagle, peregrine falcon, marsh hawk, and osprey. Once I followed a coyote along a nature trail and looked into the brush just in time to see its den full of pups. I saw a porcupine climbing a tree to eat soft seeds in the spring and a bittern swaying its long neck and beak in imitation of the windy reeds that surrounded it, camouflaging its brown streaked body. Once I glimpsed a big cat—either a large bobcat or a mountain lion—watching me from the brush, only to disappear in the blink of an eye when it saw me looking back.

I had a friend who lived on a ranch near the preserve. During one of my most trying times, she noticed that my car passed by almost every day on the way to the Bosque. "Are you watching some special bird or something?" she asked. I can't remember exactly what evasive thing I said, but what I didn't say was that I went to the Bosque to escape my own unraveling nest.

The winter of 1983–84, the last winter I spent in my first marriage, I followed every movement of the geese and cranes as if my fate were tied to them. There were a few whooping cranes still in the flock, among the most endangered birds in the world. Naturalists from New Mexico were working with scientists from Canada, where the birds summered, putting whooping crane eggs in the nests of the more populous and vigorous sandhill cranes. The whoopers from the far north generally wintered on the Gulf Coast in Texas (not far from the place I would settle in the next decade), but the sandhill population divided, with some going to Texas and some coming to the Bosque. The experimental group of whoopers, hatched from the eggs in the sandhill nests and socialized among the westward-trending sandhills, came to New Mexico. The hope was that these pioneering misfits would breed and start a new flock of whooping cranes.

The experiment seemed to be working for a while. There were about seven adult whoopers when I first started visiting the Bosque. Startlingly tall and white with sharp black markings, they stood stately in the fields among their gray-feathered, red-faced cousins, the sandhills. And there were always a few mottled orange and white juvenile whoopers. But the numbers were declining during my fateful year; I saw only three adults and one juvenile in the great milling crowds of sandhills. As I watched the cranes head north during the spring of 1984, my faith in my way of life seemed as thin as the hope of the flock that rested on the sloping back of that single young whooper.

I had gone from identifying birds to identifying with birds. The crane became a kind of totem for me, along with other endangered species—the little snail darter in the Tennessee River, the sea turtle of the Carolina coastline. My attraction to wildlife protection and to environmentalism, probably like that of many people in my generation, grew deeper from personal loss and disorientation. I wonder if all environmentalists begin as war orphans, or war-scarred vets like Doug Peacock with his grizzlies, or divorcees.

One thing my wife took with her when she left for graduate school was the bird books with the marked indexes, both volumes, East and West. We lost contact, but I know she kept up the birding. A mutual friend showed me a picture of her several years later, out on the West Coast. It was a profile shot, and she looked good, had her hair cut short. Her eye was pressed to the lens of a birding scope set up on a rocky Pacific shore.

On my return these many years later, I found myself alone in the Bosque, just as I was on the trail at Water Canyon earlier—the first time I ever remember being the only car on the driving tours. I got it. It was the down season for birding. In fall and winter and early spring, the cars will line up to view the thousands of cranes and snow geese, the wintering hawks and eagles and falcons, the scores of ducks. But on this day I saw mainly memories and a few old familiars: a covey of gambel quail flushed; a roadrunner dashed ahead of me to break my reverie; a double flash of blue light resolved into a pair of indigo buntings, which I first saw near the big lakes in Tennessee; a solitary sandpiper sounded like a messenger from the coast; floating by on a wide pond was the long-necked western grebe, which I've also seen on Klamath Lake in Oregon; nighthawks chased mosquitoes in the swampy air near the cottonwood bosque, a stunned specimen of which I once saw huddled on a low wall in the magnolia shade outside the old graduate library in Knoxville; and a small group of bachelor wild turkeys gleamed red-gold in the late sun, recalling the first one I ever saw crossing the road near my mother's girlhood home at Edgefield, South Carolina, on the way to visit my grandmother in Augusta, a solitary driver then as now, the birds capturing my attention, pulling me out of my inward dreaminess to become one with my memories.

❧ Water Canyon and the Bosque were the places I went to break the routine of work and domestic life. During the hard times, I visited the Bosque so often that it almost became a routine, like the practice of the field biologist who records minute seasonal variations of movements, growth, and behavioral adjustment of animals and plants. Both places became ritualized retreats for me, no doubt.

But the ditch bank west of town was different because I went there almost every day. It became the prototype of my daily walk, gradually becoming a morning routine until it achieved ritual status, a regular activity without which my life would have seemed incomplete. I would go out for a run or a walk, then write before I went to the office. My daughter, who was born not long after I left Socorro, doesn't remember a time during her girlhood that she didn't wake up to find me sitting at my desk, writing in my notebook or tapping the keyboard. When she was a baby, early morning was the only time I could count on her being asleep—she was a restless child, just like her old man—so I formalized my ritual and began rising at 5:00 a.m. to make sure there was time to write and run. I've changed places, moved around, taken vacations, switched jobs, slowed down from running to walking, but the morning outing, usually followed or accompanied by writing, has been a constant.

I accessed the ditch bank directly from my neighborhood, just walked out the front door of my house on Mustang Drive and was in full stride within ten minutes. The ditch bank was part of the flood control system built between the steep slopes of Socorro Peak and the river bottoms where the town and the farm lands lay in the rift valley of the Rio Grande. The rift presents a lazy opening in the southern high plains, wider than it is in the north around the Taos Box and the Gorge Bridge, where it digs eight hundred feet into the sage-covered plateau. By Eastern standards, the farmland in the Rio Grande valley at Socorro is still a narrow belt of green in a red-rock desert. It may lack the drama of the Gorge country, but with the almost imperceptibly steady sloping on either side of the river, it sometimes offers more drama than most folks care to experience. Before the flood control system was built, flash floods plagued the town. And they could still cause problems when I moved there in 1980. My first semester at New Mexico Tech, a rare September downpour washed out a bridge just south of town on the frontage road to I-25. The rushing waters carried away the car of a young woman who couldn't see the damage to the bridge because of the heavy rainfall. She drove over the ledge of the usually dry arroyo, filled suddenly with a driving stream, and was drowned. The waters were diverted to that arroyo by the dikes and ditches that saved the town. The loss of the bridge and the hapless driver showed that the system was less than perfect and could not accommodate a freak storm. But most times, the ditches worked well enough.

Along each bank-top runs a one-lane, dirt-and-gravel road like a dry ridge rising ten to twenty feet above the desert floor. The roads make a fine trail for joggers and dog-walkers in the early mornings and late afternoons when the shadows ease the intensity of the parching sun. Jogging the ditch bank first thing in the morning, then hurrying in to record my thoughts before going to class, became my habit, not as formalized or predictable, not as disciplined (or compulsive) as in later years, but the foundations were laid for my lifelong ritual on that ditch bank with the mountains to the west glowing pink with the sun rising over the mesas to the east and, in between, the green shade of the river valley whose cottonwoods turned to gold in the autumn and gray-green in the winter, providing a striking contrast to the reds and earth tones of the rocky land on either side.

I rose before my wife, then as now, and in those days took my dog Sissy along. We'd nearly always see a roadrunner and several jackrabbits. The long-legged and antenna-eared hares seemed to take an evil pleasure in drawing chase from Sissy, maybe as practice for their more serious nightly combat with the coyotes, who hunted them in packs and had a better chance of bringing one down. They'd let Sissy get within ten feet, then fire up the after-burners and leave her panting with disappointment. But she never seemed to tire of the game and usually ran two miles to every one of mine and twice as fast on average.

We got up to the ditch bank from the end of my street. Mustang Drive was in a small and undistinguished housing development southwest of New Mexico Tech. Despite the faux-Western name of the street, the houses were generic Americana, brick and close together, separated by privacy fences. Though my wife was never happy with the house, it was easy to maintain and offered good access to the town and college as well as the ditch bank. Everything was no more than a fifteen-minute walk away. It was hardly worth the trouble to crank up the car or even ride the bike—too many chances for a flat on the bike tire from the rock-hard goat-head thorns that thrive in that part of the world.

On the ditch bank, I could enjoy the sun playing over the mountain and valley, catch sight of the best birds around the town, smell the strong scent of the greasewood (creosote) bushes, and watch the cactus and yucca bloom and grow. I learned I could hold a short paragraph in my head or an outline, but not much more. It would take years for me to let go of trying to compose actual sentences and just let the ideas and images flow. In either case, when I sat down to write, still wet with morning sweat, the flood of language was like no other time of day. When I returned to my writing in the afternoon after classes, usually working in the little computer lab down the hall from my office in Kramer Hall (still the best office I ever had, plenty of natural light and roomy enough for a sofa and easy chair that didn't fit in the house), I mainly worked at typing up and editing the morning's burst of creativity. My first book and first essays in major journals like *College English* and *American Literature* came out of this emerging ritual.

The morning jog and the writing continued to sustain me through my divorce and stayed with me when Jackie and I threw in together in 1985. We had to give away her parrot, I'm sorry to say, a bird that had been with her since her Peace Corps years in Belize, because I woke him too early and set him squawking like a banshee. My ritual could never have survived with him in the house. He found a better home, believe me, with the young son of our departmental secretary. Suffering from a heart condition, the boy loved animals and merrily squawked along with Charlie, who (I like to think) gave the boy's sick heart a boost. Whatever the cause, the lad lived to adulthood and thrived, as did Charlie, who died only a few years ago. He might not have lasted so long as my roommate.

The jogging helped with another issue, too. I had begun to develop a problem with alcohol—the bane of small-town academicians. Before I gave it up altogether, with Jackie's support, I could sweat out the poisons and clear my head, breathing in the saunalike atmosphere of early-morning Socorro. It was good therapy—and bad, since it masked the depth of my alcohol dependency by keeping me sober and clean and healthy the best part of every day. I didn't realize the depth of my addiction until just before leaving Socorro.

The day of my return, August 6, 2012, twenty-six summers after I left the town, I set out at first light for the old ditch bank. I was farther away than I used to be, lodged in a motel on California Street, but still it was just an easy mile and a half to my destination. I took Bullock Street to the college campus, skirted around its northern edge, and followed Canyon Road west through the golf course—the green grasses fed by the reliable springs that gave the town its name, the waters that succored the Spanish thirsting from their march up the Jornado del Muerto more than three centuries ago. The springs were known long before the Spaniards arrived by the Indians who lived there and first welcomed the newcomers, then drove them away during the Pueblo Revolt.

I made it to the ditch bank just as the sun rose over the mesas east of the river. Glowing in the west was Socorro Peak—or M Mountain as it's called locally because of the M painted on the crest by New Mexico Tech students every year—representing the old name of the school, New Mexico School of Mines, or just New Mexico Mines. Desert cottontails and gambel quail took the place of the roadrunners and jackrabbits of the past, reminding me that, like people in their societies, nature has its different ages and shifting populations. I wondered if it has memories, too—I've heard that it does, a PBS special reporting that crows, for example, have memories that span generations—or if the old tracks and decaying fur and bones and feathers of the former inhabitants must suffice as long as they last, like the corruptible human memory that holds just so much and only for so long. I got a call from my sister Belle the night before my walk. She said that Dad had been hospitalized again. It was hard to know what was wrong because his dementia has progressed so far that he couldn't say what hurt and how bad. Now we become his memory, as our children will remember for us. And maybe, as I once read in some book of metaphysical speculations years ago, people are the consciousness of nature, or even the whole universe, so that memory is part of our business, our place in the cosmos. We are the part of nature that remembers. Then again, I thought as I walked into the sunrise, the idea seems like a sensitive, New Age version of the same old arrogance that puts people one notch below God and the angels, above the alleged ignorance of the cottontails and quail with their meaningful-seeming twitches and skitters, the coyotes who leave their scat on this one-lane road and sing in the Socorro night, the rabbit bush just coming into eloquent yellow bloom, the rocks red and yellow and copper blue that tell the tales of ages before humanity ever blinked into existence—and, like the buzzing insects and stiff grasses of this place, would likely survive a global thermonuclear war that would wipe all memory of humanity from the face of the earth forever.

I passed the old cemetery where I once attended a funeral for my secretary's husband, a war veteran and victim of lung cancer. The local chapter of the VFW came out and did the ceremony. The playing of taps on a single bugle in the dry air and the snapping of the rifles' salute in that desert graveyard with no grass but only gravel to cover the graves and the wind whistling through the cactus and yuccas made a sound unspeakably forlorn. Now the doves cooed wildly—not mourning doves, as in former days, but white-wings moved up from the south a notch, like all the birds across North America, adjusting to a warmer climate.

I had trouble finding the old outlet I used to take to Mustang Drive and had to skid down the loose dirt of a hill to walk back by my former residence. The dogs in somebody's backyard barked at me, knowing I was a stranger.

Then finally there it was, 118 Mustang Drive. The dryland gardens that two old hippies put in for us back in 1980, using only native plants (probably obtained illegally from BLM lands or the national forests), had flourished, requiring no watering and little care. The little rock-lined canal system used to direct the water around the house from the sloping front yard during the late-August monsoons—our personal flood control system—had held nicely. The greasewood had spread. The piñon and yucca palm had reached their mature heights. The ocotillos were twelve feet high and blooming beautifully, the tips of their long arms glowing red like firebrands.

I bought my wife's share of the house but lost the dog in the divorce. Sissy is long since dead, and strangers live in the house. But I'm still property-rich and cash-poor, and I can still walk the old ditch bank if I choose. Some things remain, for a while at least.

❧ Two hours after my walk on the ditch bank, I drove out of town by the same route I used when I left Socorro with Jackie, then my wife of one year, six months pregnant, in summer 1986—east on US 380 toward Roswell with Texas on the far horizon.

But this time I didn't get very far. Just past where I crossed the waters of the Rio Grande (nearly depleted at this point from upstream irrigation), on the northern edge of the Bosque del Apache, I saw a roadblock ahead with trucks and cars pulled to the side. I supposed it was an ad hoc Border Patrol checkpoint: business as usual in the Southwest, the focal point of the nation's immigration hysteria. As I approached, though, I saw that the man stopping me was a dark-skinned US Navy police officer, maybe Hispanic, though he wore no nametag and had no discernible accent.

"Hello, sir," he said. "Sorry for the inconvenience, but we've had to close the road for another hour or so. We're doing some missile testing."

Then I remembered what I always worked hard to forget when driving this way. I had come abreast of the White Sands Missile Range. I was only a few air miles from the place where (arguably) World War II ended and the Cold War began: Trinity Site, where Dr. Robert Oppenheimer, Gen. Leslie Groves, and their colleagues in the Manhattan Project came down from Los Alamos to test the first atom bomb. Oppenheimer saw the great flash and quoted the Hindu god Vishnu from the *Bhagavad Gita*: "Now I am become death, the destroyer of worlds."

Sitting in my car in that place, I was thinking, "You have an area of land impounded here the size of Massachusetts and you still need to close a US highway for testing? Yeah, right. Something must have gone wrong. One got away from you." But I remembered my shaggy beard and scruffy profile and the state of affairs in post-9/11 America and just said, "Well, that puts a kink in my travel plans."

"Sorry, sir," he said, then pointed to the pull-off on the side of the road. Several eighteen-wheelers and a few cars waited in line. "You can wait with the others if you like or come back in an hour or so."

"Okay," I said and made a U-turn. I thought briefly about spending another hour at the Bosque. Then I realized that, at this time of day, there wouldn't be much action down there, so I decided to drive some thirty miles out of my way, north to Highway 60, and cross the pass at Mountainair. Over an hour later, pressing eastward, I began to get over my irritation and started to enjoy the drive through the desolate country east of Corona. I saw Swainson's hawks, a couple of roadrunners, and a great horned owl. I sat and chatted with the flagmen at a brief delay for roadwork on the state highway heading southeast toward Roswell. They wanted to know about my hybrid car and joked about my beard ("A little warmer down here than at the North Pole, no?" Ha, ha. How original).

Along the way, I began to realize that a long detour enforced by the US military actually fit quite well into my patchwork story of déjà vu–like rips in the matrix. The truth is, I lived a good part of my life in the Land of Enchantment in a state of denial, as people say today. I was *in denial* about the true character of most public lands in America: their preservation had more to do with the nation's military and industrial needs than with a democratic revival of the commons or with the preservation of nature in a pristine state. And I was *in denial* about my own relationship with the land: it had more to do with trying to achieve a sense of freedom and success when my professional life was severely limited and my personal life was in shambles.

I suspect that most folks who use the expression *in denial* don't realize that, having started as a psychological concept with clinical origins in Freud's studies on defense mechanisms, it really caught on as part of the twelve-step programs that came out of Alcoholics Anonymous. If I had gone to AA as I probably should have back in my New Mexico days, I might have been a little faster on the uptake. As it was, my realization of the bad fit between me and my environment—my social more than my natural environment, though the two are more intimately connected than I realized at the time—came to me in little packets of truth that landed on the doorstep of my consciousness. I always found a way to go out the back door rather than stop to see what was really going on in my life.

The first package arrived early—before I spent a single night in my new hometown. Not counting our visit for the interview at New Mexico Tech, the first night my wife and I spent in New Mexico was in Santa Fe. After a couple of long days driving through the summer heat on Interstate 40 across Tennessee, Arkansas, Oklahoma, and the Texas Panhandle, we indulged ourselves in a detour to visit the old capital city that I had first toured when I came to the Glorieta Conference Center with the Baptist youth choir on tour back in 1969. She had never been, and I wanted to add some romance to her impressions of our new home state by showing her what I remembered to be one of the great small cities of the United States, packed with history, art, culture, and local color.

We turned off I-40 at Tucumcari and passed through the unpopulated high grasslands of piñon-juniper country, then gained elevation and crossed the Sangre de Cristos near Pecos, New Mexico. I was pondering why that range of the lower Rocky Mountains was named for the blood of Jesus when, at the highest elevation, we drove into a bank of fog. The weather only added to the place's mysteries. With all the Catholic monasteries and ancient churches around, I imagined I'd drifted into the medieval Cloud of Unknowing. We got out of the car to absorb the mystical air. It was cold up there, even in early summer.

We got back inside with a shiver and coasted downhill all the way into Santa Fe. We drove into town following the Old Santa Fe Trail, joking about ourselves as pioneers. The town seemed to emerge suddenly before us, among the cottonwoods and desert willows, adobe cottages, shops, cafés, and galleries the same color as the reddish earth in the surrounding mountains and desert, a town perfectly suited to its place.

We splurged on a room at La Fonda, the sprawling adobe hotel right on the town plaza. We put the bags in the room and went straight out to take in the sights. The nooks and crannies of the old town drew us down one street and then another. We examined the wares of the long line of Indian jewelers and potters on the sidewalk outside the historic Palace of the Governors. They nodded politely but had nothing much to say. We ate blazing hot plates of cheese enchiladas with green chili at Tia Sophia's and sipped more than one ice-cold bottle of Mexican beer on the balcony of the Ore House. We took the long way back to the hotel, peering into the windows of the closed shops and art galleries on Canyon Road. Delighted and charmed and thoroughly pleased with myself for getting a job in such a state, I opened the window in the room to receive the cool air blowing down from the mountains, got happily into bed between the crisp clean sheets, and fell immediately into a dreamless slumber.

The next morning I awoke to the bright sun gleaming in the window. From the bed, I could see the almost unreal blueness of the sky framing the uneven adobe rooftops. I let my eyes wander around the room. The old, dark-stained furniture was painted with turquoise and white and coral-colored images of Indian myth, stick figures of men and women with wild lines for feathered hair, magical emblems like the spiral and the zia, bears and antlered deer with crooked arrows like bolts of lightning running from their mouths to the place of their hearts.

And suddenly, out of nowhere, delight gave way to terror.

Was it homesickness? Impossible. I'd never suffered from it before, not even at summer camp. When the other kids cried as their parents drove away, I just felt sorry for them. Then again, I'd never come this far away from home on my own, never felt entrusted with another person's happiness as well as my own, never committed myself to a new life in a place so different from anything I knew back in the Southland, a place whose magic was a total mystery to me. Lying there with my wife in that strange bed, twenty-seven years old and full of self-confidence about the work I was undertaking, I was overcome for an intense moment by fears and doubts I could not deny.

I lay on my back staring at the rough vigas and latillas in the ceiling and the white plaster walls seemingly more suited to a monastery than a luxury hotel, perfectly still and quiet, overwhelmed by the distance I felt from the people who had supported me, the places I knew the way I knew my own body. I could not even bring myself to imagine the kind of dislocation that the woman beside me must have felt. She'd never lived out of her home state of Tennessee or more than three hours away from her parents and siblings and extended family. She had quit her job and left it all behind to join me in pursuing the insubstantial dream of a career at a backwater college in a place neither of us knew anything about. I convinced myself that she was a bright and sophisticated young woman who had traveled the world—and she was—but I dismissed from my mind the importance of place and family in the scheme of independence that Americans young and old hold tight and close. Unacknowledged though it was, I guess that part of the terror I felt was the crush of the pressure I felt to make this move work for both of us.

Then she sighed quietly and leaned her warmth against me, and the spell was broken. I never told her about my momentary feeling of unhinged terror. If I had, she might have told me her own worries. I never knew if she felt anything like the same. I only held her close and wished her a good morning and pointed to the bright blue of the sky through the window, a sight she received with a sleepy smile. In retrospect, I wonder what dreams the beauty of that sky dispelled in that strange place. The beauty carried us along, then and many times later.

Before we left the hotel that morning, I looked out the window again. I could see the plaza to my left. The Indians were gathering in front of the Palace of the Governors, and shopkeepers were opening their doors. The tourists were looking for breakfast. To my right stood the massive edifice of the Cathedral de San Francisco with its arches and big rose window. The old graves in the churchyard lay on its far side. In the midst of the bright bold colors, earth-toned artifices, and transparent air, I half realized that something dark and unseen regularly disturbed this place. The old histories of the Native peoples and the Spaniards, everywhere evident, were telling me that all was not revealed by the bright sunshine.

The terror had passed, but the darkness stayed with me as we checked out of the hotel, got a strong black coffee to go with the buttery croissant in the French bakery, passed the ragged beggar on the street by the parking garage, drove our faded green Volvo out of town, south on I-25, past the exits to the Indian pueblos, past the devastation of a car wreck with police cars and ambulances screaming to the scene, past the notch in the mesa where I'd heard that Conestoga wagons once passed on their way to the Santa Fe Trail.

We stopped briefly to gas up in Albuquerque, where one of my former professors now taught at the university. We had visited with him and his wife when we came out for the interview in April. From a phone booth, I called to ask if we could meet for lunch, but he told me that my new colleagues, whom I had given his number as an emergency contact, were looking for me because the moving truck with our things had arrived earlier than expected and our stuff was being unloaded into the apartment that we had rented site unseen. I got back in the car and we rushed the final seventy miles down the interstate.

When we got to Socorro, we found our belongings stuffed

into a dirty apartment located in a scruffy group of white stucco buildings, mainly inhabited by international students, who looked on curiously at our arrival. We managed to make enough space to open the pull-out couch, where we would end up sleeping for the next week, and to create a path through the dusty boxes and furniture to the bathroom and kitchen. We lifted an old rug left in the hall and found yellowish grass growing through a crack in the floor. We smelled rodents someplace but never found a nest. We scratched at fleas hopping around our ankles. We never bothered to unpack. We spent every day looking for a better place, found the little house on Mustang Drive, and put the money from the sale of our place in Knoxville into a quick purchase that we agreed would be a temporary investment. Of course, we ended up staying there for five years—I adjusted myself to the little place, and she apparently extended her sense of the temporary to the entire town (and our marriage).

❧ Adjustment for me meant welcoming everything I could about the place—the birding in the Bosque, the quietness of Water Canyon Mesa, the morning ritual of jogging the ditch bank and writing my papers—and turning a blind eye to the rest. I became a master of denial. I claimed the place with a combination of intense insistence on the beauty and even the sacredness of the land, accompanied by an angry defensiveness toward anyone who challenged my point of view.

I had not lived in New Mexico for more than a year or two when a colleague said to me one day, "I've never known anyone to become a desert rat as fast as you." I spent hours in the hot dry sun, walking with my colleagues in geology and biology and history, absorbing the science and lore of the land. I could have been a tour guide. I took special delight in the remoteness and the wildness of the place.

But people who'd known me for a long time, like the visitors I led on tours of the local wonders, could see that the changes I'd undertaken had levied their toll. They looked on me with a kind of stunned surprise when I got defensive about their mild complaints over the dryness, the sometimes harsh winds, or the relative lack of greenery in my new home.

My attitude even affected my scholarly judgment. Once I found myself arguing with the father of rangeland ecology himself—no matter that he was long since dead. I was reading Aldo Leopold's *Sand County Almanac* for the first time and came across an account of overgrazing and human mismanagement of ecology in the Southwest, based on his years of rangering in New Mexico and West Texas:

> This region, when grazed by livestock, reverted through a series of more and more worthless grasses, shrubs, and weeds to a condition of unstable equilibrium. Each succession of plant types bred erosion; each increment to erosion bred a further recession of plants. The result today [in the early twentieth century, that is] is a progressive and mutual deterioration, not only of plants and soils, but of the animal community subsisting thereon. The early settlers did not expect this: on the ciénegas of New Mexico, some even cut ditches to hasten it. So subtle has been its progress that few residents of the region are aware of it. It is quite invisible to the tourist who finds this wrecked landscape colorful and charming (as indeed it is, but it bears scant resemblance to what it was in 1848). (206)

I now see the truth in these observations, but, at the time, I simply did not want to hear it. Leopold's commentary aligned my own perspective with the historical ignorance and dandified aesthetics of the tourist. I put the book down and did not pick it up again until I had moved elsewhere.

By the time I left Socorro, I had begun to see my defensiveness as a symptom of an incomplete, in-between, provisional belonging to the land. In truth, I never overcame my status as tourist, or at best a guest. I was certainly no tried and true desert rat at home in the place. When I met Indians packing out-of-season deer out of Water Canyon; or crossed paths with rough-faced ranchers walking the trails with rifles in hand, looking for the bear or mountain lion that killed the calf on land leased for grazing from the Bureau of Land Management; or when I heard tales about the local episode in the Sagebrush Rebellion—the elderly rancher who, disregarding his own safety and armed to the teeth, squatted on land long ago impounded from his family for the White Sands Missile Range southeast of town and only gave up and came out in tears when his old buddies pleaded with him—or when I heard of the trouble on the land grants in the north, the conflicts between mainstream environmentalists and the Hispaños whose communal lands, supposedly protected by the Treaty of Guadalupe Hidalgo, had been largely absorbed by the formation of the Kit Carson and Santa Fe National Forests—then I knew I was no desert rat. The sneaking suspicion of my *turisto* status that came over me when I was reading Leopold was confirmed.

My experience in New Mexico suggests that we form sentimental (and often neurotic) attachments to places in order to soothe ourselves about some discontent that we are reluctant to face. In retrospect, the sense of beauty that I felt—and cultivated—in the desert Southwest had too much of a willful quality about it. I was always congratulating myself on being lucky enough to work in such a beautiful place. Don't get me wrong: the place *is* beautiful. But that doesn't explain the defensiveness that arose when others—whether my friends or the late Aldo Leopold—challenged my view of the place.

Could it be that our sense of beauty is always that way—possessive and defensive by turns? Like a tourist who pays a fortune for an exotic vacation and is determined, obligated, to see the beauty in the place but ultimately is beset by a feeling of loss—like buyer's remorse—and is finally glad to return to home, work, routine? Or a jealous man with a beautiful wife, who is inwardly relieved when divorce releases the pressure? Or the collector with his pride of ownership, who secretly doubts the worth of his collection and is driven to compete by others' standards, to keep adding more and more, bigger and better? Or the birder obsessing over a life list or big year count?

My professional ambition eventually pulled me away to larger universities with stronger support for scholarship in the humanities. I yielded to the academic division of labor, segregated myself in English departments, and taught specialized courses to English majors and graduate students. I lived closer to population centers where demand for higher education was greater and financial resources more plentiful. I returned to the Land of Enchantment as a true tourist, self-consciously recalling the resentment that New Mexicans feel toward cars with Texas plates, the passengers stereotyped as loud and overweight skiers, hunters, and shoppers who bring arrogance and revenue in equal measure. When the place no longer met my needs, I moved away. I sacrificed all to my own grinding need for happiness, occupation, and well-being. At the microlevel of individuality, I reenacted the ideology and practices of the military-industrial state in spite of my professed distaste for the establishment, the system, the man. I inadvertently participated in turning the place into a sacrifice zone.

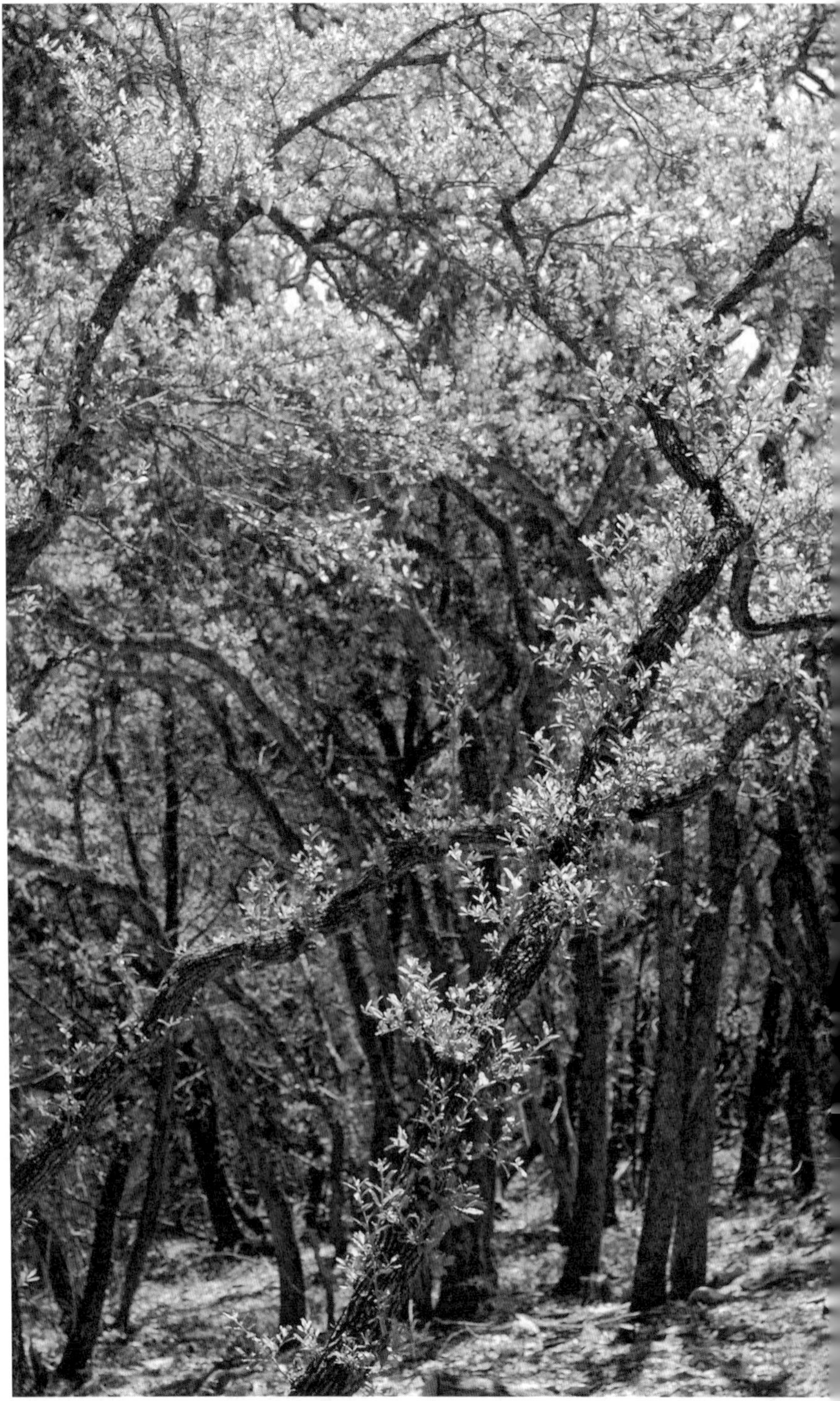

4 Dispelling Déjà Vu, Part Two

> Dixie, always regarded as benighted and backward, was now shunned and boycotted by public and private organizations, including environmental ones. This pariah status also made it easier for politicians to agree tacitly to make the Deep South a "sacrifice zone," a sump for the rest of the nation's toxic detritus.
>
> Donald G. Schueler, "Southern Exposure"

> A report in 1972 by the National Academy of Science suggested that the Four Corners area be designated a "national sacrifice area."
>
> Valerie L. Kuletz, *The Tainted Desert*

I used to joke that I was the only true pioneer in my family. After our brief life in Oregon in the late fifties when my dad was in the Air Force, I never got the West out of my blood. The rest of my family went back to the Southeast and always thought of the Carolinas and Georgia as home. I kept trending westward in some modern reenactment of a story about a children's hero, the Disney version of Davy Crockett, or one of the environmentalist heroes, maybe John Muir, a Scottish immigrant who (literally) walked away from the family settlement in Wisconsin, first going south to Florida, then heading westward and never stopping till he ended up in California, the place with which he is generally associated (though as the land tamed there, he continued to seek out wilderness in excursions to Alaska).

The joke about pioneering, I came to realize later, was on me. The image of the pioneer was part of the matrix that kept me in a perpetual state of denial, distraction, and defensiveness. I'm using the matrix as an allegory for what scholars usually call myth or ideology (as Karl Marx defined ideology: false consciousness). Myths and ideologies cover over some parts of our personal reality and highlight others. They are cultural tools of adjustment, stories we tell ourselves or theories we accept to avoid the contradictions and discomfort of living the life we have chosen or the one that's been dealt to us. They are probably necessary to mental health—a kind of psychological survival strategy—but they can really lead us astray at times.

I desperately wanted my professional and personal life in the West to succeed. My desperation threw up a screen of myth and ideology. The pioneering matrix, even as a joke, revealed my need to feel original and adventurous. It filtered out the fear and uncertainty that surfaced in the little moments of déjà vu, the breaks in the illusion when my guard was down, like the episode on that first morning in Santa Fe when I awoke in full realization of darkness in the bright-skied Land of Enchantment.

That moment was revealing in a communal as well as a personal way. It hinted at the colonialist underpinnings of the pioneering myth. Scholars in postcolonial studies these days like to say that all tourism is a reenactment by modern travelers of the colonialist adventure. We go to these places once possessed by indigenous peoples and still inhabited by remnant or modernized populations, and we claim them (the places and the people) with eyes hungry for new sites, with cameras, with consumerist and collector values, with investments. Whether I saw myself as a pioneer, a settler, or a tourist, I was reliving an impoverished version of the sad old story of exploration, conquest, and exploitation. Later I would begin to see myself as a *guest,* not only in lands I could not claim despite the desperation of my need for owning and belonging everywhere on earth. And really, aren't we all, in our mortal state of temporary residence, guests on the land (as the Wilderness Act of 1964 reminds us)?

Years of study and reflection were slow to show me the code of the matrix. And I'm no Neo. For me, the myth of the pioneering adventurer that left family and homeland behind to find fortune and success in a new world was a stubborn illusion that offset my sense of having failed to land a job near my family or my wife's family and the homeland to which I was born. The pioneering myth was reinforced by a personal element that first struck me with the uncanny force of a déjà vu one day when I was following some psychological leads in my research on Whitman's poetry in the little New Mexico Tech library.

I happened upon an essay by the psychologist Erik Erikson, the guy who invented the "identity crisis." It was a foray into autobiography and self-analysis included in his book *Life History and the Historical Moment.* Like me, Erikson was a stepson whose mother remarried when he was a young child. His new dad was a doctor, like mine. Just as I grew tall and dark in a family that tended to be short and fair-haired, Erik looked different from his parents and half-siblings. He was tall and blond, a Dane among a family of shorter, darker German Jews. He was raised Jewish but converted to Christianity as an adult and took the made-up name of Erikson to replace his stepfather's name—becoming something like a psycho-pioneer who strove to claim himself as his own father: Erik, son of Erik. Like me, he was well cared for, loved, and encouraged along the way, though his dad (like mine on occasion) discouraged his artistic leanings. As I found a compromise between the practical and the artistic in the profession of the humanities, which kept me close to literature but provided a steady income as a professor, Erikson became not a medical doctor as his stepfather had hoped but compromised between the creative arts and the health professions by becoming a psychoanalyst and biographer of the great revolutionaries Martin Luther and Mohandas Gandhi, who carried whole populations with them in their adventures of self-discovery. He was probably drawn to Christianity by the very archetype of adopted children—Joseph's stepson, Jesus of Nazareth.

Reflecting on his family status in the essay I read in the Tech library, Erikson speaks of the *positive stepson identity*, the self-assurance and belief that he could walk into a crowd of strangers and act as if he belonged. My shy sister Belle used to say the same thing about me; when we went to parties together, she would hold back and get the lay of the land while I jumped right into the hand-shaking and conversation. It was this aspect of his personality that, in Erikson's view, allowed him to have the confidence, arrogance even, to insert himself into the famous circle of Sigmund Freud and then become one of Anna Freud's most famous students in the second generation of psychoanalysis. But alongside the positive stepson identity was a negative. It involved a constant questioning of one's place in the world, a wondering if, after that easy-seeming waltz into the new social situation, you were ever really accepted, ever really belonged.

Like Erikson, my own search for spiritual identity has led me through a number of conversions, departures, and reconversions. And like Erikson, I often questioned my place in the many manifestations of the human family. I would eventually learn to claim the advantage of the positive stepson identity and accept that life in the middle of multiple influences was in many ways preferable to a hard-rock and inflexible position of identity (whether based on kinship, ethnicity, ideology, or personal choice). But at the time I read Erikson's comments on the stepson identity, I was happy just to know I wasn't the only one who seemed never quite to belong in the place or among the people with whom he found himself.

⁂ During my first four years at New Mexico Tech, I taught each summer in a program called Native Americans in Mining and Engineering Science (NAMES). The idea was to bring high schoolers to Socorro from the different tribes—Navajo, Apache, the several Pueblos, many of them remote and others with a poor record for sending students to college—to get a feel for campus life, take some specially designed courses to provide exposure to science and engineering, and consider the possibility of studying to be mining and petroleum engineers, geologists, and chemists to advise their people on the best use of tribal lands and resources—and, if all went as hoped, support the work of the oil companies and government agencies that helped to fund the summer education program.

My participation was kind of a last-minute arrangement, almost a fluke. Somebody got the idea that NAMES needed a writing workshop, and after I accepted the job at Tech in April 1980, my name came up as a possible teacher. In May, I got a call from the director, who'd read my résumé and decided I would be good for the job since I had experience teaching scientific and technical writing as well as basic composition but was also a scholar with an interest in poetry and literary history. She wanted someone to balance the interests of the technical faculty in the program. When we talked, she was enthusiastic and persuasive. I wasn't planning to leave Tennessee until late in the summer and had not yet arranged for a place to live in New Mexico. But when I realized that the salary was significantly more than I could earn in Knoxville as a summer lecturer combined with my wife's salary at the university press—and that the college was paying for my move—I jumped at the chance to get an early acquaintance with my new world, and my wife agreed (reluctantly, it seems in retrospect) to speed up the process of moving.

It all happened pretty fast, and that's how we landed in the nasty apartment that we rented site unseen and how we ended up buying a house too quickly that proved troublesome in our relationship. What I now see as an omen of the coming trouble appeared as we finally were able to unpack in our new house. One of the boxes I kept with relics of my dead father's life was lost, the one that held his medals, the Purple Heart and Bronze Star. My wife blamed the packers from the moving company, since other valuable articles disappeared too, including her collection of rare coins. The medals must have been stolen, she reasoned, as she got on the phone to the moving company. I blamed only myself. I should have kept the medals close to me, carried them with me in the car, in my briefcase with important papers. By leaving them in the hands of the movers, I had treated them as something less than irreplaceable treasures.

An image from my boyhood sought out my guilt. I must have been about six years old, because Mom and I were sitting in the little den of our rental house where we lived when Dad was an intern at the hospital in Greenville before we moved to Oregon. That was when Mom first showed me the medals, which she took down from the closet shelf that held all her most personal mementos. When I was married, she gave them to me to keep for myself and my progeny—the legacy of my father's sacrifice. At the time, I saw the passing of the medals as a sign of my entry into adulthood and my responsibility for keeping my own traditions. Looking back, I also see that it was one of many efforts that my mother made to throw off the old hurt of my father's death and get past a lifetime of mourning, of which I was a constant reminder myself. Many things about my marriage must have reminded her of her first marriage. She was about the same age that I was when she married, and the differences between our family and my wife's had to be negotiated the same way that she negotiated the differences between the life of her mill-working and farming family with the town life of the Killingsworths. My paternal grandparents were ordinary middle-class folks—my grandfather was a pharmacist who had his own drugstore and owned some farmland around town that he rented out—but my mother saw my Grandmother Killingsworth as a paragon of social grace and learned the arts and manners of the Southern lady at her side in the kitchen, in the parlor, at church, and at social gatherings in the town. I never understood this relationship until Belle told me about it years after Mom died, but now I can see it may have played a role in the way my mother always seemed to worry about losing me to my rich in-laws in Nashville and why her best feelings for my wife seemed tinged with resentment that often bubbled over into outright conflict, with extra heat added by the medication and weakness imposed by her lupus.

A couple of years before we moved to New Mexico, my wife and I came down to South Carolina from Knoxville for my Grandmother Killingsworth's funeral. She had outlived my grandfather, who died while I was still an undergraduate. We stayed in Greenville with my parents and made the short trip to Ware Shoals to attend the services. Mom begged off; she said she was feeling bad that day. After the service, my aunts invited my wife and me to choose some things from the old house by which to remember my grandparents. We chose a framed, hand-drawn family tree that I remember my grandmother tracing out for me to show me how we related back to our ancestors who first came to America from England. And we chose a framed picture of my father in his Citadel uniform. The photograph would have been made about the time he met my mother in Charleston. My aunts seemed surprised that we wanted nothing more, but the two items seemed to suffice as signs of my special place in the family heritage. (I also received my father's share of the inheritance and the money gained from the sale of the house. We used that money, a relatively modest amount after years of my grandfather's illness had depleted the family coffers, for the down payment on our first house, a little white frame cottage in South Knoxville with a shady screen porch on one side facing a patch of woods and lined with a fragrant garden. From the sale of that house, we used the money to buy the ill-fated residence in Socorro.)

On the way back to Greenville from Ware Shoals after the funeral, my wife said she would like to give the picture of my father to Mom to put in the big gallery of family photos she kept in the upstairs hall. Her suggestion was quite innocent of the knowledge that Mother's survival strategies included a suppression of memories of her life with her first husband—not a complete ban, but certainly a turning away. The only picture of my father we had in the house hung in my old downstairs bedroom. I should have understood better myself and warned against the idea of the gift. But understanding was not my forte in those days.

When we got back to Greenville, I sat in the living room reporting to Dad and my brother about the people in attendance at the funeral. My wife was with Mom and my sisters in the kitchen. The sound of breaking glass brought us to our feet. As we scrambled in, we met Mom coming out the kitchen door, her face contorted with weeping. She headed up the stairs to her room, Dad close behind. My brother and I ventured in and saw my wife standing with my sisters by the kitchen counter, shocked looks on every face. My younger sister Kathy nodded toward the trashcan sitting by the wall. On top of it lay the photograph of my father, the glass broken across his gently smiling face. Mother had cracked it on the counter and thrown it into the trash before storming from the room.

Years later, Jackie found the picture with the still-broken glass in a box of old things. She took it and placed it in a framed ensemble of three photographs—my father and my dad on either side, me in the middle. I recall carefully watching Mom's reaction to the grouping when she first saw it in our house in Lubbock during the time she came to visit her first granddaughter after Myrth was born. She turned and smiled at me, thankful that, undergirded with Jackie's wisdom, I had taken on the burden of my dead father's memory and had worked out his place in my life. She could finally let go.

I never told Mom about losing the medals. They were never recovered, and as if to compound my guilt, when I contacted the National Archives to search for the records of his citations, I found that all traces had been lost in a fire along with thousands of others from the Korean War era. It was as if fate was working alongside my irresponsibility to erase him from the story of my life.

❧ With the personal issues and mounting pressures growing with the move from Tennessee, I didn't get much time to work out a plan for teaching my workshop in the NAMES program. And so it was that I found myself one morning in early June standing in front of twenty brown faces in a strange classroom, all of them demurely avoiding eye contact, and all of us wondering what the heck I was going to do. I decided to break the ice by falling back on an old standby assignment: *write a short account of your life as if you're introducing yourself to a stranger, a mini-autobiography.* On the blackboard I listed some topics they could cover: family, education, favorite courses in school, hometown, religion, hobbies, and so forth. It was more or less the same assignment that Mrs. Bell gave me back in grade school, the one that got me started identifying myself as a writer.

The students stared at the board for a while and then went to work. While they wrote, I stared out the window at the oak-lined walkways and lawns of green grass fed by the ever-flowing Socorro Spring. I was thinking about how the landscaped campus must have looked from the air—a green postage stamp on the brown manila envelope of the New Mexican high plains, thinly bordered on one side with the green of the Rio Grande valley. At the end of the hour, I took up the papers and told them I'd read them by our next meeting, then dismissed the class. That seemed to go okay, I thought. I had another thought coming.

When I got back to my office and looked at the papers, I discovered that, without exception, the students had all copied the topics off the board in a list and written short answers as if they were filling out a government form. These kids didn't seem to know what a personal essay was. I panicked and rushed over to the admin building where the program advisor kept her office—a Native American herself, from Laguna Pueblo. I spread the papers on her desk and told what happened. She looked up at me and started to chuckle.

"You just violated about a million social taboos," she said. "These kids, especially the Navajos, are taught that it's rude to put themselves forward in public as something special or different.

Anything more than a minimal compliance with this assignment—which they did because the authority in charge asked them to, again to avoid rudeness—would be embarrassing to them. They probably assumed it would embarrass you, too."

So it was back to square one for me, this time with a lesson under my belt about what it means to be a self in a different culture. I started taking them to the library to read about the topics that their professors in geology and mining and chemistry were discussing with them. They looked up information about their home places and wrote about the land and how the people worked it. From then on, things went much better. They were a bright lot, obviously some of the top students from the tribal groups they represented. I got to know many of them quite well and in subsequent years met their sisters and brothers and cousins who also came to the program. I was invited to festivals where I met parents and grandparents, aunts and uncles, ate the good food in the homes of the hosts, and watched celebrations like the Jemez Corn Dance. A couple of times I recognized the family resemblance of a student's kin on the plaza at Santa Fe, where they were selling pottery and jewelry at the Palace of the Governors, and had a nice chat about my former students.

When I finally took the time to think about the politics of the NAMES program, any conflict I felt over the oil and mineral companies' interest in the outcome of our teaching was counterbalanced by the attitude and work of the program advisor from Laguna. She did everything she could to avoid the old mistakes of the Indian Schools—with their determination to remove Indian students from their traditions and their tribal commitments and indoctrinate them in the ways of the white world. In addition to field trips to mines and classes on mineral extraction and the earth sciences, the advisor lined up activities that reinforced Native culture and invited students to think about their place and the role of tradition in a changing world. I was always welcome as an adult chaperone on these excursions and likely learned more than the students.

We took a camping trip to Mescalero, attended the Fourth of July powwow, and watched the Apaches perform their annual dance of the mountain gods in an arena lit by huge bonfires at night (the mysterious interplay of dark and light obscuring the main purpose of the facility: it was a stadium for rodeos). "What a relief to see so many brown faces," I overheard one of the girls say to her friend as we entered the arena.

We went to a conference on Native studies in Albuquerque. In the Kiva Auditorium at the University of New Mexico, we heard the Lakota philosopher Vine Deloria Jr. exercise his famous irony and impart his teachings on Indian survival and resistance. (He stood under a No Smoking sign and smoked one Winston cigarette after another. The whole pack was gone by the end of his talk.) We heard the teacher and activist Phil Reno speak on the economy of uranium and coal mining in Navajo country, his long blond hair and pale skin contrasting with the darkness of the other speakers. (The next year, I tried to get him to come for a guest lecture at New Mexico Tech but learned that he had committed suicide. I never knew the whole story.)

We traveled to Los Alamos for a tour of the museum at the National Lab and attended a lecture by Fred Begay, the Navajo physicist who interprets nuclear science through parallels with Diné metaphysics and the old stories and myths on which he founds his identity as a scientist as well as an Indian (much as Marilou Awiakta uses Cherokee legend as foreknowledge of atomic science, both in *Selu* and in *Abiding Appalachia: Where Mountain and Atom Meet*).

In a classroom in Socorro, we heard the Navajo poet Luci Tapahonso read from her work. I remember how the kids laughed at her image of old women drinking Diet Pepsi while they ate their high-fat meals of barbecued meat and white-flour tortillas. I still have the copy I got that evening of her book *Seasonal Woman*, with drawings by the late R. C. Gorman, inscribed by the author with the blessing *Hozho*, whose meaning falls somewhere between "harmony" and "balance" and could mean "Walk in Beauty," the classic translation of the Diné blessing.

I can't say how the mixture of lessons felt to the students in the program. They always listened with the same quiet politeness and wrote many good summaries without putting themselves forward in their assigned reflections on the events (despite my encouragement for them to do so, which probably seemed to them an incitement to rudeness and the worst kind of manners). But, as for me, I was left finally with a profound sense of dwelling in the middle of my less-than-fully-informed but sincere admiration of Native ways and my troubled acceptance of much of the Western science and technology that the program encouraged us both to embrace and to question.

⁕ Not just in the NAMES program but in other social relationships as well I was an in-between figure at best, an outsider at worst. I became active in the local Catholic parish, the first time I had publicly practiced Christianity in more than a decade. Having grown up a Baptist, all but abandoned religion during my whelping as an intellectual, and declined to convert when I married a Catholic wife, now I found myself taking the catechism from the nuns who taught at the parish school and lived in a convent beside the church.

At the time, I attributed the revival of faith both to a desire for fuller participation in my new community and to an upswelling of mystical spirituality that had accompanied my study of poetry toward the end of graduate school. The feeling had begun to emerge during the long hikes in the Smoky Mountains and in my dissertation research, which involved an intense reading of Emerson, Whitman, and Thoreau's transcendentalist works of natural mysticism. The ravishing beauty of the Land of Enchantment did nothing to dispel my personal enchantment with nature, and the romance of the ancient Catholic church where the sons and daughters of the earth—the children of Native Americans, Spanish peasant settlers, and conquistadors—had sung and prayed for centuries fired my imagination. I worshiped in an old mission church whose history dated to the seventeenth century. As I hoped, my newfound faith connected me with the local Hispanic community, and I was schooled in everything from the right moment to order your Christmas tamales (Christmas tamales?) to the historical and political differences between Hispaños in my part of New Mexico (private landholders from families in relatively recent settlements of farmers and ranchers) and those in northern New Mexico (land-grant Spanish who dated their communities back to the earliest conquests and who had fiercely resented the Anglo intrusion for a century and a half). The parish nuns invited me to play guitar in the "contemporary" mass, a post–Vatican II, English-language liturgy that complemented the Spanish masses and featured songs that sounded like they were written by has-beens from the folk-rock craze, long on spiritual but short on musical inspiration. From the nuns, I also learned of the Sanctuary Movement, inspired by Latin American liberation theology, which guided refugees from the most troubled regions of Central America into the relative safety of El Norte. I offered my house as a stop on this late twentieth-century Underground Railroad, but my hospitality was never needed—or never fully trusted.

In the fall and spring semesters, I taught writing and literature to engineering and science majors at New Mexico Tech. The full faculty of the college was no larger than that of the English departments in my home institution at Tennessee and the universities where I would work later. The student body numbered a grand total of thirteen hundred. I was one of a half dozen humanities professors, so I spent as much time with physicists and geologists as with historians, philosophers, and other teachers of language and literature. The library was practically nonexistent. Every couple of weeks, I drove seventy miles to Albuquerque to use the research library at the University of New Mexico so I could keep my scholarship alive. (I was working at the time on my first book, *Whitman's Poetry of the Body: Sexuality, Politics, and the Text*. The priest got wind of my topic and asked me to give the sex talk to the boys at the parish school. "I have no credibility with them," he told me with a big laugh. I gave it a shot but didn't have much better luck—the boys referred to me as Father Jimmie behind my back, I found out later from the nuns.)

Living in the middle of so many *influences*—again in the literal sense of the term, the *flowing in* of ideas, attitudes, language, ways of life—often left me feeling swamped and uncertain. None of the new influences ran in the old channels of my identity as a white, middle-class, Protestant, English teacher, wannabe writer, and scholar in the humanities. But you could never have proved it by talking to me at the time. If nothing else, I had mastered the defensive arrogance of the academic ego that could usually pass for confidence and defiance. In my shaky sense of identity, I resorted to my distractions and relied on my defensiveness to keep from sinking in uncertainty.

❧ On first look, it seems truly strange that in the early 1980s—with the Tellico experience as part of my recent history, my increasing awareness of environmental politics, my engagement with the land and local community, and my attention to Native American studies and the connections I formed through the NAMES program—that I completely missed any coverage of the Church Rock nuclear disaster. But my reading and reflection since that time, especially in recent books and articles on the history of uranium mining in the Southwest, have shown me that in some ways the very act of walking in beauty (as I came to see my mystical engagement with the land in the terms of Navajo metaphysics) may have distracted my attention. Like so many members of the second generation of environmentalists, I became a "Deep Ecologist," trying to reclaim a quasi-indigenous outlook on nature filtered through the sentimentality and idealism of the western literary, theological, and philosophical tradition.

In this view, outdoor life not only provided an escape from my unhappy indoor life, it *saved* me from the minor hell of my ordinary existence. I forced a satisfying connection between the *holiness* of spirituality and the *holism* of ecology. Wild nature appeared as the wholly, and holy, Other. Despite the revival of my Christianity, I came to think of Nature with a capital N as a replacement for, or the embodiment of, God. I hiked and camped on sacred ground.

Rather than intensifying my encounter with the politics of ecology, as theorists of Deep Ecology like Arne Naess and Christopher Manes suggested that it should, my mysticism may have muddied my understanding of current issues. I was inclined, for example, to divide eco-spirituality from social issues other than straightforward conservationist politics and the wilderness ethic. When I taught New Mexican literature like Frank Waters's *The Man Who*

Killed the Deer and Leslie Marmon Silko's *Ceremony*, I stressed the mythic and poetic elements and the ecological sensitivity of the writing as an antidote to the excesses of the Western war machine and unbridled development of the land. Themes associated with indigenous sociology and economics were lost on me. Silko's treatment of alcoholism, post-traumatic stress, teenage pregnancy, and poverty in *Ceremony*, for example, seemed far less engaging than the mysteries of Navajo healing and the Pueblo prophecies related to witchery in the nuclear age. In the book *American Indian Literature, Environmental Justice, and Ecocriticism: The Middle Place*, the eco-critic Jodi Adamson cites a similar experience in her teaching in Arizona. The difference is that she had more Native students in her college-level classes who could challenge her point of view and awaken her to the relationship between social and ecological issues. At the time, the social issues seemed to me no different from the plight of the poor in every kind of community. It was the sense of sacredness and the earth-based mythology of the indigenous muse that *distinguished* the Native Americans and allowed me (and others like me) to ignore their connection to the global poor even as I celebrated their difference. I could use indigenous thought and lifeways to critique the spiritual poverty of the modern world, but I found it all too easy to avert my eyes from the material poverty and injustice experienced by the Indians whose stories I loved.

After moving to the urban environment of Memphis, Tennessee, in 1988, getting involved again in social justice issues, and reading the books of the eco-anarchist Murray Bookchin, who taught that "the very domination of nature by man stems from the very real domination of human by human" (Bookchin 1), Jackie and I eventually tried to repair the division of ecology from issues like poverty and race in the studies leading up to our book

Ecospeak, at which time we included ourselves in the growing movement of *social* ecology.

But I had not reached that point in the early eighties. I could see the birds in the Bosque as I admired the changing light on the faces of the Magdalena Mountains across the river, but I couldn't grasp my relation to the ongoing nuclear presence of the White Sands Missile Range that bordered the preserve. I could visit the remote marvel of Chaco Canyon, with its elaborate evidences of the Anasazi culture, but remain mostly oblivious to the plight of Navajo uranium miners living on every side of the place. I could walk the trails of Bandelier, with its carefully preserved ruins of the Ancient Ones, but I could look uneasily away from the steel doors that led into nearby cliffs, the huge antenna dishes, the government vehicles, and the other industrial fixtures of the Los Alamos National Lab, which shared space on the Pajarito Plateau with the national monument. Every step I took, in any direction, should have made clear to me what Valerie Kuletz would observe in her 1998 book *The Tainted Desert:* "the desert lands of the southwest United States have been transformed into arguably the largest peacetime militarized zone on earth . . . to what, in essence, is a military occupation." The signs of power she lists are all too familiar to me from my memories of the eighties: "high-wire fences, radar antennae, massive satellite communication dishes . . . , sonic booms, stealth aircraft, well maintained roads in the middle of 'nowhere' leading to various 'installations'" (38–40). I remember once, on a drive across a remote stretch of the San Augustin Plains on US Highway 60, seeing massive, low-flying bombers, with no insignia or identifying marks, pass through the skies, silent as owls. My colleagues told me that if I knew what to look for, I could also have seen cruise missiles flying about, common as eagles.

Even so, for me, the nuclear threat lacked *presence.* It was a matter of the past and the future—in the past, the history of the Manhattan Project at Los Alamos or the first bomb test at Trinity Site (in what is now the White Sands Missile Range); in the future, the possibility of nuclear Armageddon, which seemed so remote as to be the stuff of dreams and visions rather than reality. At New Mexico Tech, I had colleagues in physics who divided their time between Los Alamos and our college; with funding from the New Mexico Humanities Council, I hosted a screening and discussion of *The Day after Trinity,* a documentary film on the Manhattan Project, the bombing of Japan, and the subsequent work on the hydrogen bomb; I attended a lecture by the Nobel laureate Hans Bethe representing the Emergency Committee of Atomic Scientists against nuclear testing and proliferation (founded by Albert Einstein); I watched priests and nuns leading rallies for world peace and nuclear disarmament in places like Albuquerque's Sandia Labs; I read Jonathan Schell's two volumes on nuclear abolition. But, to me, the nuclear problem centered in places like Washington and Moscow. The need was to learn from the past and prevent the possible future of Mutual Assured Destruction (MAD).

It's not that nuclear issues closer to home were entirely off my radar. The proposed Waste Isolation Pilot Plant (WIPP) was frequently a topic of conversation with my students and colleagues in mining engineering and geology. With the Cold War winding down, the market for uranium was drying up, and people usually devoted to taking stuff out of the ground were now looking for ways to put it back, arguing back and forth the merits and demerits of depositing nuclear waste in the ancient salt beds near Carlsbad. The question of tailings piles and abandoned mines in Indian country also kept the issue of uranium mining alive, even at a time when the work was mostly suspended. Along with my students, I learned about the issues in the NAMES program, from the science faculty as well as the guest speakers and conference talks.

So the question remains, why didn't I know about the Church Rock nuclear spill? My habit of filtering and focusing is partly to blame, but there's more. Also to blame was a similar process going on in the public mind, which relied on information provided by the mass media. The concept of the sacrifice zone in the desert Southwest emerged hand-in-hand with the usual deflections of blame and shame—government agencies pointing the finger at companies, many of whom had sold out or gone under; companies arguing that they had acted in the interest of the government, carrying out provisions of contracts to support the military; the whole sad story recounted in painful detail many years later in books like Judy Pasternak's *Yellow Dirt: An American Story of a Poisoned Land and a People Betrayed* (2010).

Readings in such books taught me that the themes of timeliness, belatedness, and invisibility in matters of indigenous relations to modern nations—which I had learned to take notice of in questions involving the building of big dams—take on a special character in the presence of nuclear power, whether for military or "peacetime" uses. The slow-moving trauma of health effects from exposure to radioactivity in particular is notoriously hard to substantiate. A US Geological Survey study found that the health impact at Church Rock, for example, was difficult to assess. The Rio Puerco had been contaminated for decades by "discharges of untreated or poorly treated uranium mine water and municipal sewage," and "impacts attributable to the tailings spill and mine dewatering could not be determined independent of contributions from natural conditions by the early 1990s" (SRIC 1). The place was already a slow-forming disaster before the spill, and the problem was exacerbated by the lag time in response by federal agencies.

Then there's the almost unimaginable stretch of future required for radioactive substances to become inert and lose their danger. This kind of long haul contrasts with the famously short attention span of television and newspaper audiences. *Issue decay* is a conventional term among scholars in journalism for fading news value. The rapidity of issue decay makes it the polar opposite of radioactive decay, which takes more or less forever. The very word *news* hints at the weakness of the media to sustain interest in a topic over the long term. Depending heavily on news coverage, environmental politics has suffered from its "crisis" orientation (see Cox). Crises come and go while radioactivity remains and cancer makes its way slowly through affected populations. Even scholarship, usually considered molasses slow in responding to current events, especially in the social sciences and humanities, has trouble sustaining long-term interest in topics as universities demand "original" research and young scholars go on the hunt for new discoveries, new theoretical slants, new texts to study, new sites for observation, new problems to solve—thus making scholarly publication an esoteric version of the news. The sciences long ago quit providing historical treatments of their topics, rarely citing research more than five years old; now the humanities and social sciences are following suit.

Related to issue decay are the twin phenomena that we might call *issue saturation* and *issue selection*. How many stories on nuclear disaster can the media absorb, and what constitutes their newsworthiness? The few studies that have surfaced in recent years on the Church Rock incident have contrasted the coverage that it received with coverage of the malfunction of the nuclear reactor at Three Mile Island in Pennsylvania, which occurred on March 28, 1979, roughly four months before the Church Rock spill. You would think that the media would race to follow up the Three

Mile Island story with a related story that showed a disturbing trend in the nuclear industry and that in fact involved a more damaging accident. The radiation released at the Pennsylvania facility was estimated at 13 curies, while the Church Rock spill released some 46 curies, but the national press made Three Mile Island a cause célèbre while ignoring Church Rock altogether. A 2007 study in the *American Journal of Public Health* cited a similar asymmetry in the coverage involving the Karen Silkwood case in Oklahoma, which was taken up by national antinuclear groups and ultimately by Hollywood (in the feature film *Silkwood* of 1983, starring Meryl Streep and Kurt Russell), as compared to another Oklahoma accident confined to the Cherokee reservation, on which the national press was silent. The article concluded that "incidents in low-income, rural, American Indian communities have not attracted the same attention as have incidents in communities of higher socioeconomic status such as Three Mile Island or incidents that affected White victims such as Karen Silkwood" (Brugge et al. 1599).

Not only is the coverage weak or nonexistent at the time of the incident, but once it has failed to implant in cultural memory, the neglect continues as the history emerges over the years. Over the last three decades, the story of Church Rock has finally begun to make an impression in public consciousness, thanks to authors and activists like the investigative reporter Judy Pasternak, the sociologist Valerie L. Kuletz, and Chris Shuey, who was a freelance journalist at the time of the Church Rock spill and struggling to find outlets for his stories on uranium mining in Navajo country before he became a keeper of the cause at the Southwest Research and Information Center, or SRIC, in Albuquerque (Eichstaedt 105). But the impression so far has been neither deep nor wide: "When *National Geographic* released an issue in 2006 that featured nuclear power, the examples were, again, Chernobyl and Three Mile Island" (Brugge et al. 1599). The eco-critic Rob Nixon has made quite a splash in academic eco-criticism by treating "slow violence" as a phenomenon in worldwide environmentalism, but beyond Rachel Carson (for whom his professorship at the University of Wisconsin is named), he covers very few US examples and gestures only weakly toward the hope that Native American studies will take up such topics. He cites no work from that field and generally ignores the literature on North American cases of slow violence, though many of the authors use terms similar to his own to describe the effects they discuss. As early as the 1980s, comparing Church Rock to Three Mile Island, Peter Matthiessen had written, "In northwestern New Mexico, events have been unspectacular, insidious, and slow, and so far, most of its victims have been Indians" (*Indian Country* 302). More recently, in *Yellow Dirt,* Judy Pasternak refers to the "slow environmental catastrophe" (8) and the "slow-motion disaster unfolding in Navajoland" (147). I have to wonder if Professor Nixon fails to mention these examples because of the lack of coverage over the years or because of his own professional need to appear original and new. In either case, *the news* is to blame. In a very real sense, I didn't get the news of Church Rock when I arrived in New Mexico because it was no longer news—or was never news according to the usual criteria involving issue decay, issue saturation, and issue selection. There was local coverage in the Albuquerque media in the summer of 1979, but by the time I arrived less than a year later, the issue had fully decayed and the coverage was gone.

If not the analysis and attention needed to understand what has happened in Navajo country, Nixon does give us some useful concepts in addition to belatedness and slow violence—like the concept of "ecosystem people"—"those hundreds of millions who depend for their livelihood on modest catchment areas." Ecosystem people stand in contrast with "resource omnivores," the most prosperous segment of the global population, whose range of catchment is planetary in scale (Nixon 22). In the case of the Church Rock tailings spill, the Rio Puerco served as the catchment zone for the local Navajo people, who, as Kuletz points out, "were unable safely to use their single source of water, nor could they sell or eat the livestock that drank from this water" (26–27). When recommendations for how to deal with the crisis came from public health officials, they came from the perspective of resource omnivores. In Pasternak's exposé, "the authorities' ignorance of the way Navajos live" is evident in their advice that eating the meat of exposed animals "would not pose a problem *so long as the people there didn't depend on the butchered animal for their everyday food over a long period of time*" (150, her italics). The obvious assumption is that the people have some source of meat other than their own livestock, but ecosystem people like the Church Rock Navajos can't always just pop down to the supermarket and spend what would be a fortune for many on beef imported from Texas or Argentina. In addition to providing water for the local Navajos and their livestock, the Rio Puerco was central to the community in other ways: "local medicine men derived remedies from the native plants that grew along the riverbank, and children played in the river during hot summer months" (Brugge et al. 1597). Chris Shuey's colleague at the SRIC, Paul Robinson, in a 1990 paper, cites a Centers for Disease Control assessment that "federal exposure standards for the general public would be exceeded when livers and kidneys of exposed cattle were eaten over a fifty year period"; then he notes that "liver and kidney meats are regularly eaten by Navajo, particularly the elderly for whom such 'choice' meats are provided" (182). In this dryland ecosystem, the

Rio Puerco has always been the central feature on which communities (animal and plant, as well as human) depended, and the depth of that dependence has been mostly lost on public servants from state and federal offices unfamiliar with the ways of the local people.

So ignorance and neglect prevail at the moment of remote crises among largely invisible populations. Then the short attention span of the media and its public kicks in, so that slow violence proceeds unnoticed and unchecked. And neglect is not limited to the media and public but also extends to scholarly authors whose attention is diverted by the need to make academic news as well as by ideology and methodology. You may well argue that, unlike the large populations of people living close to the land studied by the environmentalists of the poor in India and Africa, the number of ecosystem people in the United States—those who depend on local water and livestock and crops they raise themselves—is very small. I have found no records even by which to begin the count, but let us say that the number probably amounts to significantly less than 1 percent of the total US population. This severe minority status compared to the huge majority who work for money and live by purchases from the grocery store could account for the invisibility of US ecosystem people in the media. But I would counter by saying that, in a real democracy, no group of citizens, no matter how small or how remote, deserves to be rendered invisible and that the very existence of downstreamers on American lands constitutes a disgrace and a potential threat to us all.

On top of that, most of us eat meat and vegetables and drink water imported to our cities and towns from remote locations (and other countries, many of which have much higher populations of ecosystem people) that go totally unmonitored by our media. As the slogan says, *we all live downstream.* When it comes to either poisoning or media neglect, if it happened to them, it can eventually happen to us. And, from the study of ecosystem people, we know that the powers that be have the means and the will to bury embarrassing issues and deflect resistance that stands in their way.

☙ Back in the 1990s, I went on a field trip to Wes Jackson's Land Institute in Kansas with three colleagues from a sustainability reading group at Texas A&M—the ethicist Paul Thompson, the communication scholar Tarla Rai Peterson, and the archaeologist Bruce Dickson, all of whom have now contributed powerfully to the literature on sustainability and sustenance. Jackson's considerable fame among environmentalists and agriculturalists had just been augmented by a chapter featuring him in William Least Heat-Moon's bestseller *PrairyErth,* so the visit felt a little like a pilgrimage. The role of guru fit the affable Jackson quite comfortably. He imparted knowledge with great authority, softened by a casual air and a twangy drawl. Like all true gurus, he refused to take himself too seriously and was an excellent host.

He took us to remnants of the tallgrass prairie, what remains of wild land in his part of Kansas (near Salinas). He showed us the acreage of the Land Institute itself, where he and his colleagues were then experimenting with the possibility of growing a perennial food grain. Finally he drove us through an all but abandoned farm town to a field with the ruins of a small industrial operation—of what sort I cannot recall. What I do remember is the question he put to us. I've long since lost my notes, but he said something like this: "We have plenty of people writing about the pristine wild lands, and a good number writing about the farms—what you might call the sacred lands. But the land you're standing on, polluted by dioxin so that it can't be farmed or developed in the foreseeable future—the *desecrated* land—who's going to write about that?"

In this sense, to desecrate (de-sanctify) a place is to render it forgettable, to turn one's back upon it, to move on, to kick the dust off our heels, and give up on it. Science fiction imagines a time when the whole earth will be abandoned as unfit for life. With each desecration, we come closer.

❧ In October 2012, as part of my hard-look program designed to shake off the haunting déjà vu of my experience in the beautiful and troubled lands I called home in the 1970s and early 1980s, I paid a visit to TVA in Knoxville and to the Southwest Research and Information Center in Albuquerque. At TVA, I looked at an archive of old news clippings on Tellico and talked to the TVA historian, Patricia Ezzell, who is also the agency's tribal liaison. At SRIC, I spoke with Chris Shuey, who has lived with the Church Rock story since it first broke.

What I learned at TVA was that the local press—the regional newspapers, the radio stations, and even the student newspaper at the university—did indeed cover the Cherokee objections to the dam at Tellico in the early 1970s, though the national press did not. And when the snail darter story broke, it drowned out all other concerns, both locally and nationally, until Walter Cronkite and other journalists in the fall of 1979 took up the plight of the farmers who lost land to impoundment, some of whom were hanging on right to the last minute.

I remained ignorant of the Cherokee story, until I read about it in Matthiessen's essay in 1980, most likely because I did not wake up to the Tellico story until it became an issue of national environmental politics and because, all along, I depended more heavily on national news, especially television news, than on local sources, which, during the Vietnam years, I had grown to mistrust deeply. The very newspaper that the antiwar activists had called the *Knoxville Urinal* covered the Tellico story very thoroughly. Indeed, the *Journal*'s editorial staff joined Gov. Winfield Dunn in opposing the project at Tellico. This position was countered by the other newspaper in town, the *News-Sentinel*. In those days, it was typical in small Southern cities with two newspapers for one to favor the Democrats and the other the Republicans and generally to divide on most issues. I didn't trust either one and looked to the national media for my news, so I didn't really catch on to Tellico until it rose to the level of national interest, even though I lived nearby.

To me, the way we get our news is part of the process that alienates people from their local lands. In a course on environmental literature that I was team teaching a number of years ago, my colleague John Krajicek gave a little quiz to find out how much the students knew about their local environment, asking questions about where they got their water and their power for electricity. I didn't mention to John that I failed the test myself. I could cite all the important work on environmental literature, rhetoric, history, and philosophy, and a great deal of work in ecological science, but I couldn't tell you the source or mineral composition of my own tap water. Embarrassment sent me searching for the answers. I've never since allowed myself to become so ill informed on matters so important. And I've always followed the local news, no matter how objectionable the politics of the local outlets may have seemed. But at the time, I was a typical case of the intellectual whose knowledge outgrows his own locale and who wakes up one day to find the world close by threatened by unacceptable transformation.

As for Church Rock, on my visit to the SRIC, I posed two questions to Chris Shuey about ecology then and ecology now: why were he and his colleagues unable to get the story out when it first broke, and why have journalists like Pasternak and others been able to get the story into print today? If I didn't know about it then, how is it that, thirty years later, I could find so much information about Church Rock, even if most people, including many environmentalists, still know little or nothing about the accident and its effects on the people in the region?

Part of the answer, he said, has to do with the invisibility of Native and rural stories in the mainstream press, as the literature suggests—a kind of neglect that continues to this day. But there's more. As a freelance journalist, he had trouble selling the original story because of the nature of the evidence. Proving environmental harm, in those days, when the only good jobs in the regions for most workers and professional people were tied to the extractive industries, meant producing indisputable scientific evidence to back up your claims. The request amounted to "show me the bodies." Few scientists were likely to corroborate claims about the connection of radiation with cancer in the absence of longitudinal studies, which had never been part of the plan among government health organizations associated with mining in the Four Corners region. The SRIC has been committed for thirty years to producing such evidence in their various collaborations, developing proposals for strong legacy studies, the motivation for which grew out of the frustration in those early days. Now people like Judy Pasternak have more solid ground for their claims, a road paved by the keepers of the cause at SRIC and other nonprofits, as well as a handful of activist researchers and public health officials.

The road to publication and public awareness has also been smoothed by thirty years of environmental communication. It all sometimes seems to have had little effect, but as Shuey says, the general public is much more savvy these days when it comes to issues involving pollution and ecological degradation. Back then, the public was less likely to question the authority of national agencies and the military. In the years between World War II and Vietnam, it was widely considered unpatriotic, if not un-American, to question the integrity of the military-industrial state. Even the post-Vietnam generation—people like me—remained at the mercy of a local and national press still dominated by older editors and managers weaned on the attitudes associated with various national emergencies and universal mobilization for the war cause. Chris Shuey calls it the "mystique" of the military, from which Native Americans are no more immune than white Americans. Native men were sent into the underventilated and otherwise unsafe mines to dig for uranium in the same "warrior" spirit that was invoked to send others to fight and die overseas, the same spirit that produced the now-famous "code talkers" among Navajo soldiers, who used their native language to foil Japanese efforts to intercept intelligence in the war's Pacific theater.

The very concept of the sacrifice zone likely had its origins in this history of the military mystique and national mobilization. Science as well as industry in those heady days of the nuclear age was so completely tied to the military that words like *sacrifice* were ready at hand. During the world wars, civilians were required to sacrifice by limiting their consumption of gasoline, metals, and meat. Families sacrificed their sons to military causes. Young men were asked to pay the "ultimate sacrifice" and die for their country. Sacrificing entire regions of the land must have seemed a reasonable extension of the concept during the Cold War.

What had been *sacred* before—livelihood, life, land—now became the *sacrifice*. It was an age-old practice, but, in modern times, people were making their sacrifices not to the gods but to the state. The fearsome hunger of the old gods that had to be appeased by offering a portion of the community's livelihood, the fruits of the land, was transformed into the rapaciousness of the nation, which demanded more and more from its citizens.

Once a sacrifice zone was declared—either explicitly (as in the case of the Four Corners) or implicitly (as in the case of Appalachia)—the tacit approval of the general public (conscious or unconscious) is expressed by rendering the place invisible and unmentionable. So it is that lands and even whole segments of the citizenry are allowed to languish while other people and places prosper. When I moved from Tennessee to New Mexico, I didn't know it at the time, but I was exchanging one sacrifice zone for another as my dwelling place.

That was then. What about now? In a time when eco-activism can be listed by the FBI and Department of Homeland Security among other terrorist threats, when "eco-terrorist" has become a favored media moniker to describe environmental activists, and when "eco-nut-jobs" regularly appear as bad guys in the scripts of some of the most popular television programs (such as *NCIS* on CBS and *House M.D.* on the Fox network, shows that happen to be among my own favorites, I admit), then the possibility is ripe for new sacrifices to be asked of the citizenry and new sacrifice zones to be declared. Full mobilization and militarization of the land and the nation loom on the horizon. But the social and cultural representation of environmentalism *as a threat*—like the gradual emergence of information relating to past environmental disasters in our history—suggests to me *not* the decline of ecology as a political persuasion but its power as a resistance movement and its potential to resonate with people's day-to-day experience in the world as we have come to know it.

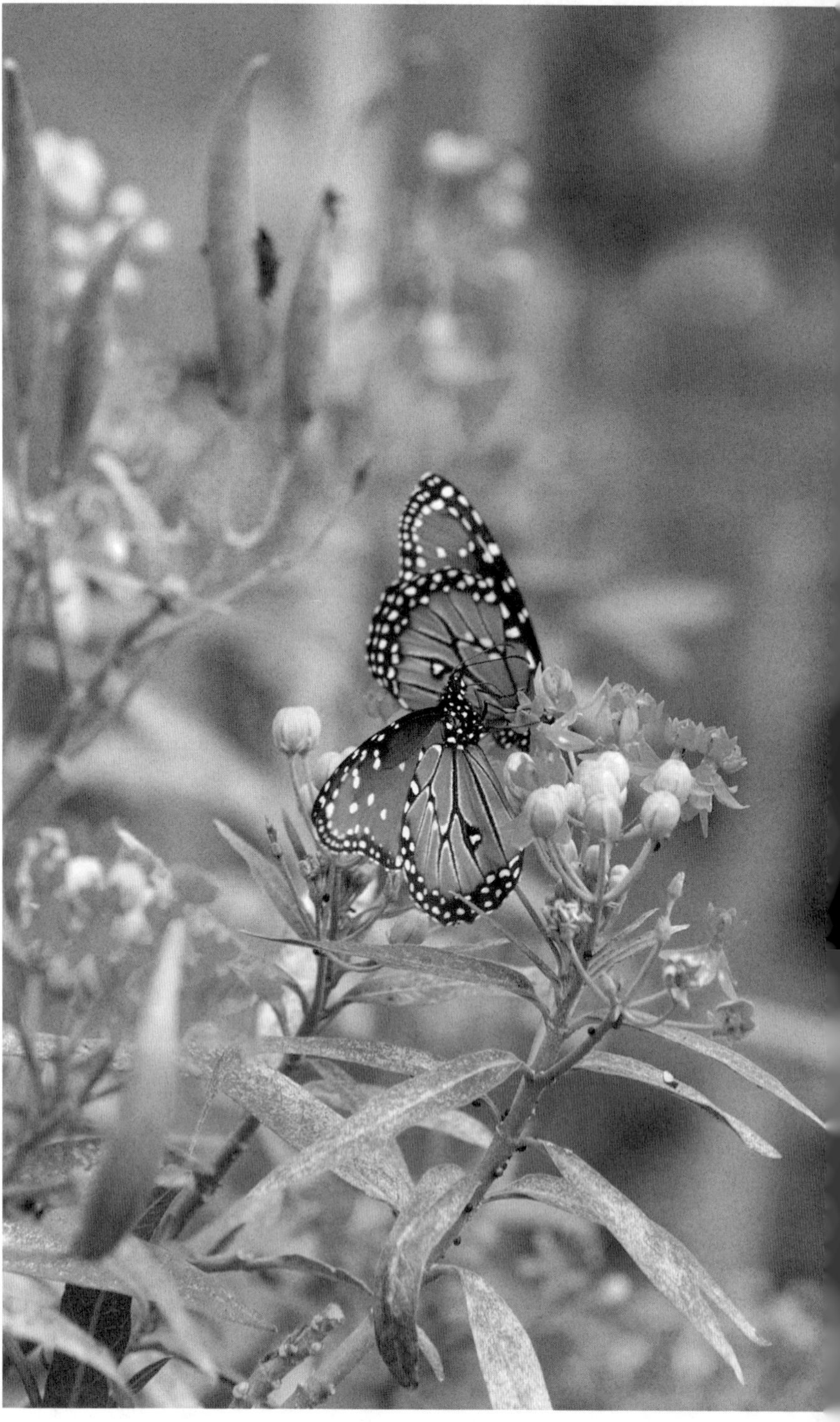

5 Defying Apocalypse

With a word he shall slay the wicked.
Isaiah 11:4

🙶 During my first fall semester at New Mexico Tech, in 1980, I was given an opportunity that ultimately proved crucial to my outlook on the writing and politics of nature. Like my role in the Native Americans in Mining and Engineering Science program and my later assignment as director of the New Mexico State Science Fair, which was held in Socorro every year, I probably got the opportunity to attend the Company-Faculty Forum on Energy Use and Development, sponsored by the Gulf Oil Corporation, because none of my colleagues wanted to go. Willingness was my main qualification. I remember thinking that, hey, at the very least, I would get an all-expense-paid trip to Denver, a reputedly cool mountain town I'd never seen.

Only after I agreed to go and was named the college's official representative did I realize that any prospects for sightseeing would be extremely limited or nonexistent. The advance schedule listed no tours or time for hiking, only speeches and discussion sessions from morning till night, then dinner at local restaurants with the other participants. The hotel for the event was not some remote mountain retreat center or a downtown haven full of history and local color but the Sheraton-Denver Tech Center. On the taxi ride from the airport, I saw that even an early-morning jog was probably out of the question since the venue was located in a snarl of interstate highways, office complexes, and industrial sites far away from any place interesting, accessible only by car, and not pedestrian-friendly by any means.

My taxi driver, as young and blond and muscled as a Hollywood Nazi, was a survivalist who'd been reading *Soldier of Fortune* magazine when he answered the call to pick me up at the airport. I saw it lying on the seat next to him when I got in. Along the way, he told me that young people like us (I was twenty-eight at the time) needed to be ready when the system collapsed. We needed to arm ourselves, train diligently, and prepare for the ensuing chaos. The guy was scary. I was glad we made it to the Sheraton-Denver Tech Center without my having to view the handgun collection he probably kept under the seat. I gave him a big tip, which I couldn't afford, something like protection money. The irony was that his harangue would set the tone for the discussions I was about to undertake over the next couple of days—and in fact, for the next couple of decades.

Despite the ugly setting and my disappointment in the daily walking and touring schedule (which did indeed prove nonexistent), the impact of the meeting was enormous. My scholarship still echoes with memories of the featured speakers, whose viewpoints ranged from strictly environmentalist to hard-core pro-development, and the ensuing discussions among the professors and the oil-company representatives who hosted each table of four or five academic guests. For me, if not for the sixteen other professors from various Western universities—most of them in fields like economics, engineering, and political science, with a professor of Chinese the only other participant representing the humanities—the discussions proved stimulating and illuminating, but also unsettling.

What struck me most solidly was the way that all the speakers on the pro-development side of the fence—most of them arguing for unlimited exploration and development of energy resources, even in sensitive and protected sites like wilderness areas—reduced the options to stark oppositions: drill for oil and mine for coal *or* freeze to death in the winter; provide jobs *or* protect the environment; submit to unlimited growth of an energy-intensive economy *or* watch the United States slip from world power and global economic leadership to third-world poverty. This reduction of options would become the focus of the book that Jackie and I published a little more than a decade later—*Ecospeak: Rhetoric and Environmental Politics in America.* The first glimmer of that study appeared in an essay I wrote about the Company-Faculty Forum for *College English* in 1981, with the title "Can an English Teacher Contribute to the Energy Debate?"

In the article and later in *Ecospeak,* the analysis drew upon George Orwell's thinking on politics and the English language. Just as the fictionalized totalitarian state in Orwell's famous novel *1984* controlled the masses by inciting fear and anxiety, largely by reducing linguistic options to fewer and fewer words and rigid forms of expression in the version of language that Orwell called *Newspeak,* Jackie and I observed that pro-development activists, as well as the majority of outlets in the mass media who seemed to follow their lead in the nonfictional 1980s, reflected the same trend. They offered oversimplified options and overstated caricatures of their opponents in public debate. The enemies were the big environmental organizations like the Sierra Club and the Wilderness Society, as well as the grass-roots environmentalists and conservationists mobilized by a decade of Earth Days and local opponents of industrial extraction, production, and pollution—the Not-in-My-Backyard (NIMBY) crowd. The federal government was also a target because of the rash of regulatory legislation passed in the sixties and seventies: the Clean Air Act of 1963, the Wilderness Act of 1964, the National Environmental Policy Act of 1969, the Endangered Species Act of 1973, and the Clean Water Act of 1977. In the days leading up to the election of Ronald Reagan, with the nation struggling through yet another energy crisis, the oil and chemical companies were clearly on the offensive. The reductive and divisive language that Jackie and I eventually called *ecospeak* ruled the day.

❧ The speakers at the forum, such as the representative from the American Petroleum Institute and the company reps who sat among us in the audience and led the discussions in our break-out groups, seemed at first blush to be paragons of good manners, open-mindedness, devotion to public service, and willingness to engage in rational discourse. But if pressed—and they were definitely pressed by the professors present—they eventually resorted to the harsh contrasts and reduction of options that allowed only one reasonable choice. (No, I don't want to freeze to death, lose my job, watch America fall. I want to drill for oil, dig for coal, and grow the economy without limits and regardless of the environmental consequences.)

But at least one speaker, a pro-development advocate from the Mountain States Legal Foundation, seemed to go overboard. When questioned about him, even the company reps seemed a little embarrassed by the rhetorical extremes of his speech. In an effort to explain the man's intensity, my table leader said to me, in so many words, that after a couple of decades of fighting an environmental movement spurred to new heights by Rachel Carson and the Club of Rome, some of the folks on the other side (his side, that is) decided that they could not merely resort to scientific evidence anymore. Something stronger was needed. Rhetorically, when confronting the general public and the politicians (though not their honored guests from academia, the man hastened to add), the pro-development advocates had made up their minds to fight fire with fire.

Hellfire, that is. The MSLF rep took to the podium with a quick step, gripped the lectern with both hands, peered at us through thick glasses, his bald head shining like a halo, and unleashed a furious onslaught of rhetoric. The speech took me back to the days of my youth, when I sat stupefied before the hellfire-and-damnation evangelists who sometimes visited our church at revival time or when I heard the anti-evolution sermon in my senior year of high school, the one that started the process of my alienation from Baptist-church-going orthodoxy. Billy Graham was mild by comparison; the old preacher I grew up with was a model of decorum. I thought instead of Elmer Gantry and the tent-revival holy rollers of my grandmother's generation. The only thing missing was the Southern accent and bad grammar. The guy from the MSLF fired up the apocalyptic rhetoric in the well-formed sentences and newscaster-free-of-dialect English that meant, to me, that he wasn't speaking out of a rhetorical tradition he grew up with and fell into without much thinking; he was *choosing* this mode of expression.

"In the West," he said, "we are at the center of a storm that is going to come over this nation." He was referring to the conflict between environmentalists and the rest of the good people of America, though his metaphors suggested the coming of the Four Horsemen of the Apocalypse. Environmentalists, he insisted, aren't really interested in protecting nature; their driving motive is to bring down the American way of life: if they were interested in protecting nature, they would realize that by restraining development and forcing governmental controls on the rational and scientifically informed activities of industry, they were bringing on Armageddon, a time in the near future when the energy crisis would become so acute that the people would be driven to rape the land and slaughter the innocents to provide heat and power to sustain themselves and their families. Don't expect the government to help, he said. The executive branch is "out of control" and Congress has "abdicated their responsibility." Keep holding back the companies with your socialistic regulations if you want. But prepare yourselves for chaos and war.

He sounded like my cab driver, for goodness' sake. Still, I must confess, he had my attention. My scientific colleagues in the professorial contingent were inclined to dismiss the speech as outlandish and emotional, not to be taken seriously among thinking people. But something—maybe my background, maybe my state of mind in those days, maybe my preparation by the cab driver—led me to receive the speech with alarm and foreboding.

As it turns out, I wasn't the only one paying attention to this man. His name meant nothing to me at the time, but within a year, it was regularly featured in the national news. The man's name was James Watt. When, later that fall, Ronald Reagan rode into the presidency on the wave of personal charisma, discontent over Jimmy Carter's ineptitude, and a flood of funding from energy companies, he chose Watt to be his secretary of the interior. It was by far the most controversial and newsworthy Cabinet appointment he made during his administration. Watt lasted only a couple of years in the position before resigning in the wake of a mocking comment he made about affirmative action. On the selection of members for a committee, he said, "I have a black, I have a woman, two Jews, and a cripple." The joke was the last of many ill-considered comments. He'd also said, to take one example, that there are two kinds of people in our nation—liberals and Americans. My own antenna for the fundamentalist quality of

Watt's rhetoric proved accurate as well. I didn't realize it then, but a taste for evangelical and dispensational theology had begun to spread across the nation. A Southern accent was no longer required. Watt frequently alluded to his theological leanings in public. A comment attributed to him that applied this outlook to environmental issues—that saving the environment doesn't matter in light of the imminent second coming of Christ—proved to be a false attribution, though it fit so well with the character he established in public debate that it was accepted as true by some usually more cautious folks in the media world. Bill Moyers repeated the quote and then had to apologize. It was also rumored that Watt wanted to change the official flag of the Department of the Interior so that the buffalo faced right rather than left. Other members of the Reagan administration gave Watt a shoot-yourself-in-the-foot award (a plaster foot with a hole in it). In general, he was viewed as an extremist and ultimately a liability to the president. But Reagan reportedly continued to favor Watt right to the end, to the point that other staff members did not dare to criticize him except jokingly (as with the plaster foot). But finally Watt proved too much for everybody involved and had to resign. In 2008, *Time* magazine included him among the ten worst Cabinet members in American history.

Even so, Reagan's choice turned out to be (pardon the pun) prophetic. Despite the dismissive contempt that my colleagues at the forum and his later critics in the media displayed toward Watt—and despite his initial failure to turn the tide against environmental protection, which had been warmly received across a wide spectrum of the American public since the sixties (as we learn from the analysis of the historian Samuel Hays)—Watt's point of view and even his over-the-top confrontational style would become a key element in the opposition to environmentalism over the following thirty years. Paired with the increasing popularity of dispensational theology among Christian fundamentalists, it would become common in the post-Reagan years for right-wing politicos to lump environmentalism in with socialism, feminism, secular humanism, ethnic identity politics, and other elements of the main enemy, which, again following Watt's lead, they called *liberalism*—without regard to the historical meanings of the term and without much regard to current political reality.

In our analysis in *Ecospeak,* Jackie and I suggested that, if anything, environmentalism constituted a *crisis* for liberalism. How could you be the party of progress in matters of labor, employment, industry, and agriculture and also the party of conservation, preservation, and protection in matters involving the natural environment? The linguistic connection between *conservation* and *conservatism* was completely disregarded in the growing division of environmentalism and developmentalism and the more general political division of liberals and conservatives. We argued that a kind of social ecology based on the principle of sustainability pointed the way to compromise on these issues, a middle way. But the trend was already in motion by that time to line up environmentalism in any form with the other "isms" that constituted the liberal threat. James Watt showed the way to the current red-blue divide in national politics and also foreshadowed the way that the politics of nature would be forced onto the left side of the divide. By the time that George H. W. Bush would claim, in his campaign for president, that as an outdoorsman he had always been an environmentalist (despite his record in the oil business and the funding he received from the extractive industries), this kind of open-handed attitude toward the politics of nature was on the way out. Where there had once been an *issue*—environmental protection or conservation—there was now an *ideology:* environmentalism. At least that was the view from the right.

From the other side of the fence, Ted Nordhaus and Michael Shellenberger, in their 2004 report *The Death of Environmentalism,* would argue that environmentalism was stuck in the position of a single-issue, special-interest group. It needed more of a grand vision and broad structure of values to attack and defeat its enemies among the neoconservatives. The neocons worked out policy from an established set of values and principles—above all, the drive to limit the influence of government and the special interests that appealed to it—while the big environmental organizations, like other liberal groups, continued to hack away at problems and issues, offering technical solutions and accepting short-term gains and even losses as parts of the inevitably slow and incremental motion taken for granted by Washington insiders. The movement, said Nordhaus and Shellenberger, needed instead to be integrated into a plan that would leave conservation and regulation behind and take up investment in alternative energies and campaigns to reform the tax structure and electoral financial rules, to get money out of politics and into cleaner new technologies and job production in new sectors. Environmentalism was dead, according to Nordhaus and Shellenberger, just as terms like *nature* and *environment* were no longer meaningful. What mattered was taking care of business and getting government on track to solve the big problems like global warming.

The fight continues to rage as I write these pages. Environmentalism seems caught in the middle, attacked as too ideological and not ideological enough. Nature is gone, people say; the "environment" is a meaningless thing. So what are we left with? The economy? Politicos like Nordhaus and Shellenberger are fighting to bring the environment into the system, to keep it from being what the economists call an "externality" that you don't have to account for in computations of costs and benefits. The internalizing of "green capital" like water, soil, air, and wind may be the answer to solving problems like global warming and preventing one energy crisis after another, or part of the answer anyway.

But even after everything is given a price, and the monetary values are set, I still worry about what will happen to the people and the places I love. Where are the mountains, the birds, the foxes, the forests, the canyons, and the rivers, and where are the ecosystem people, the park rangers, the small farmers, and the nature writers in all the abstractions of political ideology and economically determined values?

They are nowhere. They are part of nature, and nature is nowhere in that way of thinking. If that's the case, nowhere is where I want to be. Nowhere, I like to remember, is the literal meaning of Utopia.

⁂ Of course, when Nordhaus and Shellenberger say that the environmental movement lacks vision and values, they don't mean that environmentalists never had a vision. The problem, as they see it, is that the visions environmentalists cling to are outmoded, wrong, or ineffectual. One such vision is the apocalyptic trend among early environmental thinkers.

The studies I undertook in the 1980s proved that the company rep from Gulf Oil, my table leader, was right about the background of James Watt's rhetoric. In the research for *Ecospeak,* Jackie and I traced the reaction of pro-development opponents of environmentalism back to the influential writings of scientific activism in the 1960s—most notably the work of Rachel Carson and Paul Ehrlich. The apocalyptic warnings of these writers—the founders of what Jackie Palmer and I called "millennial ecology"—had produced by the 1980s an equal and opposite millennialism among the backers of the extractive industries—not only oil, gas, and mining but also the chemical companies supporting the industrialization of agriculture.

Carson started the trend in the famous prologue to *Silent Spring* in 1962. Entitled "A Fable for Tomorrow," the short speculative essay offered a composite portrait of a once-prosperous mid-America town poisoned by overuse and misuse of chemical pesticides—*composite* in the sense that it drew upon actual events from many locations, which, for purposes of drama, were located and intensified in a single site. It was also *extrapolative*—projecting a future based on the combination and intensification of current trends, like a line graph with a sharply ascending curve. In this doomed town projected onto the screen of the future, the people woke up one day to find that the birds had ceased to sing, the plants had withered, and strange diseases were afoot among the citizens. They wondered what witch or wizard had brought this evil spell upon them, only to realize at last that they had done it to themselves. The story is over within a couple of pages, and the author is explaining that no such town exists but that the effects described have happened in a number of actual places. If things continue on the same path, she warns, we could face the multiplication of effects not just in a single location but everywhere in the modern world.

The short prologue is followed by more than two hundred pages of exposé and science writing that marshals abundant evidence for her claims that pesticides need to be more carefully researched, monitored, regulated, and applied. But it was the prologue that caught everyone's attention, from the general public, who made the book a bestseller, to the administration of Pres. John F. Kennedy, who reputedly kept a copy on his desk, to the halls of Congress, where Carson would be invited to testify, to the headquarters of industry, from which a massive campaign of public relations and reeducation sped forth. Monsanto Corporation distributed a pamphlet called *Silent Autumn* that offered its own apocalyptic vision of the famine and starvation that, in their version of the future, would result from limiting the production and application of pesticides and synthetic chemical fertilizers in the Green Revolution that was on the way to eliminating hunger from the world. The rhetoric also caught on with other environmental writers. In the 1968 book *The Population Bomb,* Paul Ehrlich picked up Carson's connection of the environmental crisis with Cold War anxiety over the possibility of nuclear war. The "population explosion" became a household phrase, inciting worry and speculation over the future of food production, reproductive politics, and environmental destruction.

Jackie and I did our best to sort out the various motives and themes that passed under the banner of apocalyptic rhetoric. Our work is still cited by scholars in the field of environmental communication and in literary studies of the environment, mainly, I think, because of the thorough survey we made of millennialism in the ecological debate up to the late 1980s, when it was finally connected to global warming in books like Stephen Schneider's *Global Warming: Are We Entering the Greenhouse Century?*—which opened with a new version of "A Fable for Tomorrow"—and Bill McKibben's *The End of Nature,* which is cited these days as the first book on global warming written for the general public.

But Jackie and I never got to the bottom of the matter, I've decided, because we never fully surveyed the religious literature and traditions that undergirded millennial ecology and its opposition but that remained simmering in the background. Like everyone else living in the atomic age, with the world already divided between communist and capitalist, totalitarian and free nations on the two sides of the Iron Curtain, we were bombarded daily by apocalyptic rhetoric and never stopped to consider that it is *always* destructive and divisive, even in the hands of heroes like Rachel Carson. She made very limited use of millennial rhetoric but ultimately spawned a whole generation of arguments over who will save and who will destroy the earth. In truth, salvation and destruction of the earth are what philosophers call totalizing terms. Like the evangelical decisions to which they also attach—convert or die, choose heaven or hell—they leave no room for compromise and negotiation, complexity and subtlety. They are words of war, implying life-or-death decisions. You are either with me or again' me.

I never fully realized the inevitable destructiveness of millennial rhetoric until many years later in a very different setting. I was living in Texas by then and had been asked to lead a Sunday Bible study at a local Methodist church. Some of my friends there knew I had read a great deal over the years about the Christian Gospels. I guess I never quite got over my Baptist upbringing as a student of the Bible. Even during my absence from the church in my college years, I'd taken New Testament courses in the Religious Studies Department at the University of Tennessee. Later, as the twentieth century drew to a close, I eagerly read the new studies of the Bible, especially the work of theologians like Elaine Pagels, Karen Armstrong, and John Dominic Crossan, reporting on the discovery of ancient writings that were never included among the approved books of the Christian Bible and new interpretations based on those discoveries—the Dead Sea Scrolls, the collection of texts from Nag Hammadi, the Coptic Gospel of Thomas and other Gnostic Gospels, which I first heard about in my college courses in the 1970s, some of them handed out for the class to read on blue mimeograph.

After I agreed to take on the Sunday class, I learned that by comparison with my old friends among the Baptists and my more recent Catholic compadres, the Methodists were an open-minded lot, willing to countenance a wide latitude of interpretations and consider closely the historical background of the Bible's origins. For five years, I enjoyed teaching a long course involving detailed readings not only of the four canonical Gospels but also the Gnostic books and the then-new discovery of the so-called Gospel of Judas. I never felt my intellectual commitment to scholarship compromised or my scholarly approach to the Bible threatened. I felt I had finally found a place within Christianity where I could make my home.

Until, that is, I reluctantly succumbed to a study of Revelation, the book that gave apocalyptic rhetoric its name—also known as the Apocalypse of John, the title that uses the Greek word for *vision* or *unveiling*. One of the class members was confused by the many claims he'd always heard about the book. Why couldn't we work in our usual way to come to an understanding about the meanings of this strange text? Christian interest in Revelation had been growing since the era of Rachel Carson and Paul Ehrlich, when an equally influential and notorious bestseller was published by the Christian fundamentalist Hal Lindsey, who also capitalized on the dark mood of the Cold War. *The Late Great Planet Earth,* published in 1970, caught the attention of the Jesus Movement when it first appeared and continues to inform Christian Zionism and dispensational theology today. Concepts that I had never encountered in my Christian upbringing—like the so-called Rapture, the time in the near future when believers will be raised from the earth and nonbelievers left behind to suffer the destruction of the natural world—became a regular topic for Christian talk shows on television and radio. By the time of my

Bible class, everybody seemed to be talking about the meaning of Revelation for our times. An entire series of novels called *Left Behind*, based on the dispensational theology inspired by Revelation, had recently appeared. The series was so popular that it generated a new demand for Christian fiction. The big bookstores regularly began to feature the genre under its own heading.

I tried to deflect the suggestion that we study Revelation by saying, "Look. As I understand it, Revelation is over." I explained that, in the interpretation I favored, the book prophesied the fall of the Roman Empire just as Jesus's own apocalyptic sayings prophesied the fall of the Temple in Jerusalem in 70 AD. "It's done. It's that simple." One of the other class members, a retired minister with a long résumé in theology, agreed. "God won," he said. "End of story."

But the wave of popular enthusiasm for Revelation carried the day. We did the study, and it destroyed the class. All the politely suppressed theological differences that the participants harbored came racing to the surface. Many of the brightest and most devoted participants departed; new ones joined with motives far beyond serious study and engagement of the sacred texts. My own commitment to Christianity was questioned. I got emails trying to persuade me to see the light and let go of my intellectual pride. (The main issue, by the way, was whether Christianity was the exclusive path to God, a premise I could neither accept in my heart nor justify by my readings of the Gospels.) When I offered to step aside and let another teacher take over, the offer was accepted, to my deep relief.

Later I would take comfort for my failure as a Bible teacher, even among the mild Methodists, from the theologian Karen Armstrong's commentary: "Revelation is deliberately obscure, its symbols unintelligible to outsiders"—which would include not only non-Christians but also those outside the historical context of its original composition—including modern Christians, many of whom find whatever meaning they want in the text. For this reason, and for many others, she says, "It is a toxic book," one that appeals mainly to "people who, like the Johannine churches, felt alienated and resentful" (76). The original readers of the book were members of a persecuted sect; the modern enthusiasts are more like a sect with a persecution complex.

The word *toxic* in Armstrong's commentary brings me back to Rachel Carson. She might never have brought the attention to environmental issues that she did if she had never written "A Fable for Tomorrow." But in introducing the toxic rhetoric of the apocalypse into her book on environmental toxins, she started a war. It was the environmentalist version of the Cold War, threatening to erupt at any moment into a fistfight, a gun battle, a bombing campaign. And it's still going on. I don't know about you, but this sole surviving son, who has lived under the shadow of death that war brings over the land since the day I was born, wishes there could be another way.

❧ In reading over my *College English* article about the Company-Faculty Forum these thirty years later, one thing strikes me as odd. At one point in the essay, I claim not to be an environmentalist but to have been swayed in that direction by my revulsion from the apocalyptic rhetoric of the pro-development side. I also hint that I was not persuaded by the theory of the greenhouse effect, the forerunner of global warming, though I preferred the style and approach of the speaker who cited the theory—a representative of the National Wildlife Federation—in fact the only speaker who cited any scientific theory and who worked hardest to ground his viewpoint within the framework of a rational argument complete with solid evidence that no one in the room felt the need to dispute. I also remember a speaker who reasonably urged us to oppose nuclear power production not only because of the problems it poses for disposal of nuclear waste but also because of the way it focuses energy production in a single, concentrated area, making it vulnerable to enemy attack (no one said "terrorist attack" in those days) as well as natural disaster—a perspective I had reason to recall many times in later years, most recently in the nuclear accidents that followed the 2011 earthquake and tsunami in northern Japan.

So was it really true, after my experience with Tellico, with my deepening affinity with wild nature in Tennessee and New Mexico, and with the appeal of the environmentalist side of the debate at Company-Faculty Forum, that at the time I published the essay in 1981 I still did not identify with the emerging ideology of environmentalism? Or was I just taking this stance to set up my arguments against the toxic rhetoric of the other speakers? Was my refusal to affiliate just intellectual posturing?

In all honesty, I don't remember my exact motives. I do know that I was deeply appreciative of Gulf for sponsoring the forum and said so in my conclusion to the essay. I was disinclined to see the event only as a public relations ploy or an act of propaganda. The company wasn't appealing to the politicians (they could do that with their dollars) or what it perceived as the naïve public (advertising and price-setting could take care of that audience); it was trying to engage a cross-section of the best minds of the universities in the mountain West. The company may have understood what has become for me a real truth about political engagement: it's all too easy to dismiss people who oppose your political point of view if you only see them on television, read their quotations in the media, or watch them in formal debates. But sitting at a table over lunch, it's harder. Putting this insight to work, my colleague Tarla Rai Peterson has made brilliant use of the focus group as a way of offering expert intervention in communities struggling over environmental issues. She brings the people to the table, where they can be fellow citizens and stakeholders and not just representatives of this or that ideology.

But if I was reluctant to identify as an environmentalist at the time I wrote the article—in public, if not in my heart of hearts—by the end of the decade, I was closer to claiming the identity. During the years we lived in Memphis, 1988–90, completing work on *Ecospeak,* Jackie and I were active in the environmentalist community. We attended Sierra Club meetings. We hosted the advance agent for Greenpeace in our home when its famous ship, the *Rainbow Warrior,* passed by town on an inner-continental tour for cleaner rivers, docking at Mud Island on the Mississippi, the Greenpeace activists holding news conferences on local polluters. We helped found the Memphis Greens to promote local environmental actions like recycling, water testing, wildlife protection, and public education. For our contribution to the group, we sponsored debates between eco-activists and local representatives of the pesticide industry, held book discussions on ecological topics, and contributed to the big celebration of Earth Day on its twentieth anniversary in 1990.

But when we did commit ourselves to environmentalism, we insisted on a particular version, which in *Ecospeak* we identified as *social ecology* or *eco-humanism.* We saw this perspective as a middle way that attempted to meet the challenge raised by Watt and other opponents. We refused to be single-issue, special-interest environmentalists who (like Dave Foreman of Earth First! in those days) saw the clear separation of issues as the key to political success, who denied the connection between social justice and environmentalism, and who refused to consider the need to save jobs on the way to wilderness protection. Environmentalism was not, for us, just a matter of "saving the earth," whatever that could mean; it was rather a matter of finding ways for people to live efficiently and happily according to the best principles of ecology. Ultimately, it was about finding the relationship among what one author has called the "three Es of sustainability": *environment* yes, but also *ethics* and *economics* (see Edwards). So our work with the Memphis Greens also included the development of urban gardens for inner-city residents, advocacy for multiracial representation on the city's governing bodies, and the kind of public awareness projects that would later fall under the heading of "environmental justice," a hybridization of environmental and social justice concerns.

Not all prospective members of the Memphis Greens appreciated this direction of our work. I recall at a book discussion one night, a man angrily confronted me when I said that environmentalists should make common cause with the socially oppressed. "Do you feel oppressed?" he said. "Hell no. This is just white liberal guilt talking. We need to get on with the work that concerns us the most. I came here because I heard this group was going to promote recycling. We need that, we really do. But I don't need to be lectured about my responsibilities to the poor and oppressed. I can get that anywhere in this town." It would have been easy enough to dismiss the guy as a racist or an elitist or whatever. But to me, he was a person I encountered face to face, with whom I shared many values. I still remember his face and his voice and his frustration—and my own feeling of being unable to make a convincing case for the thing I believed in—social ecology. Even James Watt's words about the ulterior motives of environmentalists haunt me in this regard. Politics seems easy only if you're not listening to your opponents or even your partial allies.

My commitment to a social form of political ecology was driven, as always, by personal experience. After Tellico and my time with the Native American students in the NAMES program and my teaching among students of different races, there was, for sure, my wish for a world where the different races could live together peaceably, and of course there was the old connection in my writing between nature and war, a deep yearning for global peace. But all the idealism that grew from those influences was bolstered by experiences closer to home at the moment I was living in those years. That was where I found the passion that kept me going.

Jackie and I were both emerging from a time when, as we established ourselves as individuals (even individual*ists,* some would say *eccentrics*—living on the edge of society's circle, *ec-centric*). Now we were redefining our position as social beings. We were new parents who sought the company of other parents with babies and small children. I was reestablishing my connection with my family after years of difficulty and alienation in my first marriage. Our daughter was the first grandchild in the family, followed closely by the birth of my younger sister's son. Suddenly my parents were grandparents, and we were a generation of aunts and uncles.

Jackie and I continued to cultivate our love of the outdoors, but that changed too. The backpacking gear went to the attic. Car camping became the norm on weekend excursions and on visits to her mother in California, her father in Denver, my family in South Carolina. We bought a nice dome tent. Myrth took her first camping trip as a baby in the canyon country east of the Caprock when we lived in Lubbock. When the poles of the tent collapsed in heavy wind in the middle of the night, she never cried. We awoke to her crawling around to explore the change in abode. I carried her on my back for hikes at Palo Duro Canyon, Bandelier

National Monument, and the Muir Woods. Once in Rocky Mountain National Park, she sang a wordless song all the way to the shore of an alpine lake and back again. She bounced along on my back when we took the walk to Abrams Falls in the Smokies on a visit to the east. That night in the campground at Cades Cove, more cautious than I had been before, I tied our cooler up in a tree to keep from tempting the bears (a stupid idea, I know now, thanks to my grown-up park ranger daughter). A man standing nearby said, "You afraid of bears?"

"Well, we do have a baby in the tent," I said.

"Okay." He glanced over at the woods. "I ain't afraid of bears."

"Really?"

"Naw, but I'll tell you, if I see a wild hog around, I'll climb a sapling and make it stand up!"

Instead of hunts, hikes, and birdwatching excursions to escape a troubled home life, camping and hiking—and later canoeing and cross-country skiing—came to seem an extension or enhancement of home life. We still needed the retreat and refuge we found in the outdoors. Jackie and I both grew claustrophobic without it. But what became clearer and clearer to me was the satisfaction that came from companionship in the woods and the hills and the waters of nature.

So it was that, when I rediscovered myself as a family man, I reconnected to the family of man (as it used to be called) and discovered social ecology as the version of nature politics that made the most sense to me. Years later I would find the version of sustainability that resonated most clearly with me as well. It came from my reading in Native American studies—the idea of the *seventh generation*. Everyone alive at this moment in history is the seventh generation. All decisions should respect the memory of the previous three generations (at least) and account for the well-being of the next three generations. We stand in the middle, thinking of the ways our actions and attitudes reflect the ancestral values that we bring to the moment and will shape the future to which we devote our legacy.

It used to be common for old-school ecologists like Garrett Hardin to insist that environmentalism necessarily impinges on personal freedom. But freedom has many definitions, a good survey of which appears in the philosopher Brian Norton's study of sustainability. The meaning that emerges as most suggestive for a sustainable future is the concept of freedom as multigenerational, communal, and opportunity oriented. The society that offers people the greatest number of options for fulfillment while not compromising the same range of opportunities for the next generation is the most sustainable society—a lofty goal for members of the seventh generation.

If freedom no longer means only the kind of independence built on the image of rugged individualism—too easily co-opted by the Marlboro Man and the consumerist ideal of freedom as the opportunity to buy whatever you want, whenever you want—can we imagine a new kind of independence, built on a persistent questioning of our dependencies and the possibility of living free from them: the possibility of living off the energy grid, for example?

My late father-in-law strung the wires for the first electricity in rural Kansas, where he grew up on a family farm. My grown daughter, like Edward Abbey, works as a seasonal park ranger half the year. The rest of the year she lives in a solar adobe dwelling with an outhouse and wood stove on the margins of a national forest. Her utility bill is zero. In between lies my own generation, who can hardly imagine a dark night without electric lights or a home without a TV and flush toilet for every member of the household. Maybe some call of the wild reaches us occasionally in our deeply insulated dwellings, like the chortle of the sandhill cranes in the March sky of the Brazos Valley of Texas, which my neighbors might hear at dawn in the brief interval of the year when their heaters cease to kick on every cool morning and before the air-conditioners crank up to greet the early-morning warmth of late spring. A colleague remembers growing up in Fort Worth before air-conditioning, lying down for a nap on a summer afternoon under damp sheets, cooled by the prairie breeze coming in the open window of her bedroom.

The story reminds me of the honored place that storytelling has in transgenerational and communal knowledge, the passing of the legacy on which seventh-generation sustainability depends. Perhaps the stories we need to hear right now, the images of a new world, will come not only from our grandparents, but from our children.

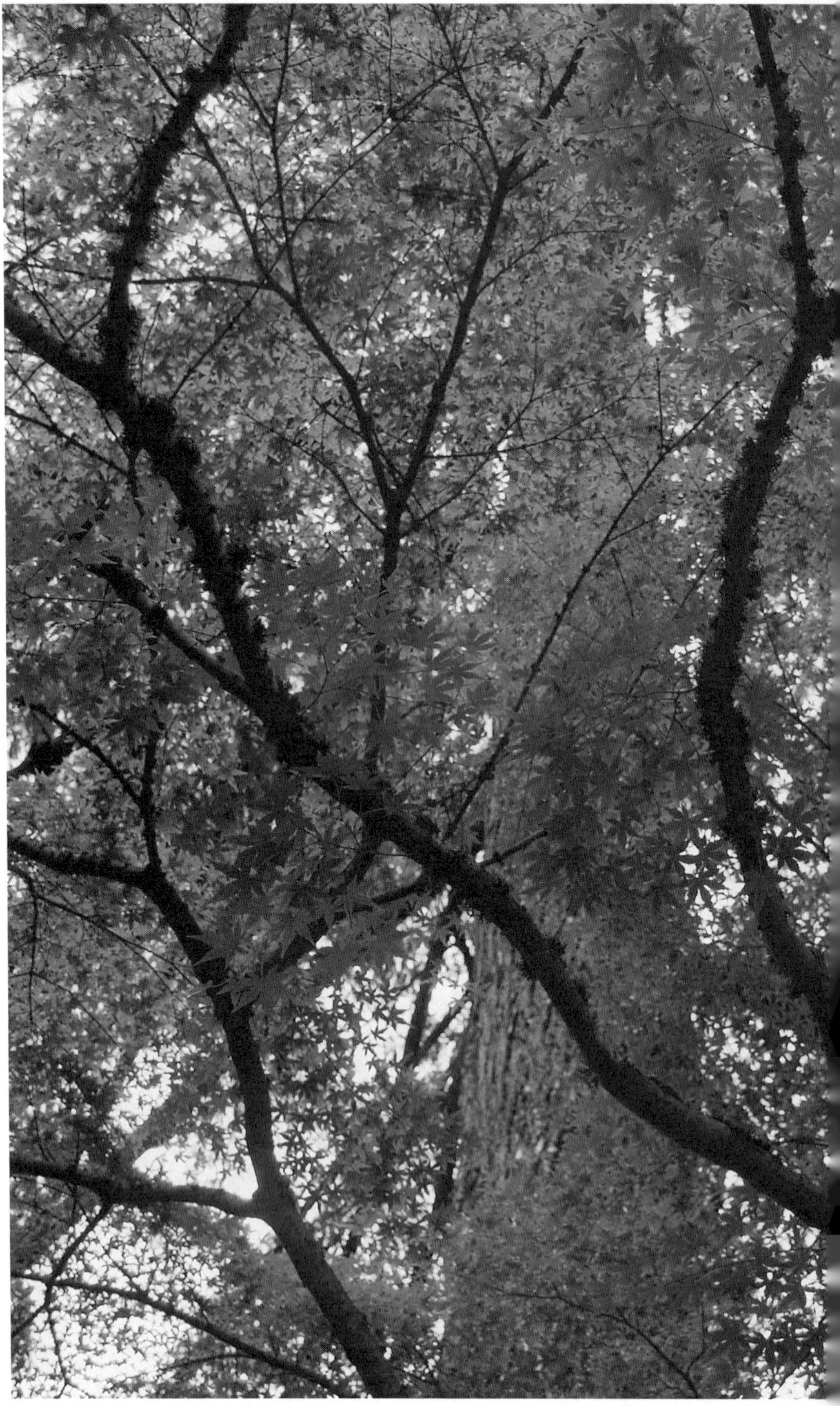

6 Apocalypse Redux and the Fate of Sustainability

. . . and then it was
There interposed a Fly—

With Blue—uncertain—stumbling Buzz—
Between the light—and me—
And then the Windows failed—and then
I could not see to see—

Emily Dickinson, "I Heard a Fly Buzz When I Died"

Rage, rage against the dying of the light.

Dylan Thomas, "Do Not Go Gentle into That Good Night"

The week after Labor Day is always an ominous time in Texas. Heat lingers from an unrelenting summer, hurricanes loom off the Gulf coast, wildfires threaten in the west. And the summer of 2011 was like summer on steroids. The number of hundred-degree days was unparalleled in recorded times, the dryness harsher and deeper than the days of the Dust Bowl during the Great Depression and the seven-year drought of the 1950s, which, as John Graves says in *Goodbye to a River*, was the worst since Spanish times according to the evidence of tree rings. Plotting rainfall against average daily temperature, one graph used in presentations by officials from the National Weather Service showed the summer of 2011 in a class by itself, almost off the charts, nearly four degrees hotter and two inches of rainfall shorter than the next closest competitor.

The heat finally broke the week after Labor Day, offering a welcome, if nervous, relief in a season that dares you to get too comfortable. On Tuesday, September 6, I stepped out for my morning walk into a fifty-eight-degree morning—twenty degrees cooler than it had been all summer when I jogged in the pre-dawn dark to keep from overheating my aging body as the temperature rose from the high seventies to one hundred degrees before noon every day.

On this mild September morning, I had the length of exactly one breath to enjoy the long-awaited cool. Then I smelled the smoke. And I felt the honest fear of one who dwells in a drought-stricken oak savannah, with brittle trees and parched prairie on every side. No air-conditioned comfort, no suburban tract of brick homes laid out on a grid of handsome boulevards could on this day expunge the fear of the animal that catches the scent of fire in a habitat prepared for burning by months of dry wind and searing heat.

This year people had actually hoped for a hurricane, at least my neighbors had, some 150 miles up the long coastal plain and away from the rising tides and heaviest winds that the people of Galveston and Corpus Christi dread in early September. Upstate we longed for anything to relieve the heat and drought that was destroying farmland, sending herds to slaughter, choking the wildlife, dehydrating the homeless who flocked to overcrowded shelters, driving utility costs sky high for homeowners, and cracking foundations in the suburbs. When Tropical Storm Lee finally came within striking range, it sent the big rains northeastward to Louisiana. Texas only got the wind. Power lines blew down, and sparks set fire to the forests of second-growth loblolly pine and native oak and juniper scrub on the edges of brown-grass prairie. Now, with an acreage the size of Connecticut ablaze, the fires were lapping at the dry land of the river valley where I make my home.

My Facebook friends posted maps of the hot spots and smoke trails. Some of them used the occasion to berate our governor's recent denials of global warming and climate science. Others mentioned the wrath of Yahweh and other gods. I was thinking yes, we seem to be living in biblical times, but, even with the scent of smoke in my nostrils, I found myself wary of this knee-jerk rhetoric.

For me, with all the studies of millennial ecology and New Testament theology behind me, Armageddon had become a tired old story. We'd heard it in 1962, in "A Fable for Tomorrow," the famous prologue to Rachel Carson's *Silent Spring;* it sounded again in 1968, in Paul Ehrlich's *The Population Bomb,* and yet again in 1970, in Hal Lindsey's *The Late Great Planet Earth.* Lindsey concludes this way: "As the battle of Armageddon reaches its awful climax and it appears that all life will be destroyed on earth— in this very moment Jesus Christ will return and save man from self-extinction" (156). For Jesus Christ, you can substitute ecological science, population management, or some other body of special knowledge, religious belief, or political ideology, depending on the version of the apocalypse at hand. The point is, we know how to be saved, but we won't accept the truth.

The Facebook prophets of September 2011 recall the complaint of Ted Nordhaus and Michael Shellenberger about the invocation of Armageddon in contemporary narratives about the fate of the nation: "The stories that the left tells about America in decline and ecological collapse and that the right tells about religious wars and apocalypse are all narratives of resentment motivated by the desire to annihilate one's enemies—to see them *get what's coming to them.* They are all revenge fantasies" (*Break Through* 186). As the old R.E.M. song says, "It's the end of the world as we know it, and *I feel fine.*"

Focusing on the left side of the story in their 2004 pamphlet *The Death of Environmentalism,* Nordhaus and Shellenberger joke that if environmental leaders had written Martin Luther King Jr.'s "I Have a Dream" speech, it would have been called "I Have a Nightmare" (31)—a quip that they had to more or less retract in their 2007 book *Break Through: Why We Can't Leave Saving the Planet to Environmentalists* after readers of their earlier pamphlet pointed out that Dr. King did in fact have a few nightmare visions of his own. The civil rights movement was based on resistance and critique as well as hope and positive planning. And in fact, Nordhaus and Shellenberger do make room for critique, but most of the negative energy they muster is directed toward the available outlooks on political ecology, from the wilderness ethic to environmental justice. They likely caught the public's attention at first and then enjoyed some measure of success because they themselves led with a version of the apocalyptic narrative—with the title *The* Death *of Environmentalism*—which, according to their own analysis, amounts to a desire to destroy their enemies.

In the work that Jackie and I did back in the 1990s on millennial ecology, our conclusions dovetailed with Nordhaus and Shellenberger's on at least one point: we saw apocalyptic narrative not as a flat-out prediction of the future (the end of the world via chemical pollution à la Carson, or famine and epidemic via overpopulation à la Ehrlich) but as the representation of a desire to do something in the present. For the political ecologists, it was not so much to destroy enemies as to mobilize public resistance to the overuse or misuse of harmful chemicals and other ultimately self-destructive behaviors. We also argued that the rhetoric was historically constrained. It worked well for one generation of activist writers—the generation of Carson and Ehrlich—because it resonated with worries about nuclear disaster in the Cold War years. But like Nordhaus and Shellenberger, we saw the rhetoric itself as the verbal equivalent of war. It was divisive and destructive. It continued to perpetuate the political divisions of ecospeak rather than healing wounds and getting on with solving environmental problems.

Our analysis suggests that we were beginning to feel some distance between our own world and the Cold War world of my mother's generation—a life lived under the threat of global thermonuclear war between the superpowers, with communal nightmares recounted not only in the discourses of military-industrialism, ecology, and religion but also in the entertainment industry, in popular novels and movies like *On the Beach, Fail-Safe,* and *Dr. Strangelove.* The growing distance we felt was typical of many people reaching the prime of life in the 1990s, in the years immediately following the fall of the Berlin Wall in 1989 and the collapse of the Soviet Union shortly afterward.

Our embrace of the sustainability ideal in the politics of ecology was also typical of these hopeful times. Our hope was that sustainability could bridge the impasse between pro-environment activists, with their demand for environmental protection and attention to the downsides of techno-economic progress, and pro-development activists, with their call for economic growth at all costs. This new middle way, we concluded, could provide the grounds for saying no to turning the world into a paved parking lot surrounding an oil well, but yes to development that makes sense according to the three Es of *environment, economics,* and *ethics,* taken together as equal partners (see Edwards). The future seemed, if not exactly bright, then at least *possible.*

❧ But, even though sustainability seems to be the one victory that environmentalism can claim, with new books of readings and programs flying its banner cropping up every day, in fact sustainability, like the relief from apocalyptic rhetoric we all felt in the 1990s, has turned out to be, well, unsustainable.

To see what happened with apocalyptic narrative, you need only look at the movies. A quick survey of the feature films in the list of postapocalyptic movies provided by the Internet Movie Database shows that such films have enjoyed an incredible popularity since World War II but that, after a lull in production in the decade following 1989, a virtual explosion of new films and remakes appeared in the first years of the new century. The list includes 106 films produced in the Cold War years of 1945–89, a mere 33 in the decade of the nineties, then 97 between 2000 and 2011, the highest number in any eleven-year period in the history covered by the list. Consider a few memorable examples:

- In the 2004 movie *The Day after Tomorrow,* a spate of worldwide superstorms brings on a new ice age, leaving the paleoclimatologist hero struggling to find family members in a deteriorating international political environment. The eco-apocalypse was repeated in films like *World's End* (2010), which imagines the fate of the United States when the world runs out of oil. Other common plots included death by plague, supervirus, and bacterial or chemical weapons gone awry.
- Along with the causes of the world-ending disaster, the effects vary. The critically acclaimed *Children of Men* (2006) projects a near-future humanity facing worldwide sterility, with bleak urban landscapes, in which gray hopeless faces greet the secret sight of a single pregnant woman with the wonder of the Epiphany itself.

- In 2004, *The Dawn of the Dead,* a remake of the 1978 film tells of a worldwide plague that turns victims into zombies. The film became one of many in a zombie craze that erupted over the next few years, covering genres from apocalyptic horror to dark humor (*The Zombie Diaries* [2006], *Zombieland* [2009], and *Zombie Apocalypse* [2011], to name only a few of the better known).
- A number of films left the cause of Armageddon unspecified and focused on the thought experiment that imagines (more realistically than the zombie allegories) what it would be like to survive. *The Road* (2009) gives us a man and his young son, survivors who tour a devastated landscape searching for food, water, and shelter among cannibalistic quasi-tribes (or virtual zombies) and proto-societies of folks making an effort to sustain civilized moral life in a gunslinger social environment. The 2006 novel on which the film is based in fact offers one of the more hopeful endings available in the corpus of the author Cormac McCarthy, among the grimmest (though most gifted) novelists currently writing. The popularity of *The Road* far outran McCarthy's earlier critical successes like *Blood Meridian* and *All the Pretty Horses,* with their evocative treatment of Southwestern history and landscapes—environments that are apparently far less interesting to current readers than the burned-over and all but unrecognizable setting of *The Road* (the popular success of which can be gauged by its inclusion in Oprah's Book Club).
- To take but one of many relevant documentaries from the period covered by the list, the high-profile *An Inconvenient Truth* of 2006 features Al Gore, the former US senator from Tennessee, vice president in Bill Clinton's administration, and failed presidential candidate, always a Washington

leader on environmental causes, campaigning to establish global warming as a scientific truth in the public mind and the greatest threat to the future of humanity presently on the horizon. The global scope of the film, with its dramatic views of threatened coastlines and collapsing ice shelves, is balanced by stories from Gore's personal experience with family tragedy and political disappointment. A memorable image in the multimedia production (a kind of over-the-top PowerPoint presentation by Senator Gore) gives us a cartoon frog that, placed into a laboratory bath of gradually warming water, cooks to death before it can realize the danger and leap away to safety. The animation offers one of the few cinematic images of a concept now common in the critical literature on environmental collapse: the slow apocalypse or gradual disaster. The film enjoyed a great deal of recognition and led to Gore's winning of the 2007 Nobel Peace Prize, which he shared with the Intergovernmental Panel on Climate Change. It also made him a convenient target for focused right-wing attacks on environmentalists' alleged efforts to undermine the American way of life with alarmist rhetoric, liberal ideology, and cooked-up science. (My neighbor in Texas, a very funny guy, has a T-shirt that says, "Al Gore didn't invent the Internet, but he did invent global warming.")

If the threat of Mutual Assured Destruction drove the engine of apocalypse in the days of the Cold War, what is it in the current age that fuels the taste for end-of-the-world narratives? It is probably not one thing but a perfect storm of related events suggesting an uncertain future and an unsustainable way of life in the present. Consider the following series of events in the history of the

United States that occurred between the time of my awakening to nature writing following my mother's death in the deep winter of 1999 and the day I smelled the smoke in September of 2011, a dozen years later:

- The new millennium turned in 2000 under the shadow of worries that a Y2K bug would undermine the global computer network—known first as the World Wide Web, a phrase that captured the wonder and excitement (and some would say the cultural imperialism) of an electronically networked planet with expanding options for communication and commerce, a term that has fallen into disuse in favor of the less glamorous moniker "the Internet" (the one *not* invented by Al Gore), the old military term for an increasingly commonplace phenomenon upon which life had come more and more to rely in the short space of a single decade. Before the 1990s, home computers and email were relatively rare in the average American household and workplace. Communication via the web is so common now that it seems to have been with us forever, but it is still relatively new. The Y2K bug threatened to bring down the whole network and, with it, a whole new way of life.
- Then, while we fussed over rumors of electronic incapacity and gossip concerning infidelity and sex in the Clinton White House, the new president, George W. Bush (having narrowly defeated Al Gore), came into office only to face the disaster known now as 9/11 in his first year of office, 2001—an attack by terrorists on the US homeland driven by religious extremism in Islamic nations and contempt for American power (economic and military) abroad.

- In the wake of 9/11, national security systems tightened their grip at home, with the PATRIOT Act and the formation of the Department of Homeland Security, while abroad, in Iraq and Afghanistan, the nation undertook wars devoted to regime changes for the ostensible purpose of fighting terrorism on a world-wide scale.
- In 2005, the Gulf Coast was struck by Hurricane Katrina, the deadliest storm to hit the United States in more than one hundred years, raising questions about the infrastructure of major cities, the ability of the poor to protect themselves against environmental disaster, and the capability of the government to deal with large-scale storms and deteriorating coastal conditions that could well be generated by global climate change. Katrina was the first of many superstorms that have wreaked havoc on coastal cities worldwide. Tsunamis have been particularly deadly and destructive, including the one resulting from an undersea mega-thrust earthquake off the coast of Japan in March 2011, which also involved a scare over widespread contamination from meltdowns in nuclear power plants (the Fukushima disaster).
- The first decade of the new millennium closed after the financial crisis of 2008–2009 left most Americans with a bleak economic outlook on the future. From the right came new voices that decried the hampering of economic potential by government regulation (including environmental regulations), laxity of immigration laws, and godlessness. From the left came concerns about increasing unemployment, inequality of income, and isolation of the very rich from ordinary Americans. The end of the American way of life, or the American Dream, was the theme on both sides

of the political divide that split the nation in two, a division reflected by the nearly equal distribution of the two parties in Congress, which resulted in what seemed like perpetual gridlock and inaction.
- The Arab Spring of 2011 brought not only hope for a grass-roots movement for freedom of the common people from the oppression of military dictators in the Middle East but also anxiety about the possibility of desecularization and new governments based in religious law.

It was in this context of political and economic turmoil that American culture responded with a fervid burst of apocalypticism that outpaced even the Cold War craze for end-of-the-world narratives. Armageddon was back.

❧ Among the products of American culture that took a turn toward the end of the world is the series of religious-themed novels that began with *Left Behind* by Tim LaHaye and Jerry B. Jenkins, the success of which spawned the considerable contemporary appetite for Christian fiction. The chronology doesn't quite fit with the narrative I've been spinning so far, since the first of these new novels appeared in the mid-nineties, when secular literature and cinema seemed to be taking a break from the apocalypse and when eco-politics was enjoying an expansionist period with the movements of sustainability and environmental justice. Very likely, Armageddon became a growth industry among American Christians at this time under other influences, which ran parallel to the earlier success of Lindsey's *The Late Great Planet Earth*.

When that book first appeared in 1970—the very year, I have to recall, that I left the church myself—it was taken up with enthusiasm by many participants in the so-called Jesus Movement. Also known as Jesus People or Jesus Freaks, the members of this movement embraced a countercultural response to Christian conformity that reproduced the hippie movement within the ranks of young believers. One of the first people I ever heard refer to "the Rapture" was a long-haired, blond-bearded, college-aged man robed in white bedsheets and standing in front of the University of New Mexico library in the fall of 1980. "One day soon," this street preacher intoned, "I'll be lifted up into the sky, and I'll look back on all you people burning to death down here, and I'll think it's a terrible bummer, but I'll keep on rising up to heaven and won't be able to do nothing about it then."

The countercultural force of end-times thinking may well go back to earliest apocalypses collected in the Hebrew scriptures attributed to prophets like Enoch and Daniel (see McGinn). This literature appeared in the two centuries before Christ as an alternative bid for authority in the face of the traditional power wielded by the temple priesthood in Jewish society. The stories told of prophets ascending into heaven to see the true God revealed anew. They were often given instructions about the ways of God toward humanity and new secrets pertaining to the course of human history. The unveiling was the point; it sought to establish new sources of authority, directly connected with God and not dependent upon priests who claimed exclusive access to a deity supposed to be housed in the temple. At various times in Jewish history, the temple in Jerusalem was destroyed and the people removed to faraway lands. Apocalyptic writings offered hope of continuing access to God, an access less exclusive and ritualized.

This interpretation of the early apocalypses, greatly simplified here, remains controversial among theologians and historians of religion, but its gist found its way into the history of Christianity. In times of great change, when the established church came under question, apocalypticism tended to thrive, both for the way it questioned authority and the way it suggested the passing of one world and the survival of a purified remnant of believers worthy of carrying on the belief in new forms.

Likewise, in secular postapocalyptic tales, the surviving remnant often represents the values and characteristics of a society that, according to the vision, deserve to be carried forward in a new civilization (in Christian terms, the New Jerusalem). So, for example, the love of family prevails in the dark scenarios of films and novels like *The Day after Tomorrow* and *The Road*. Individualism and personal ingenuity, the ability to live by one's wits and one's skills, also figure largely. In the 2008 novel *World Made by Hand*, by James Howard Kunstler, a group of folks living close to the land, reinventing low-power technologies and agricultural practices using hand tools, and linked by family and communitarian ideals, is pitted against a ruthless gang of thugs on one side (virtual zombies again) and, on the other side, an autocratically governed body of neo-peasants more or less enslaved to a property-rich leader. The book becomes a meditation on the survival of various social forms and the values associated with them (Wild West anarchy, communitarian anarchy, and neo-feudal autocracy).

Whether we're talking about apocalyptic visions of the church or society at large, what we're looking at is a questioning of authority, tradition, and conventional practices based on a desire not simply for revenge or the destruction of one's enemies but to satisfy a hunger for something new. There is a popular tale of how antiwar activists in the sixties and seventies grew up to become the "tenured radicals" berated by right-wing critics of academic liberalism today. But what happened to the long-haired, countercultural participants in the Jesus Movement, as well as the milder alternative groups of Christian practitioners that grew up in the sixties, in organizations like Young Life, which even my conservative sister preferred to attendance at the regular Baptist church once it began to go ultraconservative? These countercultural Christians grew up to become church leaders and to continue the search for alternatives to the traditional denominations of Christianity. They founded and populated the nondenominational and interdenominational megachurches that sprang up in the eighties and nineties. They inspired the growth of the charismatic movement among middle-class folks—speaking in tongues, rhapsodic interpretation, spontaneous healing—things that in my youth belonged to the holy rollers in rural and working-class churches spurned by the establishment. The end of the world in the apocalyptic tales for these new kinds of Christians signified the end of a constraining tradition of Christian practice and belief. The New Jerusalem was the reinvented form of Christianity now thriving in neo-Protestant congregations meeting in halls the size of basketball arenas in the great cities and sprawling suburbs of millennial America. Having established their place by sweeping away the competition of standard denominations—the Baptists, Methodists, Presbyterians, Episcopalians, and Lutherans, now struggling to maintain shrinking and aging memberships—many of the new Christians have now set their sights on transforming secular institutions such as the educational system as well as state and federal government. Many have joined the ranks of the so-called religious right. The apocalyptic fire of their separatist culture—not just their churches, but their schools, their literature, their cinema, their self-contained communities—now represents a burning desire to transform the whole society that surrounds them. When Armageddon flashed onto the scene in the first decade of the new century, they were ready.

❧ As literature, cinema, popular culture, and religion all feast on apocalyptic fare in the new millennium, even science seems to get into the act. When I studied science in the 1970s and 1980s—first in college and then in regular readings of popular science writing, which I taught in literature, rhetoric, and technical communication courses—classical Darwinism dominated biology and the uniformitarian tradition of Darwin's mentor, Charles Lyell, prevailed in historical geology. It was an aggressively gradualist tradition, one in which the world was said to evolve over an almost unimaginably long history, with small changes leading to big differences over time—in species development, land formations, and atmospheric trends. The gradualist predisposition replaced a catastrophicism that in Lyell and Darwin's time was still associated with Christian theories of earth's history—God's creation of the world in relatively recent times (4004 BC according to one famous calculation based on biblical sources, and in seven days), as well as the Great Flood recounted in the Bible, and so on. Some of the most celebrated scientists of the mid-nineteenth century, such as Emerson and Thoreau's friend Louis Agassiz at Harvard, remained committed to the catastrophic view and were marginalized by historians of science in the twentieth century after uniformitarianism and Darwinian evolution became the preferred theories.

Over the course of a century and a half after Darwin, a slow shift has occurred that has favored the reintroduction of catastrophe as a nature-shaping force. I'm not talking about "creationism," the attempt to substitute religious orthodoxy for science in the schools, which is part of the business of the religious right and has little, if any, support among adequately credentialed scientists. Catastrophe certainly maintains its place in this doctrinal way of thinking. But it also has a place in mainstream science.

Late twentieth-century paleontologists studying the great extinctions and other relatively rapid developments in geo-history came to revise Darwinism with such theories as "punctuated equilibrium," a kind of synthesis between the catastrophic and gradualist views of earth history. Accordingly, life and geological change proceed gradually over eons at a time, then undergo extraordinary events that speed things up considerably. To take perhaps the most famous case, the extinction of the dinosaurs could well have been advanced by a collision of a large asteroid or comet with the earth that raised a great cloud of dust, lowering temperatures and changing the climate worldwide. Other factors such as increased volcanic activity likely contributed as well. But in this, as in other extinctions in the fossil record, global catastrophe almost certainly played a role in the evolution of life on earth.

Science works hard to maintain its distance from other cultural developments, to secure an objective truth about the natural world, but even so, science and culture—like nature and culture—are mutually influential and tend to coevolve in history. The relationship of gradualist science to its cultural and geographical context is specifically addressed in the work of Mike Davis. In his 1999 book *Ecology of Fear: Los Angeles and the Imagination of Disaster,* Davis explains how nature writers and city planners alike have cultivated an imagination of the world based on the temperate zone of western Europe, New England, and the middle Atlantic states—places where four seasons define a fairly predictable annual cycle and concepts like the balance of nature match nicely the experience of flow and balance between hot and cold, wet and dry, city and country, urban and rural markets, plus a distribution of people over the entirety of available land with concentrations of population at ports and market centers. It is the imagination of a mainly agricultural and mercantile people living in a fairly stable environment. It conforms quite well to the worldview of Lyell's uniformitarianism, a principle that, in Davis's words, "conflated the constancy of natural laws with uniformities of rate and state." This view of geological history and biological evolution harmonized with the taste for gradual change and reformist politics that thrived in Great Britain during Darwin and Lyell's day. Just like the ideal political state, the earth was viewed as "a conservative steady state system" (15). "Catastrophism of any sort, biblical or Jacobin"—religious or revolutionary—was "branded as nothing more than prescientific superstition" (16). *Evolution, not revolution* could have been the bumper sticker for this worldview.

If you hear echoes of this way of thinking in the analysis of Nordhaus and Shellenberger, with their claims that the time for conservation and regulation has passed and that the time for wise investment has arrived (along with reform of tax laws and election funding), don't be surprised. Ultimately they are as interested in preservation as the environmentalists they criticize; what they want to preserve is not only wilderness or natural beauty but the status quo of the current political economy, which demands continuous growth supported by the constant manufacture of hope, even if it means denial of catastrophic potential and the treatment of disaster as variation from a norm that does not really fit the reality it describes. As Davis says, this "doggedly uniformitarian mindset . . . still conditions most environmental expectations" (16).

The problem is, just as the economic vision doesn't describe the experience of most Americans in an economy of shrinking wages, tighter credit, and increasing joblessness, the uniformitarian vision of ecology doesn't describe the environmental experience of Americans living west of the Mississippi. And I would add, given the earthquakes, hurricanes, and floods in the summer of 2011 on the East Coast, or the increasing unpredictability of drought and heat in places like the "normally" mild and wet-summered Southeast where I grew up, the uniformitarian eco-political vision is on the verge of failing across the board in North America.

The residents of Los Angeles, who have a long history of having uniformitarian expectations dashed by earthquakes, flash floods, mudslides, and wildfires, become an advance study for the rest of us in an age of global warming. And as Mike Davis says, "Southern California at least by Lyellian standards is a revolutionary, not a reformist landscape. It is Walden Pond on LSD" (16).

⁂ Walden on LSD, summer on steroids—name your place, your time, your drug of choice. Life is scary and getting worse. The question for nature writers and other artists of environmental politics is how to get people to face it.

Many popular critics writing today follow Nordhaus and Shellenberger in saying that environmentalism is too depressing and negative, that people need a positive outlook to motivate them to consider a sustainable lifestyle and solve environmental problems. I will be the first to concede that hell-fired, self-righteous sermonizing may not be what we need. I will also concede that a good deal of environmentalist discourse makes people want to curl up into a fetal ball, pray to God for release, or spend their time watching reruns of *Leave It to Beaver*. I get it, I really do. Even Jackie, my ever-patient wife and coauthor, sometimes finds my thinking depressing these days, so how am I going to convince strangers to join me in taking a hard look at our consensual nightmares, if not our impending deaths, to smell the smoke in the Texas subdivisions?

I guess I would start by asking a question about our rhetorical options: What if the I'm-okay-you're-okay, cheerleading rhetoric of the motivational speaker (even the ones I admire the most, like Frances Moore Lappé) is unethical in creating the false optimism of a sunny and mild outlook on our environmental future, not to mention current conditions? Who is going to write the bad-news letter when the news really is bad, right here, right now?

I would also say that I don't find the argument compelling that people resist environmental rhetoric only because it's negative. The news on television and in the newspapers is famously negative, so much so that psychologists and popular medical advisors like Dr. Andrew Weil often advise their depressed patients to take a "news fast." And yet millions of people read the news every day, become news junkies, and appear to thrive on negativity. They find good news boring, and it's a slow news day without a few tales of mass slaughter and destruction. They listen to the fear-inspiring, angry monologues of talk show hosts every hour of every day and have a wonderful time. They lap up apocalyptic sermons and rush to movies like *The Day after Tomorrow, Children of Men,* and *The Road.* They read novels like *Left Behind* by the thousands.

A recent article in the news magazine *USA Today Weekend* features a cover story with the teaser "The End of the World Is *Not* Near: You're in luck! Maya calendars to killer asteroids, experts tell why you have nothing to worry about." The story is titled (with an allusion to *Mad Magazine* that wayward readers from my generation will surely recognize) "What, Me Worry? Scientists Explain Why the End of the World Will NOT Arrive in 2012." It quotes a series of high-profile physicists, astronomers, and anthropologists. They are happy to state their views colloquially for the masses. One says, "Bull. It's all bull." Another says, "Crazy. People always worry about the wrong things."

What are the wrong things? The article dismisses the near-future likelihood of a series of world-destroying scenarios taken from futuristic fiction, popular science writing, and pop culture—impending collisions with planets, asteroids, and comets, the expansion of the sun, the prophecies of various ancient peoples channeled by New Age seers—then concludes, "This year, we've already survived a drought that affected 80% of U.S. farmland . . . and a super-storm named Sandy, which flooded New York City and much of the East Coast, *all things nobody predicted*" (Vergano 12; emphasis added). Nobody predicted? Apparently *USA Today* didn't check with the climate scientists who've been worrying about the prospect of megadroughts and superstorms for decades now.

It's time to consider the possibility that apocalypticism has nothing to do with facing our problems. Cultural critics agree that, from the Cold War to the War on Terrorism, apocalypticism has to do with widespread anxiety about the inability to sustain life against the forces of death, about our sense of powerlessness and our worries about the future. But they don't always say that the underlying purpose of the stories is not to increase anxiety but to soothe it.

The heroes of postapocalyptic narratives walk away—not unscathed, but with a deeper awareness of what counts most. Usually it's family, community, or God. Even in the stories with the harshest conclusions, when everybody finally dies—as in the dark narrative of *On the Beach,* still one of the most moving of the Cold War apocalyptic tales—we put down the book, we walk out of the theater, maybe give an extra hug to our loved ones, then get on with the business of life. Maybe we have a nightmare here and there, but we have survived Armageddon. We do it again and again. If you play video games, you can endlessly vaporize zombies and monsters that are out to snatch you up in your prime. You can switch the game off and have a snack.

The increase in the number of apocalyptic tales and the frequency of references to Armageddon may well suggest the need for a more frequent and compulsive purging of the fears and anxieties that drive the popularity of such fictions. While many of the scenarios we contrive to survive are not real, the worries and fears that move us to contrive them are. As the real terror mounts, the need for a purgative experience in the theater, library, or video game increases apace. But the tales of Armageddon are not about facing it; instead they feed the old three Ds of distraction, defensiveness, and denial. Like the laxatives taken by compulsive eaters or other forms of bulimic purging, we need more and more and feel less and less satisfaction from the relief they offer.

Purging is one definition of the word *catharsis,* the term Aristotle used in his *Poetics* to describe the feeling we get at the end of a tragedy that we watch in the theater. Suffused with the emotions of pity and fear (either brought with us to the theater or inspired by the events we watch, or both), we confront the death of the flawed tragic hero, but ultimately we see that the death foretells the return to order and balance in the society. In Shakespeare's *Hamlet,* to take a famous example from English drama, the minor character Fortinbras delivers his final speech about the survival of the social order while the stage is strewn with the bodies of the main players in the tragedy. We walk out of the theater sadder but wiser, the overweening power of pity and fear purged and our emotions restored to their proper balance. At the end of Cormac McCarthy's *The Road,* the boy must let go the hand of his dying father but take the hand of the remnant community that offers hope for a sustained civilization. We put down the book and feel sad but hopeful.

The modern dramatist Bertolt Brecht objected to catharsis more or less because it promoted distraction, defensiveness, and denial, allowing a temporary adjustment in the psychology of the viewing audience that aided social conformity and political inaction. He felt that Aristotle's kind of theater rendered the audience passive and self-satisfied. He strove for a drama that would create alienation in the audience, engage viewers intellectually and politically, and send them into the streets, not only sadder and wiser but determined to remake the world that had inspired their anxiety and fear. Catharsis allows us to sleep better and rise refreshed. Brecht longed for a theater that would wake us up and put us to work.

❦ The work of a wide-awake nature writing has become partly a matter of distinguishing among competing end-of-the-world scenarios to determine the right things to worry about. One book that does just that is Craig Childs's 2012 *Apocalyptic Planet*. Childs's version of nature writing blends the study of earth science with the adventure story, mingling lucid explanations and interviews of prominent scientists with a narrative of his travels to fascinating places that ultimately reveal something about the nature of places everywhere. In this book, Childs courts Armageddon by traveling to sites that already suffer the fates that science, religion, and culture imagine as end-of-the-world scenarios: the deep desert of Mexico, the threatened coastland of the Bering Strait, the genetic wasteland of an Iowa cornfield, the ice sheets of Patagonia and Greenland, the high volcanic moonscapes of Hawaii—many of which also show symptoms of environmental damage currently associated with human activities (glacial shrinkage and rising seas from global warming, decreased biodiversity from genetically engineered and chemically treated crops).

Childs is an even-handed analyst reluctant to place blame on any one factor, draw hasty conclusions, accept grand theories, or make sweeping pronouncements about the fate of the earth. His scientific informants vary in their views on the overall effect that human beings can ultimately have on the earth, ranging from the long view of geologists who see humanity as a scratch on the surface of deep time to biologists who lament the reduction of biodiversity from human causes and refuse to let people off the hook with the view of extinction as part of a natural cycle (which it is, but not to the extent currently unfolding as people destroy habitats at rates and on a scale they could not have managed in the days before the era of the great technologies).

The overall view that emerges from *Apocalyptic Planet* is that human activity is only one factor in the changes we are facing in the new nature but that it definitely makes a difference and may well be complicating and augmenting natural changes such as global temperature increase, the onset of extensive droughts, and possibly the latest great extinction in the history of life on earth. I come away from the book better informed, sadder, wiser, and haunted by something like a naturalist's version of Pascal's Wager. Pascal, the seventeenth-century French philosopher and mathematician, famously said that, since the existence of God cannot be known for sure, a rational person would believe in God because to do so was to risk nothing (except perhaps the contempt of one's fellow rationalists) whereas to fail in belief, with hell looming on the horizon of the afterlife, was to risk everything.

For me, the New Naturalist's Wager says it's worth the risk to make the economic and technological adjustments necessary to reduce the possibility that global warming (including the megadroughts, superstorms, and increasing sea levels, not to mention loss of habitat and reduction of biodiversity) is caused by human activity. To fail in this effort is to risk everything, if not for ourselves, then for the next few generations.

❧ Unlike Childs, I don't travel the world in search of apocalyptic landscapes and famous scientists. I just read the books and smell the smoke in my Texas neighborhood. Recently, both my reading and the simplest observations suggest that the idea of sustainability, in which Jackie and I put so much hope back in 1992 as a middle position between environmentalism and developmentalism, has begun to seem at best a stop-gap measure for making the transition to a new way of life and at worst a lost cause. I worry that sustainability masks contradictions and lacks the conceptual punch needed to drive a new way of thinking about how we live on the earth right here, right now. It seems as if everybody has jumped on the sustainability bandwagon these days. But they mean many different things when they invoke the word, and too often they mean something that has nothing to do with ecology. When my dean tells me that our budget is unsustainable—and he uses the word all the time—he's not talking about ecology at all; he means he can't continue to pay at the same rate. When economists talk about sustainability, they divide between the neoclassical approach and the ecological approach. Neoclassical sustainability models rest on "two underlying assumptions: [that] created capital can substitute for natural capital in production, and [that] technological progress will uncover these substitutes as natural capital becomes scarce" (Goodstein 98). Ecological economists refuse to accept these assumptions and the standard conflation of monetary and natural capital. Instead they focus on "problems arising from both population and consumption pressures on . . . natural capital—from fresh water, to planetary temperature, to biodiversity" (122). In other words, contrary to what Jackie and I hoped in our conclusion to *Ecospeak*—published in the same year (1992) as the United Nations Conference on Environment and Development in Rio de Janeiro, commemorated in 2012 with the United

Nations Conference on Sustainability (Rio + 20)—sustainability has not resolved the differences between developmentalism and environmentalism, which now travel under the new names of neoclassical and ecological sustainability within the field of economics. The division remains an intractable challenge to both liberal and conservative policy makers and analysts.

❧ In addition to masking contradictions, sustainability as a concept has been stretched to the point of meaninglessness and now is often used to imply a milder version of environmental politics that requires less action and even less thought than that which is really needed. Consider the case of David Owen, the author of *Green Metropolis,* which proposes Manhattan as "a utopian environmentalist community" (1). Owen is the guy I quoted earlier who connected environmental literature with the fear of death by quipping that most environmentalist books were so depressing that he was saving them for reading in case he was found to have a terminal illness. The subtitle of his book invokes sustainability— *Why Living Smaller, Living Closer, and Driving Less Are the Keys to Sustainability*—and pretty well covers all you really need to know about his argument unless you're a New Yorker and want to enjoy having yourself held up as a model of green living, albeit a model that is unconscious of itself, that only involves going about business as usual and managing through that lifestyle to set the pace for sustainability worldwide.

The unconsciousness of the ecological New Yorker is, in fact, for Owen one of the great points in favor of his argument. We can only behave sustainably, he suggests, if we don't have to think too much about it because thinking is depressing. His reasoning reminds me of an exchange I had with a New York textbook publisher once. We were talking about the good communication practice of putting important information in headings and picture captions where fast and careless readers are more likely to get it. I said, "If only I could write a book that students didn't have to read!" The response? "Can you do that?" I know, it was a joke, but even so, jokes about not reading and not thinking wear a little thin on a person like me, especially when the jokes come from a region touted as the intellectual mecca of North America.

Owen could well be right that Manhattanites require less space and less energy because they live in small dwellings situated close to what they need in the neighborhood system that has evolved in New York; that they drive less than most Americans because of bad parking and good public transit; that they are more fit because they walk more than my neighbors do down in Houston (which has for several years enjoyed the dubious honor of ranking as the fattest city in the world). But Owen's calculations about the overall ecological footprint of most New Yorkers seem to be based on factors like individual utility usage and not on factors that account for the global transportation network required to deliver energy as well as all that healthy gourmet food and wine and coffee to Manhattan.

Nor does he provide much geographical analysis of the kind that Mike Davis gives for LA. New York is a port city that benefits from access to a worldwide trading system. It is built in a temperate zone that doesn't require the heavy energy demands of Dallas in summer or Minneapolis in winter. And even so, it's expensive as all get out. I couldn't afford to live in Manhattan—or, for that matter, in San Francisco, or even in Davis, California, with its wonderful small-town, eco-friendly environment. I won't bore you with the figures; it's easy to do the comparisons with the cost-of-living calculators on the Internet. Suffice it to say that all of these places have costs of living more than twice as high as my humble hometown in Texas and that even if they were sustainable in environmental terms, a possibility that I seriously doubt when it comes to New York, these places don't meet the economic criteria for sustainability. Excepting those who live in the slums or on the streets (who also live small, live close, and drive less, by the way), these cities are mostly havens for the rich and well-to-do—including, it would seem, the author of *Green Metropolis*.

Using the simple technique of critical analysis that scholars in feminist and indigenous studies have taught us, ask yourself who David Owen is referring to every time he says *we* in his book. I assure you he's not talking about the people of New Orleans trying unsuccessfully to escape the ravages of Hurricane Katrina; he's not talking about the Paiutes and Navajos living in what Valerie Kuletz has called the "Tainted Desert"—the militarized sacrifice zones of the American Southwest; he's not talking about the great majority of the people living in the Global South, not single mothers in the Bronx, not people sleeping on the heating vents of Manhattan streets, not even a well-paid senior English professor living in Texas, and certainly not those pesky environmental activists. Environmentalists are always referred to as "them," not "us," in his book, though he uses the adjective *environmentalist* to describe the Manhattan utopia. For Owen, *we* refers to investment bankers, lawyers, stockbrokers, people in the trades and professions, and staff writers for *The New Yorker* like himself. This *we* includes the "golf buddies" that nobly carpool with Owen (since he moved out of the green metropolis to take his family to the suburbs). This *we* does not include those whom the environmentalists of the poor call "ecosystem people" who depend directly on the land of their home places (Nixon 22); this *we* includes only "resource omnivores" who seem to depend, as Owen himself points out, on the power of energy-intensive machines that leave them the freedom to browse their investment portfolios on their iPads but who also depend, as Owen neglects to say, on the back-breaking labor of underpaid men and women picking their strawberries in places like Watsonville, California—at least until they are replaced by the latest strawberry-picking technology or rendered unnecessary by imports from Central and South America, where labor is even cheaper. The success and continuation of the oil industry mean as much to this *we* as to the oilmen and politicians in Houston and Dallas, since New Yorkers depend so heavily on fuel oil for heating, airplane fuel for travel (yes, they do leave their utopia quite frequently), and diesel fuel for the trucking that brings their food and bottled water from farther and farther away every year.

In short, with his long historical digressions on the baleful influence of the automobile on urban planning and his treatises on how there is no viable alternative to oil because of the depth of *our* dependence on it—the no-alternative argument being always inclined to leave things as they are, the conservative recourse of those who are currently benefitting from the system in place—David Owen barely begins to address the problems with urbanization that Lester Brown, the founding director of the Worldwatch Institute, outlined thirty years ago in what remains one of the definitive studies of sustainability, or at least one version of sustainability, the book *Building a Sustainable Society:* "The premise that urbanization . . . will continue unaltered until most of the world's population is concentrated in huge urban conglomerations rests on the assumption that food surpluses produced in the surrounding countryside or imported from abroad can sustain urban expansion, that energy will be able to underwrite the higher costs of urban living, and that ever more people can find productive employment in the cities. There is now reason to doubt whether any of these assumptions will hold" (268–69). More recently, from a very different perspective on sustainability, the critique is echoed in Joan Martinez-Alier's *Environmentalism of the Poor:* "A world where urbanization is increasing fast is . . . a more unsustainable world. Cities are not environmentally sustainable; by definition, their territory is too densely populated with humans to be self-supporting" (153).

※ The smoke I smelled in September 2011 is the scent of the end of a world. It tells me that my way of life is unsustainable, just as my parents' way of life was. We are unable to pass it forward to the next generation, much less the next three. My parents' generation of the American middle class thrived in the postwar boom of the 1950s and '60s. As income growth slowed down, people in my generation opted for two-worker households to make up the difference. A neighbor couple I knew when we lived in Lubbock back in the 1980s held down a combined total of five jobs to be able to own their own home in our modest subdivision. Many members of the next half-generation, a little older than my daughter, learned to live on easy credit, which offered a way of keeping the economy afloat on consumer spending, with the smaller and smaller financial elite first underwriting loans for people with the aspiration but not the means for social mobility and then depending themselves on government bailouts when the loans went bad.

After the financial crash of 2008–2009, with 9 percent unemployment nationwide and the crazy antics of easy credit revealed and undermined, unsustainable debt became the order of the day. I happen to be one of the lucky ones with a mortgage I can afford, but could I sell my house if I wanted to? The number of For Sale signs in my neighborhood suggests not, at least not at a price that would allow me to move to a comparable dwelling some place else. Unlike my friends in West Texas and the Hill Country, I live over a reliable aquifer, but how long will it continue to produce the water we need if this drought lasts as long as the one in the 1950s, but with this added intensity of heat and the demands for economic growth? And what about the prospect of eating local food—which right now is a pretty good, if relatively expensive option? In the summer of 2011, it was not as good as it was in 2010. I still need the supermarket, with its worldwide distribution networks, and I need to remember that all the food I eat, and that most everybody eats in America, is *surplus food,* as Lester Brown reminds us. We middle-class Americans are resource omnivores that feed at many troughs, none of which we maintain ourselves, except by spending money.

As the number of resource omnivores increases worldwide (with the growth of megacities, where the poor join the rich in becoming resource omnivores), the pressure on the ecosystem—and on ecosystem people—becomes greater, more and more land needs to be capitalized and developed to serve those far away, and the resource omnivores themselves need more and more money as prices outrun wages and debt deepens. In this literal and figurative climate, sustainability seems farther and farther out of reach.

For those of us who depend on money to buy our livelihood, the economic element of the "three Es" tends to swamp the elements of environment and ethics. When Jackie and I asked a local green designer to give us a plan to refit our house for solar and wind power, he told us, in so many words, to sell it and start over. Or, he said, we could spend a small fortune making it somewhat more efficient in using standard utilities. Replace all the windows, the furnace, the air-conditioner, the insulation—the bill was staggering and the outcome still not sustainable in the strictest sense;

that is, the resulting house would not be a legacy worth passing to the next generations as a livable dwelling for the long haul. Our daughter certainly wouldn't want it and probably couldn't afford to maintain it. What have we done about this house so far? Nothing. That's the usual response to the task at hand, I'm afraid. It's overwhelming.

The reason that most people run from environmentalism is not its negativity but its cost, its difficulty, and the scale of the change it requires—both personal and social. We resource omnivores need to rebuild our living spaces—our cities and our homes—and adjust our expectations. And we need to realize that, even if we all make the individual changes we desperately need to make—for our own welfare and for our communities—those changes probably will not be enough to effect large-scale reforms but will at best serve as the means to commit us personally and politically to supporting the big changes that are needed.

In their book *Too Many People?*, published in 2011, the Australian eco-socialists Ian Angus and Simon Butler make a strong argument "that individual consumption is not a major cause of environmental destruction and that changes in individual behavior can make at most a marginal difference" (137). To illustrate their point, they offer the case of one of the world's wealthiest men, Ira Rennert. At the level of individual consumption, his lifestyle is excessive by any standards (multiple huge mansions, private jets, the works). He leaves a Sasquatch-sized ecological footprint. Even so, "where ecocide is concerned, Rennert the consumer is a piker compared to Rennert the capitalist" (167). His wealth comes primarily from the Renco Group, whose holdings include some of the world's largest producers of magnesium and lead. One of these companies, U.S. Magnesium LLC (MagCorp), was named "the number one polluting industrial facility in the United States" by the EPA (167). Pollution from Renco facilities in Peru resulted in the poisoning of thousands of local citizens, including children: "99 percent of children tested in La Oroya had blood-lead levels that vastly exceeded EPA and World Health Organization limits" (168). The conclusion: "As an individual consumer, Rennert represents hyperconsumption at its worst. His way of living is a gross insult to the earth. But as the owner of Renco Group Inc., he has shortened the lives of tens of thousands of people and laid waste to entire ecosystems" (169). As Angus and Butler go on to show, even the work of industrialists like Rennert pales beside the destruction of life and land perpetrated by "the world's worst polluter": the US military, which in 2009, the year of our worst economic trials, used "5.7 trillion gallons of oil, just under 16 million gallons a day" and "produced an estimated 7.3 million tons of greenhouse gases" (174). In short, military-industrialism is alive and well, and when enacted in the context of the harsh conditions of global climate change (whether natural or human induced), its practices are so destructive on the grand scale as to dwarf the environmental impact of individual consumers even in the Global North, the heartland of consumerism.

But what Angus and Butler don't quite realize is that all these facts and figures won't be convincing to the seasoned deniers that form the distracted and defensive majority of the population in my world. The process of facing fears and admitting the truth is harder than many environmentalist writers will admit. I don't know about your world, but the climate science deniers are everywhere in mine. It's not just the governor and his oil industry supporters. Even my physical therapist has a theory about solar flares and El Niño, for goodness' sake. Most folks can't be bothered with our rational arguments. They are like deniers everywhere: they don't want to be convinced or to convince me of their arguments; they just want to carry on, doing what they're doing.

They are far more likely to accept the arguments of a writer like David Owen. The desire for comfort and the resistance to intellectual and ethical challenges—as well as the fear of death, the wild reality of life, within us and outside us, and all the things we can't control—turn sustainability broadly defined as the three Es into the kind of sustainability the dean is talking about, purely a matter of economics: the one E, the big E. The one E, for all its volatility in our times, remains the easiest of the three to control or tame or talk about. It is the closest, most comfortable. It acts like a closed system, with environment and ethics scratching at the door but not allowed inside.

For me, the best metaphor for economy is the insulated, air-conditioned, self-contained, suburban house. We think we can live there in self-sufficiency, safe and secure from the trouble outdoors—until the environment stops flowing in the channels that feed the system (water in the pipes, power in the outlets, food and clothing from the online stores) or breaks open the doors and cracks the foundations (wildfire, drought, hurricane, tsunami, flood), or until ethics comes knocking and asking hard questions (about the neighbor in need, the homeless, the prisoner, the community, the nation). Then things can get a little wild, and the time has come to face it.

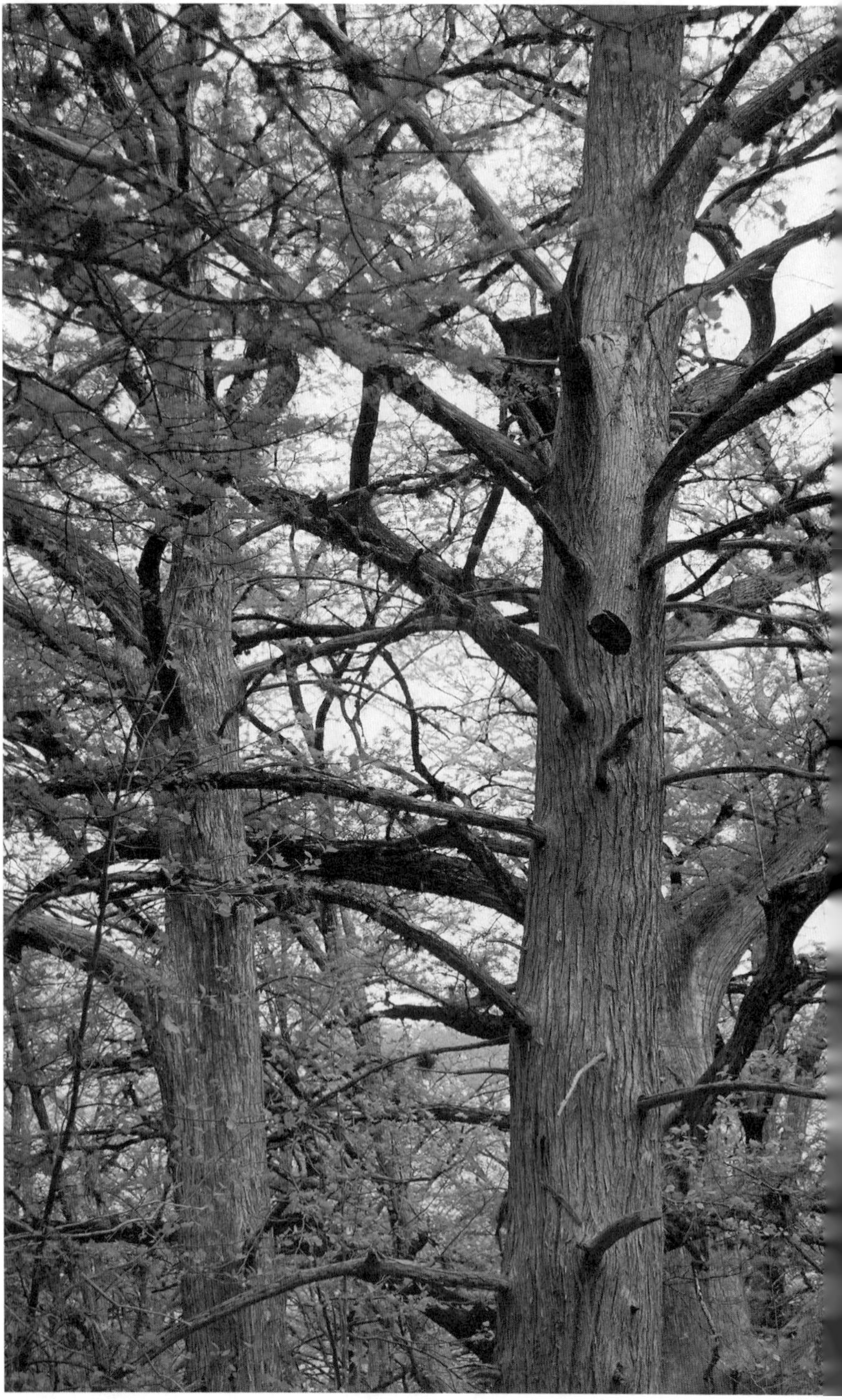

7 No Illusions, No Fantasy, No Melodrama
The Legacy of Rachel Carson

> Shams and delusions are esteemed for soundest truths, while reality is fabulous.
> Thoreau, *Walden*

🕊 Rachel Carson's biographer, Linda Lear, tells how readers of the bestselling and award-winning nature book, *The Sea around Us*, published in 1951, wrote to thank the author for providing relief from "man-made problems" like the nuclear arms race, the McCarthy hearings, the Korean War. Carson took little comfort from these grateful readers. She had always insisted that "natural history never provided an escape from reality or the problems of twentieth-century life" (Lear 205). Shortly after the publication of *The Sea around Us*, Carson began to use her success as a nature writer to win a forum for issues in environmental politics, work that culminated a decade later in *Silent Spring*, the one book that may be said to have sparked the modern environmental movement. Her head-on engagement with the political issues, which incurred the wrath of the chemical industry, also must have flummoxed a good segment of her former fan base who counted on her for peaceful and reassuring accounts of life viewed on the grand scale, human affairs reduced to a blip on the big screen.

Now, a half-century later, the drama of audience response continues to confront the issue of escape versus engagement in such problems as how to combat denial on questions like global warming, how to see the world with eyes clarified by scientific research, as it is and not as we wish it were. As Bill McKibben has said, we need to take a hard look at what is going on between the earth and ourselves: "No illusions, no fantasies, no melodrama" (*Eaarth* 100).

Illusions and fantasies involve disturbances in the way we see the world; they are psychological terms that are often used in political language as well. But there's an overlap in McKibben's terminology that hints at the place of nature writing and other arts in developing new ways of seeing the world, of facing up to what's wrong with our world. Fantasy and melodrama are used not just in psychological and political language, but also in the study of the arts. They are what we call modes, styles, or, most comprehensively, *genres* of artistic expression.

Genres are categories used to arrange the arts on the basis of subject matter, style, audience appeal, motive, and context. Genres of the novel include mysteries, romances, and science fiction; in nonfiction, we have biography, science writing, and travelogue; painting and photography give us landscapes and portraits; in cinema, we see documentary, action and adventure, anime, among many others. Nature writing like *The Sea around Us* may be considered a different genre from the writing of environmental activism, such as *Silent Spring,* though both were produced by the same author, Rachel Carson.

Scholars in rhetoric know that genre is more than a simple classification. Carolyn R. Miller has taught that genres imbed attitudes and imply certain kinds of social action. They stimulate communal activity and create audiences as much as they meet needs and desires. Walter Beale draws attention to the ad hoc quality of genres. No list of genres will ever be fully reliable over time. I tell my students to think of genres like the categories by which the bookstore is arranged. They emerge, shift, combine, separate, and disappear. The shelf for "nature" is often, though not always, separated from the one for "environment," to keep books like *The Sea around Us* separate from books like *Silent Spring*. A good number of readers want their natural history kept free and clean of environmental politics—or somebody does.

In interviews and marketing materials, the producers of big-budget nature films, such as the extraordinarily successful *Planet Earth,* have worked to distance their art from political turmoil. As my associate Lisa D'Amico shows in her ongoing studies of the genre, issues like species decimation and extinction, global climate change, and habitat destruction are depoliticized and forced into the background as the nature documentary works to remove the human face from animal portraiture and panoramic landscape coverage. Who are the people living in such remote climes? What forces have caused the reduction of habitat that makes these animals and scenes so rare and thus so valuable to the buyer of home theater technology? The films avoid these questions and eliminate the troublesome human element from the beautiful images delivered in high-tech formats to the eager gaze of worldwide consumers. The images are so lovely (and so politically innocuous) that the films are regularly featured as demos in appliance outlets that specialize in high-end, big-screen TVs. Commodification of nature is the name of the game, and part of the process is cleansing away the environmentalist taint, which potentially breaks the spell of enjoyment for the contented viewer.

To take a homelier example, consider my experience with Texas Master Naturalists, an organization of volunteers that extends the reach of the understaffed parks and wildlife administration in my home state by providing public education and service in state and city parks, natural history museums, schools, and other sites promoting understanding and enjoyment of the natural world. The chapter newsletter on which I worked in my first year was urged not to include an article a colleague wrote on the local controversy surrounding the placement of a new coal-fired power plant. "Too political." In one training session, I answered a question put to us by a seasoned park official with reference to global warming. He gave me a hard look. "Now that's politically touchy in this state," he said. Then to the whole group of trainees: "Remember to stick to the science and steer clear of the politics." Science, as we all know, tries to describe the world with language and methods designed to eliminate human bias. But, in the interest of explaining science to general readers, the genre of science writing on the model of John McPhee, Craig Childs, and David Quammen often repopulates the story of science with the people involved. Instead of the technical, value-free language of scientific research, they use ordinary language with its value-rich figures of speech and associations with everyday activity. The park service uses the same techniques but feels the need to draw the line when it comes to politics and certain hot issues, even if it means calling back an attitude of scientific disinterest as a rationale. In an atmosphere of shrinking budgets, state agencies cannot risk alienating clients who come to the woods and fields to enjoy nature, not to have their politics challenged. Likewise at the national level. My daughter tells me that 2008 was the first year interpretive rangers in the national parks were allowed to use the phrase "global climate change"; "global warming" was still taboo.

🙞 The assumption is that people go to the woods to escape and relax, not to think hard about their lives. The history of the most enduring nature writing argues against the claim. Authors from John Muir and Aldo Leopold down to the Edward Abbey of *Desert Solitaire,* Terry Tempest Williams in *Refuge,* and Janisse Ray in *Ecology of a Cracker Childhood,* while drawing on good science and offering careful depictions of natural history in their regions, do not shy away from engaging politically and ethically hot topics. Likewise, the biography of Rachel Carson stands as a testimony to the meaningfulness of the relationship between retreat to nature and political engagement with nature.

As Linda Lear shows, Carson grew up in the former farmlands of Pennsylvania, "the once wildly beautiful valley of the lower Allegheny," and witnessed the effects of coal-fired power production on the land. "Industry had brought technological progress, higher income, and regular work, but it had also produced environmental blight," and "the memory of the defilement . . . would remain" with Carson after she moved to the eastern seaboard (Lear 55). As a child, she dreamed of a life by the sea, the wide expanse of ocean providing relief from the whiff of dirty air and the sight of damaged lands. When she finally made it to the shoreline, she was moved to devote her life in science to the study of marine environments. In her government work as what today we would call a technical writer, she dreamed again of getting free of the cramped office to collect specimens, watch birds, observe the movement of the tides and seasons, write in her notebook, and meditate on life against the background of the expansive marshes and beaches cooled by the breezes and storms rolling off the open ocean. The very title of her first book, *Under the Sea Wind,* suggests the refreshment the ocean brought to a woman hungry for a breath of clean air to clear her head from the clutter of the daily commute and government office.

The title of her second book, *The Sea around Us,* suggests a growing awareness of the concept of *environment,* literally *that which surrounds.* The new book increasingly relies on ecology as the science of relationships among the elements of nature. Early in the book, she notes that "through a series of delicately adjusted, interlocking relationships, the life of all parts of the sea is linked" (19). She still saw the sea as a place of refuge from the controlling hand of modern humanity—or as she said in the style of the day, the hand of *man*. Her use of the generic masculine pronoun in retrospect seems rhetorically charged, for one of the many struggles throughout her career was to win acceptance as a woman scientist and author. After millennia of evolution as a land animal, she says, "eventually man . . . found his way back to the sea. Standing on its shores, he must have looked upon it with wonder and curiosity." He could not return completely to the sea, but "invented mechanical eyes and ears that could re-create for his senses a world long lost, but a world that, in the deepest part of his subconscious mind, he had never wholly forgotten." "And yet," she insists, "he has returned to his mother sea only on her own terms. He cannot control or change the ocean as . . . he has subdued and plundered the continents. In the artificial world of his cities and towns, he often forgets the true nature of his planet and the long vistas of its history" (15).

Looking back on these words from an era facing ocean acidification, pollution of the seas, overfishing, and giant floating islands of plasticized garbage, we may think of Rachel Carson as outdated or naïve in her faith in the power of the sea, living in a fantasy world where mother ocean still rules over her restless and hungry human children. But hold that judgment.

Midway through *The Sea around Us,* we find what would become in *Silent Spring* her fully developed prophetic voice. Reflecting on Darwin's crucial topic, island biogeography, she tells how depletion of native species in the sensitive environments of remote islands followed from the introduction of livestock, rats, crops, and human settlers. "Most of man's habitual tampering with nature's balance by introducing exotic species," she writes, "has been done in ignorance of the fatal chain of events that would follow" (95). Clearly, Carson's retreat to the sea and the study it inspired sharpened her sense of the problems that human ignorance, combined with a thirst for control, could bring to the natural world. Her deep admiration of science, with its clever methods and technologies for dispelling ignorance, was already in conflict with her concern over the human temptation to use science and technology to conquer nature without realizing the consequences of the applications devised.

Mindful retreat or refuge, then—such as we find in Rachel Carson's legacy—is ultimately not the same as *escape* in the way the word is ordinarily used today. Refuge and retreat create the space—mental and physical—to sort things out and allow the quiet moments needed for imaginative engagement with one's world. Retreat relaxes and re-forms a mind too much distracted by the chatter of the global village.

❧ You may say that I am *romanticizing*, but please wait. It's true that the attitude of retreat and refuge I'm posing as an alternative to escape and as a complement to political engagement derives from the values of solitude and closeness to nature cultivated in the classic romanticism of Wordsworth, Coleridge, Thoreau, and Whitman. But when we say *romanticize* today, we are actually conflating two worldviews inherited from the nineteenth century—romanticism and sentimentality. Romanticism is not just about romance, and sentimentality suggests far more than just sentiment or feeling. They are shorthand terms for a whole set of attitudes toward the life of the individual in relationship to the rest of the world.

The romantic differed from the sentimentalist in the way that each valued the inner life of the individual and the outer experience of nature (see Douglas)—what we might call inwardness and outwardness. The romantic turns inward or reaches outward to nature to seek insights, the better for which to return to society with new ideas and with passions and energy recharged. The sentimentalist turns inward or goes to nature to indulge in good feelings and intense experiences, all the better to avoid or even deny the crushing realities of politics and the demands of daily life. The romantic seeks alternatives; the sentimentalist seeks relief and momentary delight. Romanticism produces rebels; sentimentality produces neurotics. The old romanticism was known to inspire the move from illusion to disillusion, the dispelling of unreality in the clear light of nature. Seen in this light, romanticism may still have a place in the campaign to defeat denial, even if similar processes—turning inward or turning to nature—undertaken with an attitude of sentimentality might reinforce the psycho-social mechanisms of denial.

Romanticism does not, I admit, always help us to get from disillusion to action. But what many activist writers these days fail to realize is that you can't just wave scientific consensus like a wand—say, for example, that the best authorities in science agree that global warming is the result of human actions—and dispel the illusion and fantasy and melodrama that keep people denying the reality of problems like climate change, species depletion, and ocean pollution. Nothing sells so well as illusion, fantasy, and melodrama—or sentimentality and escape.

To the sentimentalist, escape feels like freedom, but it's not the same. Think of the runaway slave or the escaped prisoner—stock characters in nineteenth-century romantic and sentimental literature, the era of *Great Expectations* and *Uncle Tom's Cabin*. The threat of the return to confinement is always at the heels of a person on the run, the escaped slave or prisoner. Sentimentality settles for the condition of escape, but romanticism seeks full freedom. "If dogs run free," says the Bob Dylan song, "then why not we?" But the dog has its leash, and we have our limits. Escape is a walk on a leash. Freedom considers the option to join the pack.

※ Of the various contemporary forms of escape from reality—illusion, fantasy, and melodrama—illusion might be combated by reason or, failing that, therapy and medication. Fantasy and melodrama are a bit subtler. They are genres—cultural as well as psychological phenomena. They require constant critique and readjustments of aesthetic taste and imaginative vision. Illusion falls within the province of psychiatry and hard-nosed science and social science. Fantasy and melodrama fall more in line with the arts, including the art of nature writing. So let's go there.

I teach a course in science fiction, and my students always want me to do more with fantasy. I have to explain why I resist the trend to join the two genres together in the hybrid of "sci-fi-and-fantasy," the predominant shelving preference in most bookstores these days. I follow Ursula K. Le Guin, who's written both sci fi and fantasy, in defining science fiction as a *thought experiment*—similar in intent and form to the kind of thinking made famous by modern physicists like Einstein and Schrödinger. Science fiction runs on a "what-if" premise that generates the story. The premise usually comes from topics in science, engineering, and social science: What if we could travel in time? What if we could build a thinking machine? What if there existed a humanoid race without gender or sexual differentiation? The thought experiment generally produces a commentary on what it means to be human or to live in the world as it is, in contrast to the world that might be. The commentary often reveals ethical and political truths or conundrums worth further investigation.

Fantasy, by contrast, posits a world that is stable and rule governed. The characters behave according to well-established traits determined by class, race, and kindred. The plot is generated when someone violates a rule or otherwise disturbs the order of the world. The lines are drawn between good and evil, the defenders of order versus the agents of disorder and destruction.

Science fiction is not defined as a story about the future with space travel and aliens, and fantasy is not limited to medieval settings, swords and sorcery, elves and witches. Space operas like *Star Wars* fit my definition of fantasy better than they fit the sci-fi genre. Time travel tales that send modern characters to medieval times might well earn the science-fiction label.

The politics are different, too. Sci fi, because of the way it fosters an appreciation for difference and a taste for change and novel situations, tends to promote an attitude of progressivism and a skepticism that challenges social and psychological norms. Fantasy, because of the way it works within a relatively stable world whose established order the hero fights to protect, favors a conservative outlook. As a way of thinking that gets picked up in the fiction that bears its name, science is open to the possibility of falsification, of having cherished premises proved wrong in the interest of advancing truth. As a literary genre, fantasy is like the psychological state that bears the same name: it trades in wish fulfillment and hero worship. On these grounds, sci fi tends to be romantic—a trip into another world that brings you back with deeper understanding and a propensity to question received wisdom—while fantasy trends toward the sentimental: a momentary escape into a world where good predictably prevails over evil and the world works according to rules and customs known in advance, from which readers return to accept their place in a very different world. Escape is addictive. You need it more and more because you never adjust to the world in which you are forced to live. Fantasy satisfies the addiction with its endless series of stories based on the same characters and themes. Readers eagerly await the tenth book in the series. They can fly off to Hogwarts and leave the Muggles behind. Engagement, on the other hand, of the kind promoted by Romanticism and sci fi, may well be "depressing" at first. That's the way it feels to move from illusion to disillusion. In her famous introduction to the sci-fi masterpiece *The Left Hand of Darkness,* Le Guin says that reluctant readers have told her that science fiction is like environmentalism—too depressing.

❧ The almost off-handed connection Le Guin makes between sci fi and environmentalism brings us back to Rachel Carson. Her first critics dismissed her as a hysterical woman and a purveyor of science fiction rather than true science. The charges drew upon the prevailing sexism and social paranoia of the times. In the era of the Red Scare, the arms race, and the feminine mystique—and in the aftermath of Nazi fanaticism—the charge of inciting mass hysteria was a serious one.

This was also the age of high modernism, when authors such as T. S. Eliot and William Faulkner stood like high priests in the secular religion of literature and critics regularly drew harsh distinctions between highbrow and lowbrow productions in the cultural arena—genuine contributions to civilization versus mere distractions for the sake of entertainment. The characterization of *Silent Spring* as science fiction played upon the low estimation of sci fi as a cultural product. Sci fi was rated at the same level as cheap westerns, drugstore romances, television comedy, and children's lit. The idea of teaching a college course on science fiction like the one I teach now (or a course on the romance novel, children's lit, or television) was unthinkable back then. And yet, in the decade framed by the publication of *The Sea around Us* and *Silent Spring,* science fiction was enjoying its classic period, with authors like Ray Bradbury, Isaac Asimov, and Robert Heinlein producing their best work. And a new wave of science fiction, with all the complexity of literary modernism and influenced by such artistic and philosophical movements as surrealism, psychoanalysis, existentialism, and feminism was also emerging in the work of writers like Arthur C. Clarke, C. L. Moore, and Philip K. Dick (whom, by the way, Japanese critics have long rated with Faulkner as one of the great American novelists). The new wave of sci fi foresaw the emergence in the next decade of such socially and psychologically complex writers as Frank Herbert, James Tiptree Jr. (Alice Bradley Sheldon), and Ursula Le Guin.

The critics of *Silent Spring* were not likely to have read the best science fiction available in their own day. They were probably thinking of the B movies then associated with the genre—the aluminum foil robots, clumsy special effects, ridiculous dialogue, bad acting, and above all, the connection to another genre—the horror movie. As a boy in the sixties, I watched the 1955 version of *Invasion of the Body Snatchers,* based on the classic novel by Jack Finney, with my sister Belle on a local Saturday afternoon television program called *Shock Theater.* Belle still remembers nightmares inspired by the birth pods of the alien invaders who took over the bodies of ordinary citizens, so that the characters never knew who was an invader and who was the guy down the street. Now recognized as an allegory for the threat of communist takeover from inside—an artistic production actually *engaged* with the politics of the 1950s—the film was received by viewers like Belle and me as something else entirely. Call it cheap thrills. The activation of social paranoia remained below the surface for us, though it must have worked subliminally to heighten the psychological terror that kids evince when faced with such questions as "Is Mommy really herself or some impostor?" If you happen to have a moody parent, the effect is even stronger. One day, it's Mommy or Daddy; the next day, some alien is inhabiting their bodies. Good science fiction works at both levels—social commentary and psychic thriller or adventure story. But notice that escape actually plays no part at either level. You're left with a new outlook on the world (whether the world of the primal family or society at large). Sci fi engages the reader, inwardly if not outwardly.

In the early twentieth century and on through the classic period at midcentury, science fiction was also a literature of recruitment. It was aimed at young and inexperienced readers for the purpose, often explicit, of teaching them how to reason scientifically, to work out the consequences of premises and laws, to be wary of simplistic explanations, to gather evidence patiently, and not to leap to unwarranted conclusions. Sci fi is the romance of science, and more than a few young fans have grown up to be research scientists or engineers.

In *Silent Spring,* Rachel Carson wanted to recruit the general public to defend nature and the nation to fight the misuse and overuse of synthetic pesticides, so she borrowed the literary form of sci fi for that purpose, especially in "A Fable for Tomorrow." The critics who dismissed the work as science fiction were really saying that it was illusion, fantasy, melodrama—or just bad science and bad writing. They were wrong about everything except its relationship to science fiction. The truth is that the legacy of Rachel Carson shares a great deal with sci fi, while its opposition attacks it as if it were fantasy and melodrama.

Science fiction feeds the sense of wonder that Carson's early works also inspire. Think of the language associated with the early outlets of twentieth-century sci fi, with titles like *Amazing Stories* and *Astounding.* Both Carson and the purveyors of sci fi cultivate what might be called the scientific sublime. They unfold the mysteries of nature and the discoveries of science before the audience's admiring and awestruck eyes. But the unveiling is not an end in itself. Once the imagination is engaged, it is put to work in the thought experiment of premise-testing.

Increasingly in the 1950s and 1960s, drawing on the gothic tradition of Romantic writers like Mary Shelley, E. T. A. Hoffmann, Nathaniel Hawthorne, and Edgar Allan Poe, science fiction writers like Philip K. Dick and Alice Bradley Sheldon found themselves engaging the dark side of the scientific enlightenment—the neglect of emotional life and human feeling, the monomaniacal pursuit of power through knowledge, the unintended consequences of technological development, including the production of monsters and the destruction of nature. Hence the connection with the horror genre, as wonder and awe gave way to shock and terror, illusion melted into disillusion, and hubris yielded to horror. This tradition formed the background for Carson's "A Fable for Tomorrow." Some evil spell seems to have settled over the community she depicts, but no wizard or witch has done the harm. The people have done it to themselves. Chemicals misapplied or overused take the place of the witch's brew. And here's the premise: what if the people do nothing and allow the process to continue? The birds cease to sing, the sedge withers from the lake, and, zombielike, human beings walk to their graves. The merciless unfolding of the premise is the hallmark of science fiction and *Silent Spring*.

Part of the skepticism that runs deep in the sci-fi genre blocks the possibility of melodrama—the division of the world into the forces of good and the forces of evil, heroes and villains. European sci fi has always been more ruthlessly antiheroic than the American version. My students generally hate *Brave New World* and *1984*, complaining that they find nobody to admire and attach to emotionally, but that's just the point. Aldous Huxley and George Orwell despise hero worship and sentimentality. Frank Herbert was advised by his famous editor at Ace Publications, John W. Campbell Jr., to end the first volume of *Dune* with the protagonist Paul at the heroic height of victory, before he succumbs to the hunger for power as the dogged pursuit of the premise demands. It was good marketing advice, which Herbert accepted, and the book sold millions of copies. My students love it—and to be honest, so do I. None of us are immune from the need for escape and hero worship on some days and in some times of life.

Rachel Carson originally considered a melodramatic title for *Silent Spring*—*Man against the Earth*—but her editors wisely talked her out of it. The proposed title would have undermined the actual complexity of her treatment, which shows that people are not a single unit but a diverse community pulled in many directions. Science itself is divided. What she calls Neanderthal science and industrial technology use chemistry like a club to beat down rather than solve the irksome problems of agricultural pests. Other scientists, like the emerging ecologists of her time, strive for a subtler understanding of nature. And still others are blinded to the ethical issues by silos of specialization. The public ranges in scientific understanding from the engaged amateurs of the Audubon Society, who were among Carson's main correspondents, to those totally unaware of what was happening to their world, lured by the soft sell and hidden persuaders of the advertising industry. Even the best candidates for villain, like the Monsanto Corporation, are allowed to have good intentions—feeding the world, saving the growing population from the disease and destruction brought on by the insect hordes, providing jobs in an expanding postwar economy. Carson's complex outlook demands something more careful than the division of the world into heroes and villains and victims. Her conclusion is not that we should abandon pesticides but that we should regulate them and look for applications of scientific knowledge that are more limited and targeted in their effects, that we should learn from the law of unintended consequences and be ready and flexible enough to make constant small adjustments in our technologies, that we should respect the lives of all organisms that we affect by our actions and be aware of issues involving biodiversity, and that we should strive to educate the public rather than try to sell them on power-brokered solutions promising the quick fix and the fast dollar.

But the attacks on *Silent Spring* represent a curious case of genre switching that continues in public discourse today. Ignoring the subtlety and complexity of the case that Carson mounts, the attacks reframed and reduced the book to a fantasy story, a melodrama with heroes and villains, then sought to attack the heroes and defend the villains. Having a hero identified opens the way to the fallacious ad hominem attack. You don't deal with the facts and the issues, just with the person. The same techniques have characterized the opposition to environmental regulation, from Ronald Reagan's notorious secretary of the interior, James Watt, who said that environmentalists didn't really care about nature but only wanted to destroy the American way of life, to the Rush Limbaughs of today's media, who focus on personalities rather than issues and ideas. If you can bring down Al Gore, you can bring down environmentalism, right? Only if you see Al Gore, or Rachel Carson, or Bill McKibben, or whomever, as the hero of the cause, the champion whose defeat will send the troops running with their tails tucked.

Why does the American public continue to be swayed by this kind of rhetoric? Partly because we love a story with heroes and villains, even if it means the fall of the hero. We clamor for fantasy and melodrama. If the person who conveys the idea is evil, then we don't have to take the idea seriously; we don't have to test the premise; we don't have to learn enough to make an informed decision; we can be comfortable in our hatred of the public enemy who's trying to change our way of life. Demonization rules the day. The victim is not Al Gore; the victim is democracy.

The effort to defeat denial doesn't need a hero, even a Rachel Carson. It needs to overcome the need for heroes and the division of the political world into good and evil that hero worship demands. It needs to wean the audience from the feel-good story, from the sentimental nostalgia that makes us think we still live in the world of *Leave It to Beaver* and *Father Knows Best*. It needs to open our eyes to the postapocalyptic landscapes of our world—the *Blade Runner* settings of our cities, the monocultured lands of the countryside, the rising tides, the floods, the heat waves, the heavy weather.

There's a huge debate going on. It's not about whether global warming is caused by humans or not. The real debate is about how to fix the problems we've caused. Nuclear power may be fast enough, but is it safe? Can wind and solar energy compensate for a reduction of dependence on coal and oil? Can large-scale organic farming, which might replenish the earth and reduce carbon emissions, still provide enough food for a hungry earth; or do we need to continue the work of the Green Revolution with synthetic pesticides and fertilizers, at least in the developing world? But before we can test these premises, we must get over the illusion, the fantasy, the melodrama of a people whose sentimentality runs deep and who have sustained themselves for decades now on a culture of escapism and denial.

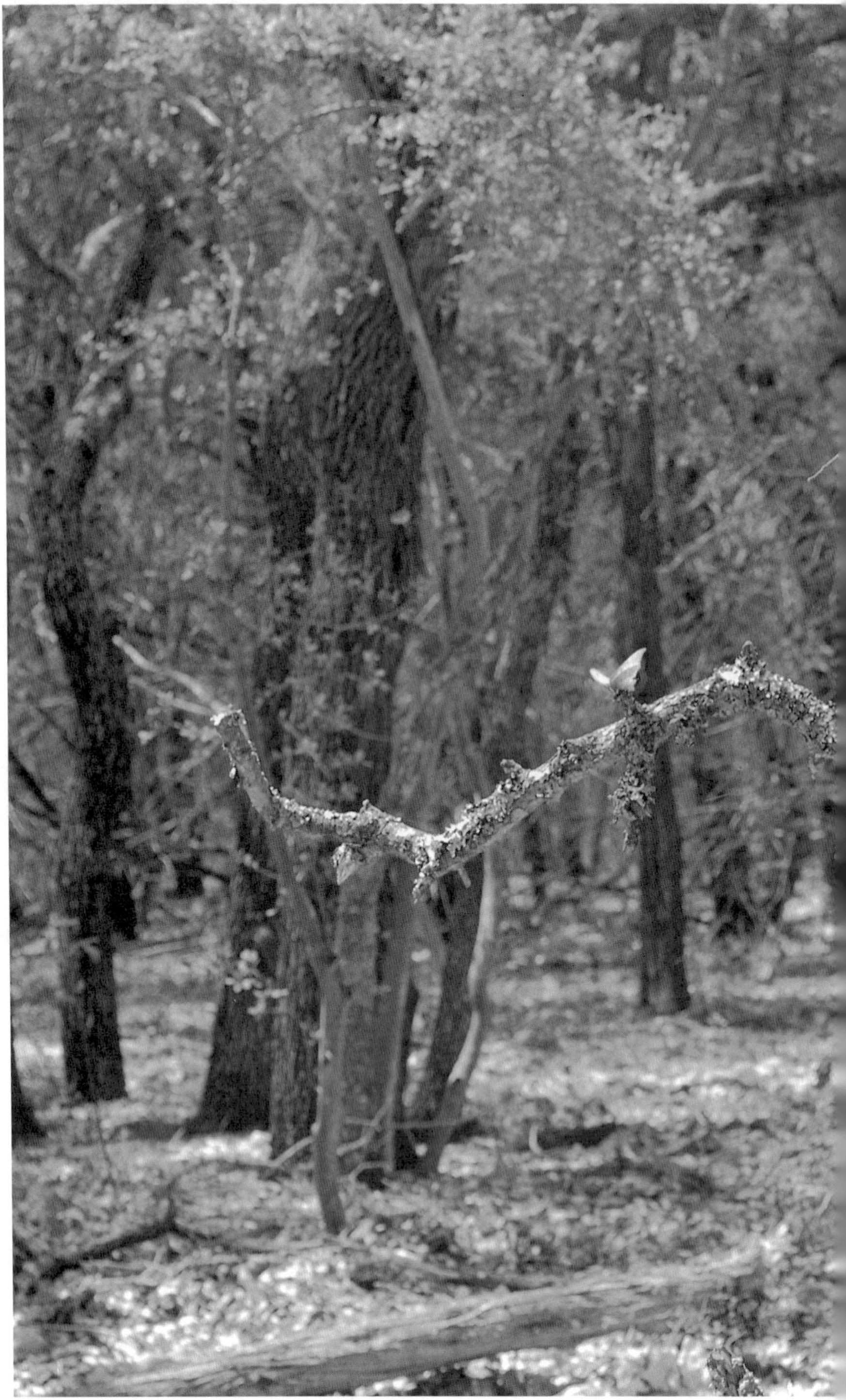

8   Epiphany Matters

> Epiphany—I want it to mean simply a rare and free showing forth of vital presence. But it's an ancient term and won't be easily stripped of its religious associations; the presence, by its sudden intensity, will seem not just extraordinary but supernatural. Perhaps that's not inappropriate. Birds seem radically different from other creatures.
> Leonard Nathan, *Diary of a Left-Handed Birdwatcher*

> I resisted hard the temptation, borne of a Roman Catholic upbringing, to describe it to myself or to others as the feeling of being connected to God, and the wonders of Creation. It seemed to me truer to the experience to be simply astounded that a small bird floated out there in this century, as its forebears had done for thousands of years before either Jesus or any of the rest of us. Nature had no moral imperative; nothing helped the bird; there was no fellow love for it out there; the water didn't help it, save harbouring its food source; the other birds wouldn't mourn its passing; the weather was just the weather. A man stood on the beach, watched it pass, and spoke out loud its name, in wonder and intense joy.
> Luke Dempsey, *A Supremely Bad Idea: Three Mad Birders and Their Quest to See It All*

❧   I mentioned in the overture that the experience of smelling the earth of my front yard following my mother's death in 1999 was both an epiphany and an apocalypse. I could have said the same thing about the moment I smelled the smoke of the Texas wildfires on my morning walk in 2011. The epiphany and the apocalypse—

usually understood as kinds of *vision,* though I suppose smells may count as well—are both forms of revelation or unveiling, involving a sudden discovery, realization, or sensing of a truth about the world. They both involve the alignment of insight and sight, of inward and outward perception. They can both change your outlook on the world and energize your engagement with it.

The difference is that the apocalypse usually results in a questioning of values while the epiphany inspires an affirmation of values. The two may work together, of course, apocalyptic longing leading to epiphanic affirmation, or the epiphany affirming values that stand as alternatives to those questioned by end-of-the-world thinking.

For me, an epiphany is like a version of the sunrise I dreamed of one morning before dawn in Taos, and then was stunned to see it replicated in waking life that very day on my morning walk.

I went out at first light, the day mostly cloudy, but with an opening around the edges of the horizon, a circle of clear sky between clouds and land. As the sun emerged in that narrow space, rising in the V between the flanks of two mountains, the cloud cover overhead was suffused with color, the world suddenly enveloped in a red-gold-pink-purple quilt of sky. Just as suddenly, the sun lifted above the clouds, and the world went gray again.

When the gray comes back in times like this, apocalypse looms, but with the rays of light shining through, you can feel the presence of epiphany. The moment contains the color, the depth, the promise of a life worth living, a world renewed. It's what the poet and birdwatcher Leonard Nathan calls "a rare and free showing forth of vital presence." It involves a seer, an attitude or frame of mind, a moment in time, and, for the nature enthusiast, a place somehow endowed with special history, energy, or personal commitment. Seen from another's perspective, it may not seem like much, but for the seer, it's somehow everything.

🕊 My earliest memory of such a moment (at least the full-blown experience) happened on a family vacation at Hilton Head. It must have been 1968 or thereabouts. I'd gone off on my bike, irritated with my parents, missing my friends, feeling sorry for myself, living inside my head.

At dusk I stopped by a black water lagoon beside a golf course. I was the only person around, just watching the day fade into night, when I noticed movement in the water on the other side of the pond around the foot of a half-submerged stump of gray wood. I was thinking that maybe an alligator or big turtle was stirring the surface of the water when, all at once, the stump straightened up, took wing, and flew away over the dunes toward the beach.

It was a great blue heron that had frozen under my gaze.

Another day at Hilton Head, I set off by myself, walking the beach. I walked in the same direction every day, toward the northern point of the island, so I knew the main features of the terrain. On this day, something was different in the distance, a large boulder sitting near the dunes. How could it have gotten there?

As I approached, its true form emerged and its identity dawned on me: a sea turtle, dead, covered with flies, its enormous body swollen with midmorning heat, head turned toward the sea it would never reach again, eyes plucked clean by gulls and crows.

I ran back down the beach and got Mom and Dad and the kids to come and see. My sisters complained of the stink. My dad and little brother gazed on it quietly, almost reverently, it seemed. My mother told how she'd heard the turtles would come up at night to lay their eggs and then crawl laboriously back to the ocean. She pointed at the carcass. "She didn't make it."

Years later, at Pawley's Island, we came upon a female loggerhead laying her eggs in the dunes at night and watched with Myrth and the other children as the huge animal struggled back to the sea in the light of the full moon that fell like a silver carpet along the wet sand. Seemingly exhausted, the turtle used her flippers to drag herself slowly along until she entered the surf and the waves hauled her bulk back to the place to which her limbs were better adapted—her home in the sea. My mind reeled with the memory of the boulderlike presence on the sunny beach at Hilton Head.

In the spring of 1986, I was driving northeast out of New Mexico, going for a job interview in Lubbock. Darkness had just fallen. Up ahead, somewhere near Brownfield (one of those aptly named West Texas towns, like Levelland and No Trees), I saw a brightly lit dome. I thought it might be a basketball arena. As I got closer and it loomed larger, I was thinking that basketball must be pretty big in West Texas; this place was huge.

Then the dome began to round out at the bottom, and I realized my mistake. It was the full moon rising, red-gold and half filling the broad horizon.

In January 1991, having just moved back to Texas from Memphis the fall before and while exploring the coastal region on a family trip, we stopped at the San Jacinto Monument, which commemorates the last victory for Texas independence in the war against Santa Anna's Mexico. Jackie remembered the place from her childhood in the Houston area.

It was nearly dusk when we climbed up into the tower of the monument, the sky partly cloudy, the setting sun casting a pink glow here and there. Near the edge of the big tidal river that flowed down to the nearby Gulf, among the golden grasses in the surrounding marsh, I saw a group of shorebirds feeding in shallow water, snowy egrets I presumed, reflecting the sunset.

Then the sun fell behind a cloud on the horizon, and the landscape went gray and white like an old movie—except for the birds, which magically retained the pink. I dropped a quarter in the scope that the state provides to get a better look.

They were roseate spoonbills. I'd never seen them before in

nature but knew their names and their image from Audubon's watercolor.

In February 2007, about the time I committed to taking on the job of department head in English at Texas A&M, I was out on my morning walk in the neighborhood—an expanse of middle-class housing built on an old Texas prairie—just after sunrise, the air cool and clear.

A yellow-rumped warbler flying out of a hedgerow caught my eye, and I stopped to watch it cross my path, then saw movement on the ground in my peripheral vision in the other direction—little gray birds over on the church lawn. Could they be a flock of the warblers, the kind of gathering I had seen the week before at the park? But no, they turned out more brown than gray—sparrows. What kind? I couldn't tell without the binoculars, so I picked up my pace again and got back to the business of walking.

Then dead ahead, coming fast over the horizon, I spotted a hawk winging in my direction—a red-shouldered, no, too sleek, maybe a Cooper's—coming straight for me, thirty, forty feet high. Almost directly overhead, it folded its wings and dove headfirst—right at me. I froze in my tracks.

Only at the last moment did it swerve and sweep gracefully into the group of sparrows I'd been watching not ten yards to my left. It missed the target, recovered flight inches from the ground, and swooped back skyward, lighting briefly on the low branch of a live oak nearby, showing silver-blue back feathers on the way up, rufous-striped breast on the perch. Resting a half minute, as if to nurse its pride, the hawk resumed a low course across the wide lawn, scattering sparrows in every direction.

Later, with the bird book, I decided it was a sharp-shinned hawk, a male. But at the moment of its dive in my direction, all inclination to identify was burned up in pure experience. Self-consciousness fell to ashes. I felt something like the paralyzed dismay of prey looking up to find a hawk coming at me, then puzzlement, and finally delight. It was a day like any other day, but it was magic.

All my life there have been these moments. Perception comes unhinged, and what I thought I was seeing morphs into something else. I puzzle over the glance into an alternate reality or join the universe in laughing at a little joke at my expense. I was nothing to the hawk, after all, but he was everything to me.

❧ The dreaminess of the dawn or twilight settings, the sense of mystery or new life awakening in dull routine, and the power of lasting memory are among the things that make me want to call these episodes epiphanies. The ones I've singled out all happened at crossroads in my life story over the four decades: the passage out of adolescence at Hilton Head (the adjustment to seeing myself as an individual, at the edge of the circle of friends and family); the midstream change in professional direction on the road to Lubbock (leaving one college to join the faculty at another, a wife six months pregnant with my only child); the inaugural year of another new job in College Station (which would become my longest-lasting academic post, the place I settled to raise a little family and establish myself in the profession); and finally the assumption of the leadership role late in my career at Texas A&M.

In these times, I tended to turn inside, close myself off in my own ego, which is for me the psychological analog of the self-contained and climate-controlled suburban home or academic office. I want to call the episodes epiphanies because they pull me out of myself and place me in the presence of something at least momentarily grander and more colorful, more delightful, more hopeful than the ordinary circumstances of my life, the sort of presence that mystics call God, or the life force, or ultimate Being. The effect is a restoration of balance, perception, and wonder that allows me to release whatever anxiety, pettiness, depression, or worry that haunts me.

I open myself to the epiphany on my daily walks, which makes the walking more than an exercise to keep me healthy, more even than a therapy to keep me sane. I can't say that I seek the epiphanies, because they usually surprise me when I'm composing a sentence in my head, working out a problem, fretting over a conflict. I'm sure their effect is healthy and therapeutic. They often give me back my sense of humor, relax my anxious nerves, and likely lower my blood pressure. But the gift is greater than all that. It is mystical by being partly inexplicable and incapable of being fully captured in language—ineffable. "The Tao that can be spoken," says the Tao Te Ching, the classic text of Chinese mysticism, "is not the true Tao" (quoted in Mogen 162). I can speak of the epiphany's effects on me, but not exactly of the thing itself. My greatest hope is that, by writing down the episodes or telling them to my closest companions, I can relay some of the feeling they bring and open others to the experience of the world from which they arise. For me (if not for all mystics and connoisseurs of the epiphany), the world that shows through in these moments of intensity is a decidedly *natural* world.

And yet, like other recent nature writers who've considered the term (such as my fellow birdwatchers, the nature writers Leonard Nathan and Luke Dempsey), there's a part of me that's reluctant to call my anecdotes epiphanies. Even within these moments of great personal significance—with the larger presence of nature snapping away at my self-consciousness—the experiences seem too trivial to withstand my moments of doubt, too ordinary to merit the mystical designation, too earthy and mundane to rank as revelations. And yet the term haunts me.

The word *epiphany* was first used, and is still used, in the High Church calendar of Christianity as the name for the feast celebrating the coming of the magi, their vision of the star signifying the birth of the Christ child. My visions just show me herons and hawks, ponds and prairies. But the way they *feel* to me, the attitude they inspire, suggests reverence and awe—as if they have broken through the crust of plain life and touched me with a new reality that makes me more humble, more open, and more happy.

❧ There are places you can go where you expect to be thrilled and witness wonders at every turn—Yosemite, Yellowstone, the Giant Forest in Sequoia National Park, the Muir Woods, the Bosque del Apache, the desert in bloom at Big Bend. These places we call *sublime,* a term that overlaps with epiphany. For me, the difference is that the sublime lacks the thrill of the unexpected experience that suddenly couples sight with insight. Thoreau's experience on Mount Ktaadn, reported in *The Maine Woods,* has been called an epiphany, but I would think of it instead as an encounter with the sublime. He went hunting for the shock of the raw wilderness and found it. For his epiphanies, look instead to *Walden* and his journal accounts of seemingly unmerited surprises in the tame environs of Concord.

Once I took a swamp tour with Jackie and Myrth near Slidell, Louisiana. Hearing me say "prothonotary warbler" when a bright yellow bird streaked across the bow of the boat we were riding in, our guide marked me as a birder and told us he had seen a purple gallinule earlier in the day and would try to find it again. As he steered the boat into the shallow water among the cypress knees, we concentrated our attention. When it actually appeared, iridescently purple with a bright orange-and-yellow beak, the living bird seemed like a Disney creature, a mechanical cartoon planted out there for the tourists.

The enjoyment of sight mingling with insight did not come for me until the gallinule managed to disappear into the background, a miracle of camouflage or escape for such a brightly colored trickster. I enjoyed losing sight of the bird more than catching sight of it.

The epiphany is like wildness leaping out of tameness, asserting its undeniable presence in a place and for a person rendered utterly domestic by the human transformation of the world. Ralph Waldo Emerson famously tells of walking in a common pasture and suddenly enjoying "a perfect exhilaration": "Standing on the bare ground,—my head bathed by the blithe air, and uplifted into infinite space,—all mean egotism vanishes. I become a transparent eyeball; I am nothing; I see all; the currents of the Universal Being circulate through me; I am part or particle of God" (*Essays* 10). The language seems silly if you look too closely. The notion of the transparent eyeball seemed a joke even in Emerson's day. It was the subject of a famous caricature by Emerson's fellow transcendentalist, Christopher Pearse Cranch, about whom my professor, F. DeWolfe Miller, wrote the definitive book back in 1952, with Cranch's funny drawing on the dust jacket: the huge eyeball topped with a little hat is the whole head of the figure, a grotesque globe wobbling on the insubstantial, long-legged body of the philosopher striding over an open field.

But if you look with a measure of forgiveness, kind of squinty-eyed, at the language of the passage, its value appears. First of all, there is the notion that "all mean egotism vanishes" (10). The negation of ego—the key moment in classic mysticism, in which the self is lost in contemplation of a larger being or power—offers an alternative to the competitive bolstering of ego in a society that values aggressive self-aggrandizement at all costs. The concept of ego-negation resonates with my candidates for epiphany experienced during times conventionally accompanied by self-doubt or self-absorption (adolescence, job interviews, career shifts). I feel nature pull me out of the morass of selfishness and return me to my senses.

But the Emersonian epiphany lacks something important. While it seems to inspire humility and the diminishment of ego, it ultimately yields to an infusion of power and elation. In the stretch of a single sentence, Emerson goes from saying "I am nothing" to affirming that "I am part or particle of God" (10). That's why the passage can provide the eco-critic Christopher Hitt with his best example of the "egotistical sublime" (607).

A problem more important for me is that, while Emerson's epiphany happens *in* nature, it is not prompted *by* nature. There's no heron, no rising moon, no hawk, no purple gallinule, only a bare common and snow puddles. It is as if God lifts Emerson out of the ugly setting or that the Self transcends the ordinariness of the tame and uninspiring scene. The word *common*—meaning the pasture open to all citizens but suggesting the ordinary and undistinguished—speaks volumes. Associating dull routine with the common place (or the literary *commonplace,* more or less another word for formula, convention, or cliché), not to mention the *common man,* Emerson arises to the status of the natural aristocrat. Nature channels through him but disappears in the process as he expands to a godlike stature. For me as for Emerson, the epiphany always arrives unearned and unannounced, without any effort on my part and in an unexpected setting—appearing like a royal baby in a Bethlehem cowshed. But in the process, the place becomes more than a setting for action; it becomes a character in the story, an active element in the scene.

And one more thing: the epiphany is meant to be shared. It is not only an inflation of the individual—not just one illuminated philosopher, one magi, one shepherd, one angel. It involves a holy family surrounded by visitors from the East, shepherds with their flocks, and angels descending from heaven—a blessed community. If a gathering of friends or family is not always actually present at the moment of my epiphany, they appear in my mind's eye as the ideal community to whom I direct my candidates for epiphany in conversation and writing.

By contrast, Emerson's romantic solitude seems almost a requirement of his enlightenment. His experience takes him out of community. "The name of the nearest friend sounds then foreign and accidental," he says of the time of his transcendence, "to be brothers, to be acquaintances,—master or servant, is then a trifle, and a disturbance" (*Essays* 10). Over the century and a half following the publication of Emerson's *Nature,* solitude (a value he inherited from Wordsworth and the English Romantics) becomes such a part of the formula for the literary experience in nature that we find many of our modern writers not only valuing the egotistical or antisocial sublime but even crafting their work to make it appear more individualistic than the experience actually warrants. In *Desert Solitaire,* for example, the impression of Edward Abbey's crusty independence results partly from the author's decision not to mention the frequent presence of his wife and other companions. Similar omissions occur in John Graves's *Goodbye to a River.* And it's not just a "guy thing." Annie Dillard—the queen of the eco-epiphany, whose candidates for epiphany are the subject of an entire scholarly monograph (by Sandra Humble Johnson)—also focuses on her response to nature as an individual, a loner. She minimizes the presence of her husband and other close companions in her excursions and observations. Her cat plays a larger role in *Pilgrim at Tinker Creek* than does her husband despite the fact that she shared her house with both at the time of the writing.

❧ Remembering the time my family lived in Oregon during my dad's Air Force service, I've been inclined to think of my dad as the one who saved me from the endless hours of indoor boredom enforced by school and homework when I was belatedly learning to read and to associate my mother with my schooling and my taming because of her insistent lessons at the kitchen table over the accursed texts of Dick and Jane and Dr. Seuss. But that's not fair; it may even be sexist. The contrast is too simple and stark. The truth is that Mom presented me with what seem, in retrospect, my first proto-epiphanies, experiences that complemented the sublimity of Dad's more conventionally masculine world of hunting and adventure.

One early morning, Dad had left for the dispensary, the little kids were still asleep, and I was doing my lessons at the kitchen table before it was time to go to school. (I was an early riser then as now, much to my mother's chagrin, I imagine, though she never said so.)

All of a sudden, Mom said, "Quick, come here and see."

I looked up from the yellow linoleum and saw her staring out the storm door. I scraped the chair back and hurried over to have a look.

Mount Shasta raised its snow-covered head and shoulders on the distant horizon. But she was looking at something closer. She leaned down and pointed toward the irrigated field just beyond the edge of base housing. I followed her pointing finger and saw what looked like a large brown dog running across the field. How I could see it so clearly at that distance, I have no idea. Maybe it had something to do with the perspective created by our perch on the hill.

I turned to look at her. Her face was radiant, smiling, looking at me now.

"It's a wolf," she said. I don't know how she knew what it was, but her animation was convincing. Even if it was not a wolf, it was the very image of wildness lighting her eyes. I could see it there and feel her excitement.

Another morning, I was ensconced at the table again. The little kids were asleep. Dad was off to work. Mom was looking under the kitchen sink, probably to get out some cleaning products or something. I nearly jumped out of my seat when she slammed the cabinet door.

I looked over to see her standing straight up. She looked at me, embarrassed, it seemed. "It's nothing," she said, "just a mouse. It surprised me." Her pride was talking now.

She came over and put a broom in my hand. "Now you help me get it out the door," she said. She added in a whisper, like a conspirator, "Daddy doesn't like mice, so let's take care of it before he gets back." She giggled a little about that, so I did, too. "You stand by the outside door and hold it open. Just brush him out if he comes your way. I'll head him in that direction."

"Yes ma'am." I felt the excitement. Mom and I were taking care of the wild intruder that "Daddy doesn't like."

She went over to the cabinet and leaned down. "Ready?"

"Ready!"

She pulled the door open and stepped back fast. "Shoo!" she said.

Then I saw it, a brown spot of fur on the yellow and white tiles at her feet. "Shoo!"

Then it moved. Did it ever! In two big hops, it landed on top of the kitchen table where I'd been studying. I was holding the door and staring in disbelief. It had to have covered six feet with each hop, and there it was, squatting on its haunches beside Dick and Jane, supporting itself with two rear legs cocked for action, its forepaws held out in front, nose twitching. It was looking at me, and I was looking at it. I had just enough time to think, "Its ears should be bigger"—the cartoons were my only source of mouse imagery—before it took two more hops and was past me, out the door.

Mom and I looked at each other. The radiance was there again. And we started laughing. "I think they call it a kangaroo rat. Do you see why?"

"I sure do!"

Forty-five years down the pike, Jackie would find a little hognose snake in the swimming pool. By the time she fished it out of the skimmer, it was stiff as a pine plank. She laid it out on a tree stump in the sun for Myrth and me to pay our respects. We came out and admired its distinctive turned-up nose, its brown and tan markings lovely as inlaid wood on a fine musical instrument—like a native flute brought to life, but now dead. We touched its quilted scales and nodded to one another.

Later Jackie went out to bury it before the stink set in. But it was gone. Maybe a bird got it, or just maybe it came back to life, as snakes will sometimes do, and crawled away.

The next morning she opened the garage door, and there beside the house, partially hidden by a little hawthorn shrub, was a brown-and-tan hognose snake, about nine inches long, looking up at her—if not the same snake, then its perfect twin. They locked eyes for the briefest moment before it slinked back into the greenery.

When Jackie told me the story later that day, I saw the delight in her face, the same old radiance I remember on Mom's face, the snake's resurrection lighting her eyes.

People are hungry for epiphanies these days. I know it because the word and the phenomenon are almost as common in popular culture as the apocalypse. Even my sister Belle has epiphanies.

A couple of months after we put Dad into a care facility in

Columbia, close by my other sister Kathy's house, because his dementia and other ailments had gotten so bad that home care was impossible, Belle and I were talking on the phone. Dad had gone to the facility on Labor Day weekend 2012, and now Christmas was coming on and Belle was dealing with her new independence. The single sibling in the family and a cancer survivor herself, Belle had continued to live near the old home in Greenville and, while working as a schoolteacher and athletic coach, had cared for Mom in her illness and Dad in his decline her entire adult life. I was calling to say that the Christmas presents she sent had safely arrived in New Mexico before the onset of the next winter storm, due to arrive that night, December 18. She was still living in Dad's house, where she had taken up residence full time the year before, when Dad got really bad. A professional caretaker came during the day, but Belle spent every night there. Then came fall, and the busy season at school, and between that and her travels to Columbia for visits, she had not found time to move back into her comfortable condo down the street. It had been hard for her to let go and allow Dad to be moved. It made her sad that he had to leave the house he loved, his place of greatest comfort. But we finally convinced her that she had reached the end of her capacity in the care-taking role—losing sleep, worrying constantly, continuing to teach school full time, organizing the daytime caregivers, sacrificing social life and personal satisfaction, and risking her own precarious health. Belle and I talked almost every day—among other things, about how she would have to remake her life in a world without sick parents who needed her daily attention. She was fifty-six years old, with enough time in the school system to retire, but looking again at the old hard questions of identity and purpose. The day before we talked in the week before Christmas, Kathy emailed to say she had signed the papers for hospice to come in for Dad.

That night, Belle told me that, as she was cleaning up the kitchen in Dad's house, she found herself staring at a plate with our mother's china pattern—a defining feature of a married lady's identity in the culture we grew up with, as old as her life in the family that the woman made for herself and that she bequeathed to her survivors. Suddenly Belle was overcome with a thoroughgoing sadness, deeper than any she'd known since Mom's death. The realization hit her that for the first time in more than fifty years, neither Mom nor Dad would be present in this house for Christmas. A world a half-century old had come to an end.

She got herself together enough to call her friend and talk a little, and soon she was feeling better. What she said to me was "I guess I had an epiphany."

She had no idea that I was writing about epiphanies. Belle has a lively intelligence and an artistic imagination, but she's not a literary or philosophical person by nature or training. I don't share much of my writing with her. She's a physical education teacher for elementary school kids, a former basketball and softball coach, a Baptist by upbringing and a practical-minded, occasional church-goer as an adult. So I was mildly stunned by her use of the old High Church, mystical, and literary term. I respected her feelings too much to stop the story and ask her how this word came to be part of the vocabulary of her personal life.

But a few days later I did ask. She said that she couldn't remember where she first heard the term. She didn't recall using it as a young woman, only more recently. Then she told me about other flashes of insight that had hit her lately, often when she was working in the yard and just letting her mind roam free.

❧ By the time Belle told me about her epiphanies, I'd decided I already knew where she got the word. Probably TV, magazines, or even the newspaper. Since I first started collecting my own candidates for epiphany, I'd heard the word everywhere. When Belle said it, it was the crowning moment of a long search.

Like stories about the end of the world, epiphanies are everywhere. The TV character Dr. Gregory House speaks of breakthroughs in diagnosis as epiphanies. I've read the word on the sports page of the local newspaper. The author Neal Stephenson says of an observation made by the protagonist in the recent novel *Reamde,* "The epiphany—if this wasn't too fine a word for some crazy-ass shit that had popped up in Richard's brain—had occurred in a brew pub at Sea-Tac" (132). The word attaches to things not only secular but mundane to the point of insignificance—a wardrobe choice, a decision about where to eat lunch, whatever. Usage verges on cliché.

The TV scriptwriters, sportscasters, novelists, and consumers who use the term may have learned it not in church but in English class. That's where I first encountered the word, back in the early 1970s. By that time, it was already going out of fashion among professional scholars, though it never quite disappeared from the classroom and the literature textbooks. Its usage among literary scholars peaked during the heyday of the New Criticism, the movement that dominated Anglo-American literary studies in the postwar years. Unlike the competing agendas of American studies and British cultural studies, the New Criticism tended to ignore the historical and political elements of literature and focus instead on its universal meanings and its status as an artifact of high culture. This systematically antipolitical version of literature must have felt comfortable to many American professors working in the high-growth prosperity of the first two decades after World War II. Maybe it muted the general anxiety of the Cold War. Why drag poetry into the fray?

The New Critics took heart from William Faulkner's famous

acceptance speech for the 1949 Nobel Prize in Literature (which I first read in high school in the sixties). The celebrated novelist cautioned fellow authors against submitting to the fear of nuclear destruction, worrying too much over the question "When will I be blown up?" Instead, he urged them to attend to the "old universal truths" that have sustained literature over the centuries—"love and honor and pity and pride and compassion and sacrifice." In this list, the values of *honor and pride and sacrifice*—appropriate to the battlefield and to a warrior nation or world power—are balanced by *love and pity and compassion,* necessary for peacetime living, for the making of homes and towns and productive lives. This balancing act was the great aim of literature in the New Critical way of thinking and was also the stated goal of world politics at the time, with its interest in *balance of power* (American versus Soviet, capitalist versus communist, and so on).

Many of the most influential New Critics—John Crowe Ransom and Cleanth Brooks, for example—were the sons of Southern ministers who learned to read the Bible closely and brought something like biblical interpretation to bear on the study of secular literature. Others, like Allen Tate, followed their hero, the poet T. S. Eliot, into the Catholic Church and made peace with Christianity during an era dominated by advances in science and technology that seemed to leave religion behind. Though never enamored with Romanticism, the New Critics seemed determined also to realize the aspirations of Shelley and Emerson and Whitman to elevate poets to a kind of secular priesthood and turn poetry into a modern scripture. So when authors like Eliot began to follow Wordsworth in depicting particularly intense moments of something like revelation, and when the quintessentially modern novelist James Joyce followed Emerson in using *epiphany* to describe these "spots in time" (as Wordsworth called them in *The*

Prelude) or some "still point in the turning world" (in the language of Eliot's *Four Quartets*), the literary epiphany signaled the convergence of traditional religion with the advent of a secular religion in the halls of literature. The New Critics embraced the epiphany and made it a staple in the interpretive language of modern criticism.

As with so many such terms, it eventually suffered from overexposure—like a movie star who takes on too many bad roles, or a pop song overplayed on the radio—and by the time of my entrance into the profession, its day seemed to have passed. The definitive work was already done, and summative studies had begun to appear that would continue to trickle out over the next decade or so, as I passed through graduate school and entered the world of the junior professor. I can't remember ever using the term in my professional scholarship.

Trends in academic studies may come and go, but language follows its own course in ordinary usage. So why should I have been surprised—some time after the turn of the twenty-first century—when everybody seemed to be talking about epiphanies again? I suppose it was partly a matter of lag time. It takes a while for knowledge to find its way from the lectures and monographs of academe to the scripts of television programs (and vice versa). But the belated exchange is often quite striking. The episodes of *House M.D.* in many ways involve textbook uses of the epiphany, at least as a plot device. They share with Joyce's fictions the sudden introduction of a culminating insight that seals the plot of the narrative. The story is pretty much over after Dr. House has his diagnostic epiphany. A similar pattern appears in many of Joyce's best stories, like "Araby" and "The Dead."

Belle's epiphany with the china pattern was, in its tone and content, even more Joycean than the epiphanies of Dr. House. Her story shares an overwhelming sadness with the works of the great Irish novelist. The insights of the Joycean epiphany are world-shifting or, if not world-consuming, mildly apocalyptic. And that's one thing that makes them different from my own eco-epiphanies, which tend to be joyous or amusing moments. There are other differences as well.

🌿 I remember the first time I read the kind of story I would now consider a candidate for my version of the epiphany, though I didn't know the word at the time. It was not too long after the episode of the flying stump at Hilton Head. The story appeared in the anthology used for my first-year English class, the same one in which I first read Asimov's essay "The Eureka Phenomenon." Asimov's title describes the kind of thing that Dr. House experiences in the TV show better than the word *epiphany*, in my view. The essay tells of how Archimedes discovered the buoyancy principle after first giving up on solving the problem of finding a way to measure the amount of pure gold in the king's crown. He goes off to the baths to relax. When he sees the water slosh over the side of the bath, a flash of inspiration about displacement comes over him. With this tiny hint from the world outside the mind, when he is not consciously engaging the problem at all, the solution hits him. He jumps out of the bath and runs through the streets naked, shouting "*Eureka!*"—the Greek word for "I've got it!"

I recall that I liked the story and admired Asimov's crisp prose (which I also enjoyed in his science-fiction stories), but the essay that really got me going in that anthology was written by another scientist, the anthropologist Loren Eiseley. It was an excerpt from *The Immense Journey*, a book about evolution published in 1962 (the same year that Eiseley's friend Rachel Carson published *Silent Spring*, with its prototype for the environmentalist apocalypse).

Like the Asimov piece, Eiseley's essay must have appealed to me because I was a science major at the time but also wanted to be a writer. The editors of the anthology for English composition students might have chosen it for the very reason that it included an episode that could pass muster as an epiphany. The 1960s were the heyday of the epiphany in literary studies. I read the piece in my first term of college, fall of 1970.

Eiseley tells of floating down the Platte River on a solitary expedition during his young manhood—at least he says he was by himself, though as we've seen, some authors in the epiphany tradition edit their companions out of the story to intensify the mystical experience of the individual. (I amuse myself with the image of Eiseley actually joining a group of his scientific companions in a decidedly unscientific and unmystical skinny-dipping excursion that he later revises into the epiphany.)

Overcoming an aversion to water stemming from a traumatic experience in childhood, he slips anxiously into the shallow Nebraska stream with its occasional depths and threat of quicksand. Lying on his back, he yields to the flow of the river: "The sky wheeled over me. For an instant, as I bobbed in the main channel, I had the sensation of sliding down the vast tilted face of the continent. . . . I felt the cold needles of the alpine springs at my fingertips, and the warmth of the Gulf pulling me southward. Moving with me, leaving its taste upon my mouth and spouting under me in dancing springs of sand, was the immense body of the continent itself, flowing like the river was flowing, grain by grain, mountain by mountain, down to the sea" (13).

Eiseley's story shares with Emerson's the sense of losing the ego in the contemplation of something larger than oneself; here the floating humanity of the speaker yields to oneness with space and time. He is both negated and enlarged. In this sense, it is classically mystical, though not in the least religious. Probably without my knowing it at the time I read the piece, the mysticism appealed to my Christian background, which I had consciously shed in my newfound independence from my parents but which probably left a void that I felt the need to fill. It also provided an image of outdoor release, the escape from boredom, which I had need of again in the schedule of required courses I was facing at the time—endless stinking labs and homework problems and textbook readings. The idea of floating away on a distant river tugged at my longing. It likely played a part in sending me on frequent excursions to the nearby rivers, lakes, and mountains.

If Loren Eiseley was my first model for the eco-epiphany—the favored image of my youthful independence, the reclaiming of my wildness, and the escape from what I found most oppressive in my socialization—my latest model is Kathleen Dean Moore. Moore returns me to the responsibility of mature engagement with the community. She adds the social and ethical layer that often seems missing in the mystical romanticism that runs from Wordsworth and Emerson to Eiseley and Dillard. The best of many good examples comes from her book *The Pine Island Paradox:*

> Rocking in my kayak, I watched my son perched at the crest of the island. His attention had been caught by something far out at sea. . . . He raised his arm and pointed. I turned my binoculars to that place. It was a pod of dolphins, silver curves jumping in unison, shining just for a moment, then sliding into the sea.
>
> I believe that the most loving thing you can say to a person is "Look." And the most loving stance is not a close

> embrace, but two people standing side by side, looking out together on the world. When people learn to look, they begin to see, really see. When they begin to see, they begin to care. And caring is the portal into the moral world.
>
> "Look, there, almost to the edge of the sea. Can you see them?"
>
> Jonathan pointed to a far place on the horizon where light leapt and leapt again. (49)

Moore understands oneness with nature as something that people can experience together. Outside of Moore's writing, my favorite image for the sociable epiphany is the scene from Steven Spielberg's film *Close Encounters of the Third Kind,* when the aliens finally land and the crowd of people looks together up into the bright light of the ship descending to earth.

A more recent example, one perhaps more pertinent for the aficionado of nature writing, is the coming together of an estranged father and son in the film *The Big Year.* In the epiphany that consummates the repaired relationship, the crusty old workingman dad (played by Brian Dennehy), weakened by a heart attack, manages to take a walk with his birder son (played by Jack Black) and spots a great gray owl for the son's big year list. The son has pushed ahead on the hike, encouraged by the father to fulfill his goal and not be held back by the old man's inability to keep up. But then the son is overcome by a sudden worry about his father's well-being behind him on the darkening, snowy trail. Rushing back, he finds the old man safe, pointing up into a tree at the stately owl. They stand side by side, grinning and looking.

Strolling by myself on the beach early one morning during a brief vacation at Hilton Head in the nineties (a Father's Day gift from Jackie and Myrth), I paused absentmindedly to watch a man fishing in the surf with a boy about twelve years old. Out of nowhere, a dolphin erupted from the water not ten feet from the boy, coming right out of a wave near the shore—the full body there in the air before us and then gone in an instant. The boy's head snapped around to see if his father had seen. The joy on that kid's face when he caught the father's eye had the old radiance. Then they both looked around to check to see if anyone else had seen. I stood there open-mouthed on the beach. When our breath came back, we all began to laugh.

The story suggests another quality of my candidates for epiphany—the vague sense of dissatisfaction that comes when no companion is along to see what I see. Birders know one version of this disappointment: will anyone believe that I just saw a golden-cheeked warbler so far out of its range? But lovers of nature also know another kind of disappointment at not having the best companion nearby, the person who really gets it, when the wonderful thing happens. The sense of longing produced by such disappointment could well be the main motive for writing down the epiphany in the first place. The writer wants to engage in that most loving of acts, according to Kathleen Dean Moore, to point and say to the companionly reader, "Look!"

❧ I should tell you that a month or so after I smelled the smoke of the wildfires the week after Labor Day 2011, it finally rained in Texas—not enough to end the drought, but some. On a cool October morning, I went out the front door for my walk and found a light drizzle falling, the streetlights reflecting off low clouds moving rapidly from north to south across the sky.

In the predawn air, cooled by the north wind and the storm from the night before, I saw the form of a cottontail resolve in the driveway. As I watched the rabbit keep still so that maybe I wouldn't see it, I heard a sound high in the cloudy darkness. It was the geese heading south, always a big moment in my seasonal life. I looked to the sky and, squinting hard, I finally made out their dark forms, moving fast, as they came almost directly overhead beneath the low clouds in a rough V.

At that precise moment, about a mile away at the high school practice field, the marching band began to beat and blare out their music, as if to celebrate the arrival of the geese.

I went back inside and got my notebook. In the dim light of the back porch, with the martial strains of the drum line and trumpets mingling with the fading chortles of the geese, I wrote it all down. I was thinking, "When Jackie wakes up in an hour or so, I'll tell her."

I guess I had an epiphany.

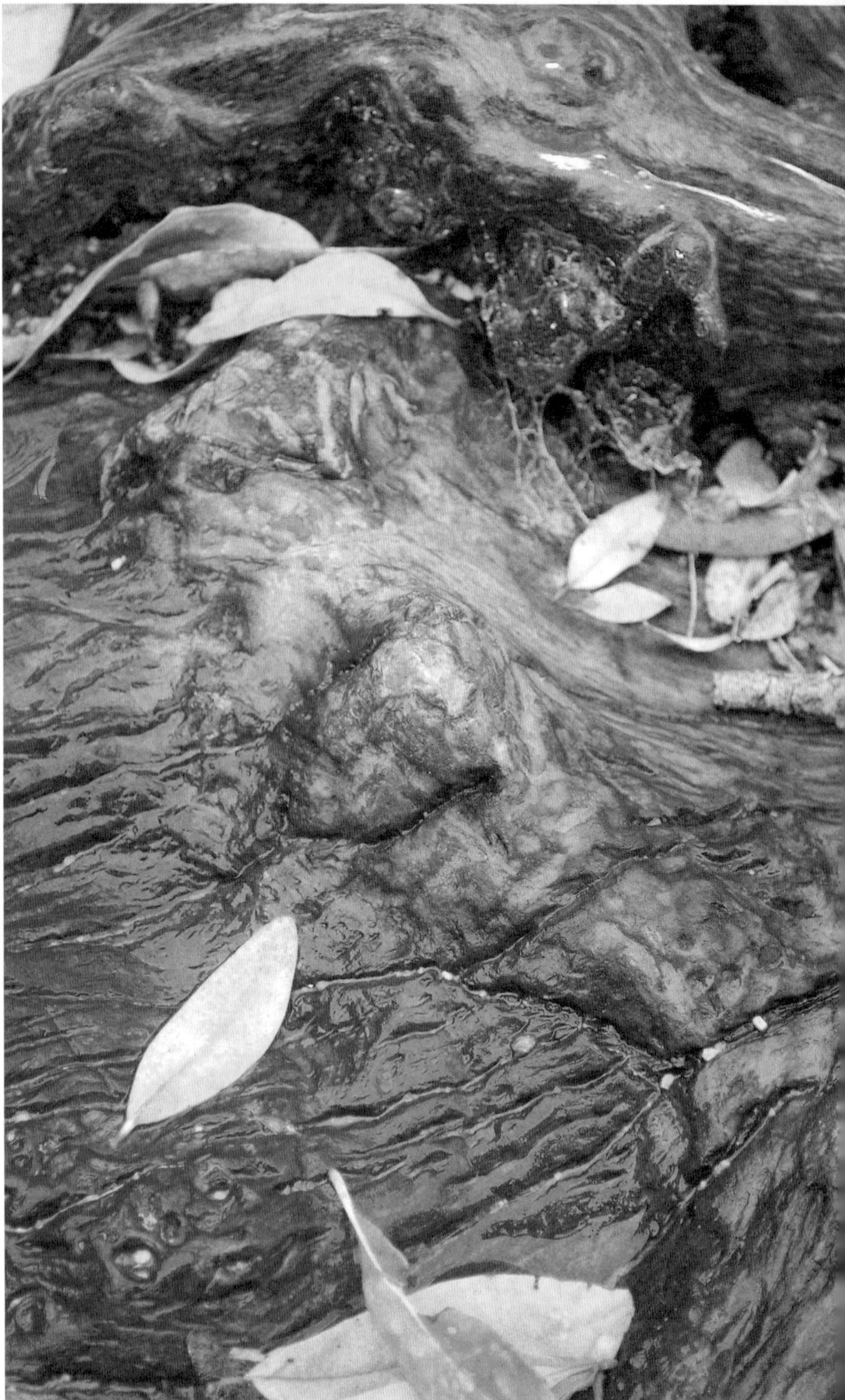

9 Imagination Wild and Tame
The Smell of Money

> I too am not a bit tamed, I too am untranslatable,
> I sound my barbaric yawp over the roofs of the world.
>
> Walt Whitman, "Song of Myself"

Jackie retired in 2010 from academic life and now makes jewelry full time. She still thinks hard about the ecological questions we've done our best to face in almost three decades together. Disturbed by the frame of mind she found me in when I resorted to my darkest thinking on sustainability as a lost cause, the trapped feeling I sometimes experienced when I served as a department head looking at the culmination of my career as a series of endless indoor meetings, the return of apocalypse when Texas started to burn in 2011, she decided to do something about it.

She realized that we were aging fast, that we had been living an unsustainable life in a place where global warming means almost intolerable heat and drought in an ever-longer summer, that we were barely able to afford a vacation anymore though we had achieved most of our career goals (in salary as well as position and accomplishments), that we probably couldn't sell our Texas house or afford to decrease its ecological footprint, and that what everyone is now calling the Great Recession of 2008–2009 had hit my life in the university very hard. My graduate students were struggling to find jobs. The university was admitting ever more students, and the administration was offering incentives for retirement but authorizing fewer new hires every year. Still, she did not accept that we were stuck. She cashed in what was left of her retirement account at the end of the year in 2011, and we bought a small place near Taos, New Mexico, where Myrth had been living for a couple of years in the off-season for park rangers and where we all have a history together, a place of memories where we want to live out, as far as nature and the economy will allow, our future. From my perspective, the timing was good because, in my term as department head, I'd earned a research leave to catch up on my writing—including this writing. The hope was that, by my retirement time, we could sell the Texas house (or rent it to the increasing number of our neighbors who can't afford their own place) and move to this downsized house where our ecological footprint is smaller and our need for vacation is quenched by the local beauty.

Now here we are, our financial resources stressed to the max, living for a year on an overgrazed, sagebrush-blanketed acre of mesa just west of town, perpetual cool air in the window on a summer morning, hoping the wildfires in the south of the state don't bode ill, laughing nervously when we hear our next-door neighbor worry over the dependability of our water wells and talk about moving his whole extended family to sea level (from which we have just taken flight), but doing what we can, at some risk, to walk in beauty. I'm still the same old professor, thinking through the same themes, but then, one morning, I find imagination awakening, and the desire comes over me to think wild thoughts.

❧ June 11, 2012. The coyotes wake me at 5:30 a.m. I drift back to sleep till 6:00, and they're at it again. On the edge of a dream, my mind first registers the wild cries as a siren from a fire truck or police car. I smile when I realize my mistake. It's happened before. Once at midday on a hike in Bastrop, Texas, I heard a pack of coyotes crank up out of nowhere and thought I was hearing a crowd of little girls squealing somewhere over by the lake. It takes a while for a mind tamed by suburban life to recognize wildness for what it is.

After first light, the dogs of the neighborhood join in. My neighbors keep dogs for the reasons that everyone in America does, for emotional comfort and companionship but also, here, for protection. They feel exposed out on the open mesa, especially those in the nicer homes whose beautiful lines and up-kept exteriors all but shout, "I collect art and Navajo rugs and have a fortune in electronic gear and other stuff behind these seemingly quaint adobe walls." With dogs to protect them from human intrusion and theft, they build fences to protect the dogs from the coyotes—those charming confinements actually called "coyote fences," built from unfinished, sapling-sized stakes with the bark left on, spaces in between the stakes big enough for the dogs to see out but not for the wild dogs to get in and kill them. My friend from Texas told us that, near his house at the lake, construction workers uncovered a coyote den and found dozens of dog collars, the wearers of which long ago disappeared from the yards of their doting owners.

I get up and pull on my clothes, head out for my morning walk, down the "improved road"—more dirt than gravel because of regular gradings by the county and the constant migration of dust and mud in this place. The neighbors don't want the road paved—better to face the dust in summer and mud in spring than increase the access and speed by which the cars can come zooming through. Rocks and gravel crunch under my shoes. The place is so quiet that I can hear the sound of my own feet, unlike my old suburb back in Texas where traffic begins to growl well before first light and drown out the subtler sounds. Now the sun comes up over the mountain and spreads yellow light to replace the pink of dawn.

I'm too late today to see the scaled quail on top of the big sage bush (or perched on the sage-green electrical box), greeting the sun with the characteristic call of mating season—*chip-churr, chip-churr,* over and over. I'm about halfway down the dirt road toward the blacktop of the county road when the coyotes go off again, wild and loud, off to the northwest at the shady foot of Taos Mountain. Another group answers from down the rift valley to the south, maybe where Jackie and I hiked last week and where I paid for my view of the cactus blooming in the desert by sacrificing my bare calves to the sage flies that bit so bad at the top of my sock line that my legs still itch and burn a week later.

Confined within the coyote fences, the dogs around me sound their warnings (of me for sure and maybe the coyotes as well). The sound the dogs make seems muted by contrast to the coyotes, their voices lower, smoother, more mellow to the ear. The coyotes sing like the Northern Plains Indians at the powwows, high and yodelly. I once heard the cowboy poet Henry Real Bird of the Crow people perform a Northern song and slip seamlessly into the yodels of Hank Williams's "Lovesick Blues." The coyotes could well have been the source for this style of singing (Henry's Indian songs and Hank's cowboy-inflected country music). The dogs in their fences sound like Bing Crosby or some other crooner. They try hard to howl and yodel like Henry or Hank or cry out like the wildest rockers, from Little Richard to Robert Plant of Led Zeppelin, but they are badly in need of a microphone or an electric guitar screeching with distortion. The dogs are able only to soothe the worried ears of their masters, who need that homey sound as they slip down for another forty winks under the light summer comforter. The coyote cries like an ambulance headed for someone else's door, rendered forgettable by the familiar woof of old Shaggy or Maggie out in the yard.

Temple Grandin—the animal scientist you always hear on National Public Radio, the one who's used her autistic imagination to redesign most of the nation's slaughter facilities to improve the final moments of the cattle's lives—tells how dogs and humans coevolved. The forebrain of dogs shrank as they came to depend on their human companions to do the thinking, the planning, the directing—what we (with our special brand of arrogance) call the higher functions of cognition. The midbrain expanded to fill the available space in the canine skull. This arrangement left the dog to do more of the work of smelling and hearing and feeling the difference in the wind when the wildness closes in after dawn and the coyotes keep howling even after the moon has set and it's broad day—for what reason I can't tell you; you'll have to ask the dog. I can't tell you partly because, as if to compensate, the midbrain of my ancestors shrank to make room for more forebrain and leave the finer business of sniffing and hearing to the dogs.

I own no dog these days, but many of the neighbor dogs know me, and when they come out of their coyote fences and meet me on the road, some graciously accept my scratch behind the ear, my greeting that calls them by name if I know it, as if they know that man and dog, only together, make a whole being, a living system of mutuality. The coyote in its pack is utterly foreign to us both—wild and alien, whole-brained and unspecialized. I imagine it feels contempt for us partial beings, the way my psychologist friend sniffs derisively at the people he calls "codependent."

And yet we call both dog and coyote *animal.* How can that be? The dog and the coyote tell us who we are, but we don't always want to hear the news.

🙞 In a journal entry dated June 13, 1851, Thoreau writes of walking at night. His sense of sight—always dominant in the hunter brain of the human—is impaired or limited by the dark, though Thoreau claims to enjoy the muted light of the moon not quite full and takes the pleasure of an artist in the way it lights the branches of the white pine and the surface of Walden Pond and the flowing river; even puddles on the path become charming.

But more than the sights, it's the sounds that come alive for him as they never do in the day. He hears the "dreaming frog" (toad), the "peeping hyla," the bullfrog, each dominant in a given season but "heard at last occasionally together." He hears the familiar hoot of the owl and this time too the rarer drumming of the partridge: "What singularly space penetrating and filling sound!" Engulfed with sound, he cries out more than concludes: "We live but a fraction of our life." We are like a stream dammed to turn the single mill wheel of work at a mechanical pace, he says. "Why do we not let on the flood, raise the gates, and set all our wheels in motion?" He can't resist the recourse to scripture, to the voice of one crying in the wilderness, but with a new emphasis on the words that invoke the neglected sense: "He that hath ears to hear, let him hear. Employ your senses" (*Journal* 55).

But it may not be as easy or as natural as you might imagine, my old friend. If what Temple Grandin says is true, our senses are impaired not only by the night but by the way our brains have evolved. We need our dogs—and our poets and animal scientists, who work harder at sensing than the rest of us do—because our power to live in our thoughts and our dreams without the distraction of a world deeply sensed is partly what makes us human. To see it another way, if the power to live in our thoughts and dreams and fantasies is the one that leads us down the path to destruction, don't we need our poets and animal scientists and dogs to say, "Wake up! The wolf is at the door"?

We may even need them to help us breathe. I mean really breathe. In his nighttime meditations, Thoreau finds himself talking about breath. He puns on the notion of "inspire," meaning literally to breathe in, but also be filled with inspiration or spirit: "We do not inspire and expire fully and entirely enough, so that the wave . . . of each inspiration shall break upon our extremest shores, rolling till it meets the sand which bounds us, and the sound of the surf come back to us. Might not a bellows assist us to breathe? That our breathing should create a wind in a calm day!" (55). Then he goes on about living fractionally and failing to employ our senses.

Even if he is punning and speaking metaphorically of breath as spirit and inspiration, it's funny that it's the sense of hearing that leads to Thoreau's thoughts on the need to breathe more fully and deeply. For me, it was always the sense of smell. The dog is very good at it; the human has become very good at avoiding it.

※ Sometime back in the late 1980s when our home base was Lubbock, Jackie and I, too late for lunch at the local cafés and just passing through, stopped at the corporate pizza franchise in Hereford, Texas, a town named for a variety of beef cattle rather than the English ville from which the cow originally got its name. Directly across the road was a massive feedlot. It could have used some help from Temple Grandin. All the way to the horizon, bellowing cattle crowded shoulder to shoulder, fattening for market.

The smell was staggering—nothing like the smell of cows I remembered from my uncle's dairy farm, the grassy fragrance of open pastures and well-kept barns. The feedlot stink reminded me instead of how dogs and cats smell in a vet's office, nothing like their home scent even in the worst of times. I guessed it was the chemical reek of crowded, cornered fear.

"That's quite a smell out there," I said to the waitress inside.

"I hardly notice it anymore," she said, putting out the menus. "Around here we call it 'the smell of money.'"

Back in the car, after eating, then again negotiating the almost visible stink in crossing the parking lot, we repeated the phrase, "the smell of money." I recalled that people in the Southeast used to say the same thing about the sulfurous stench of paper mills.

Jackie had heard it from her dad. His ingenuity in electricity got him work in the petrochemical industry that carried the family off the farm in Kansas into the oil-rich lands to the south. Jackie spent her early childhood in Pasadena, Texas, a Gulf-ward suburb of Houston. Because it was downwind from the big refineries, the locals called the place "Stinkadena."

I know significance awaits in the phrase "the smell of money" and its connection to the remembered scene of a man and woman rushing through a parking lot to feed themselves in a low-ceilinged, climate-controlled concrete bunker decorated with the icons of corporate familiarity while large mammals in the open air across the road fed flank to flank, emitting the stench of dread as they prepared to become the toppings of the doughy disks we ate with melted cheese made from milk their own mothers may have produced. Significance awaits. It approaches allegory—maybe something about our kinship with the animals and our consequent cannibal guilt, or better yet, something about the way people will endure assaults on the senses to survive in a culture of contradictions—but for me in this remembered place, significance seems to be struggling to arrive at the easiest of allegories. My thoughts fail to harmonize with the grand narrative of human dominion over the animals, delivered ironically or straight up. The story isn't even finished. We stop, we smell, we eat, we ponder. What happens next? Why would I tell this fragment of a story to others or to myself, then stop short of the big meaning that allegory implies?

After years of mulling it over, I fitted the story with two endings, or rather one ending—a completion of the allegory—and one non-ending. The non-ending leaves the truncated story as an *image* that stops short of allegory and that stands as a lesson in wild thinking, the environmental imagination. To make best sense of the image, and to understand why I have come to prefer the non-ending to the ending, I need to start with the allegory. So the ending comes first to show the way to the non-ending. One lesson of the whole business is that an unsuccessful allegory appears to a knowledgeable audience as a fantasy that says more about the author as an individual person than about the topic communally considered, more about psychology than politics or ethics. The unfinished story invites the audience to engage the politics and communal storytelling involved in seeking an always-deferred sense of closure in the way we live our lives together.

❧ First, then, the ending, the allegory: you can call this version of the story "The Great Inhalation."

It's common sense that, if you smell something bad, you do something about it. If you smell a dead rat in your pantry, you get it out before disease spreads from the carcass. If you smell sewage in the backyard, you check the septic tank. Jackie told me about a woman in the office where she used to work who had lost her sense of smell. One day she was cooking some leftovers in the break-room microwave, and the smell alerted her coworkers—or rather pushed them to the edges of disgust. Without their help, the lady might have made herself sick by eating food that looked perfectly fine (no apparent mold or discoloration) but was spoiled to the point of serious stinkiness.

My engineering friends tell me that the smell in a place like Stinkadena or Hereford, Texas, is not necessarily a sign of danger to human health (and, they sometimes add, places that smell perfectly fine are often more dangerous). But, in the allegory I have in mind, I wonder if they've got the whole picture.

Without thinking much about it, people who are constantly exposed to a bad smell could be living in a perpetual state of shallow breathing. To live like that is to live in spiritual impoverishment in an almost literal way. If (like Thoreau in his journal) we take words like the Latin *spiritus* literally, the Holy Spirit literally means Holy Wind or Holy Breath. The God of Genesis breathes on Creation to bring it alive, including the human being made out of clay (or more generally, earth). In turn, we enliven the body, this personal plot of ground, by breathing into it a sustaining force taken from the atmosphere of the living world. To be inspired literally means to be filled with breath. Breath sustains community as well. I've heard that certain indigenous folks blow in the hand before offering it in friendship or greeting.

Without breath, we crumble and return to the earth. My mother fought through many forms of affliction during her twenty-five-year battle with systemic lupus. She endured open sores on her skin and in her mouth, body-racking seizures, an irregular heartbeat, kidney and bladder malfunctions that made her urine run red with blood. But when the disease attacked her lungs, leaving her tethered to an oxygen tank twenty-four hours a day, she looked me in the face and said, "It can't go on like this."

When I was growing up, I had to learn to breathe. It's a lesson some people never learn, taking breath for granted, a thing learned at the moment of birth and considered an involuntary reflex thereafter in the healthy animal. But many of us found new ways to breathe back in the 1960s and 1970s, my formative years, an era that I (perhaps naïvely or nostalgically) associate with an attitude of spiritual openness, including a literal expansion of the collective breath.

It was the Age of Aquarius, the songs on the radio proclaimed. In America, Asian mysticism flourished as never before. The standard versions of Christianity yielded to new versions. Islam became a force to be reckoned with, especially among African Americans. Many of these changes began earlier or crystallized later, but in the popular mind and the mass media, the sixties appeared as a watershed of spiritual transformation. Yoga classes formed and

Zen centers opened in the cities. The Beatles got a guru. Many of the new spiritual leaders taught that breath should be intentional and deliberate; new breath meant new life.

So there we were, learning to make our bellies rise and our nostrils flare, feeling our muscles lengthen and relax, discovering our bodies in strange new postures. These days, yoga has become an exercise class, a health routine, a market niche. But then it was different. It was an awakening, an alternative to business as usual. Many classes were free, and all were cheap, unlike now when the smell of money mingles with incense and peppermint in suburban gyms and city studios. The teachers today—and many of the adepts—look like magazine models. Back then, the arrangements were a bit more informal, the people not so well groomed, the atmosphere edgier.

I learned hatha yoga on the floor of a fellowship hall in a Knoxville Unitarian church. The teacher was a psychology graduate student and former gymnast who had sought out an Indian guru to teach him. Instead of factory-minted mats made of some soy or petroleum product, we used old bedspreads and army blankets to cushion our hard Western joints and sore muscles. If we had any money, we left an offering in a coffee can by the door on the way out. The new spirituality was less like a fitness plan and more like a collective gasping for fresh air. Having held our breath and ignored the stink of fouled air—going back for generations, at least to the advent of the Industrial Revolution—many Americans experienced a sucking need for *spiritus.*

Whole families got involved. After years of living ordinary middle-class lives in places like Stinkadena, Jackie's clan found themselves growing weary in the stale old atmosphere of Protestant Christianity and soon were caught up in her parents' enthusiasm for faith healing, Christian Science, the Unity Church (which built a huge pyramid-shaped worship center in Houston), and psychic readings. Her father paid for the entire family to take a course in Silva Mind Control—a meditation technique developed by a Mexican American entrepreneur from Laredo, Texas. José Silva fused Dale Carnegie's power of positive thinking with something like kundalini yoga to create a system of mental adjustments that promised the power to program your life for success. For obvious reasons, the idea that the soul worked like a computer program appealed mightily to Jackie's engineering dad, who went on to become a certified Silva instructor and taught classes from Texas to California, and then on the frontiers of Alaska (where he also worked on the oil pipeline). Jackie's mother studied Jungian psychology and, after moving to (where else?) Marin County, California, took up practice as a counselor and spiritual advisor.

My own family stuck with Protestantism back in the industrial South, where paper mills blew their stink over the marshes of the Low Country and chemical plants with their acrid odors replaced cotton mills in the Piedmont as the textile industry moved to the Far East (and we imported yoga, as if in exchange). But I partook in the Great Gasp. I went from reading Hermann Hesse and Carlos Castañeda to experimenting with Eastern mysticism and vegetarianism. Yoga proved the most lasting influence. I had heard that it offered a druglike experience, a "natural high." Yoga taught me just to breathe, to practice consciously an act that all my life I thought was involuntary—*pranayama,* as the yogis call it (from the Sanskrit word *prana,* meaning, again, both breath and spirit). People would ask me to reveal my mantra and share my experiences of meditation, which they supposed to be mind-altering to the point of psychedelia. I would say, "I just breathe. Sometimes I start by counting my breaths." Most would look at me as if I were a fool and turn away bored. But some stayed with me. At one point I found myself leading a yoga class in New Mexico. I'd come a long way from the old church pew and football team, which neatly divided soul and body.

With the new breath came greater endurance. I took up hiking in the mountains and running in the park (running was always punishment at football practice, but now it was almost fun). My senses seemed to grow sharper: colors dazzled, smells enticed, music seemed more subtle, varied textures greeted every touch. From then on, whenever I caught myself anxious or troubled, I noticed that the breath was tight in my throat. If I would only breathe, I could come back to myself. It didn't always work, but often it did.

By the Orwellian year of 1984, I was living in New Mexico. I had just met Jackie, who joined the yoga class I had ended up teaching. As we got closer, she and I discovered our mutual interest in environmental studies—she from the perspective of biology and science education, me from the perspective of literature and language, both of us with a lifelong background of hiking and camping. We both had collected a box of articles on environmental science and politics. We merged boxes and began working together on a book about environmental rhetoric.

It was about that time that I realized, along with many other students of literature and the environment, that the new spirituality, the Great Inhalation, coincided in history with the advent of the environmental protection movement, reaching a new intensity in the period between the publication of Rachel Carson's *Silent Spring* in 1962 and the first Earth Day, in April 1970. It took a decade for me to see the connection between my environmentalism and my spiritual enthusiasms, and even then—and still now—I'm not always sure what to make of it. Only the general outlines are clear (as the edges of fantasy are always a little fuzzy).

It goes like this: If the body is our little part of the earth, and breath is the wind that animates it, then it's no wonder that our search for new sources of spirit should go hand in hand with a renewed interest in the outer world that comes into our bodies with each breath, resulting in a determination to protect our interest. One day I found myself scratching notes about yogic metaphysics into my old copy of *Silent Spring*. Rachel Carson understood how our minds and bodies and breath are caught up in the dance of creation with the rest of nature. Like yoga—the word for which derives from the Sanskrit equivalent of *yoke*—ecology says that everything is connected, *yoked* together, all part of a great whole. By breathing, we participate in the chemistry of the world around us. By breathing consciously, we become more deeply aware of the connection. Call it spirit, call it breath, it's all the same.

In *The Spell of the Sensuous*, the philosopher and naturalist David Abram tells how, on returning to his home in New York from a venture into southeast Asia, nature seemed to recede from him. When he was living in the jungles and caves and huts of the Indonesian people, with their shamanistic and preliterate outlook on life, nature unfolded before him and drew him in. Back in the United States, he gradually felt a pulling away. The insects and animals no longer called to him, or even appeared regularly before him. The forest seemed remote even as he walked in it.

He blames the phenomenon on the literate experience, on reading and writing, the work that consumed much of his time upon his return. Reading and writing do create some problems for the person who desires a transcendental immersion in nature. Literacy leads us to inhabit worlds of our own making. From living too much in the world of the mind and the text, you can grow insensitive to your place in the world of wind and smell and touch. Written language differs in this way from speech. When you speak (or sing, alone or with the coyotes), you form wind into words that go back into wind as soon as they are spoken. The force of the waves you make in the air resounds off the membranes of listeners' ears. Most of the time, speaker and listener will not be able to reproduce the same version of the conversation. Not so with writing. In allowing us to "converse" with ourselves and with others at a distance, it forms a reliable, objective-seeming record that can consume attention, draw us out of circulation both social and natural.

While I admire David Abram's thinking on the issue, I have a different theory about his problem. I think that when he got back to work and started to hurry himself, worrying about the promises he had made to the foundations that gave him his travel money and his publishers' deadlines, he stopped breathing as deeply as he had in the slow time of his life among the Asian spiders and shamans. You lose your breath when you get in a rush, and one of the symptoms of anxiety is shortness of breath and tightness in the chest. Nature wasn't receding from Abram so much as he was taking in smaller portions of it with each breath. He pulled himself out of circulation. At least figuratively, it was the smell of money—the foundation funds and the advances from the publishing agents—that took him away from contact with the oxygen-rich, slow-moving earth. (Having apparently recovered his breath, David is now giving workshops and writing books on living an animal life. I hear he lives in northern New Mexico somewhere, so I guess he's my neighbor.)

Even breath itself has a price these days—not only at the yoga studio, but also at the oxygen bar. If you had told my grandfathers that one day they would be paying for air to breathe and water to drink, they would have stood gaping at you, waiting for the punch line. Current generations have adjusted all too easily to the idea of paying a dollar or more for a little plastic bottle of water. And now, at tourist attractions in Gatlinburg, Santa Fe, and Fisherman's Wharf in San Francisco, we find the oxygen bar—perhaps the first step toward an air economy. The sniff of pure O2 you buy at oxygen bars includes a dose of "aromatherapy" so that a pleasant or stimulating smell is marketed along with a high-grade source of the breath of life. Here is a new take on the smell of money.

What is it about money that makes it attach to everything? The question has a spiritual side that connects to the way we understand our place on earth. When, in the Christian Gospels, Jesus said, "You cannot serve God and money" (Matthew 6:24)—using the Aramaic word for money, *mammon,* which has become a code expression in modern English for money with a suspicious odor—he may have been promoting the interests of his home region. Galileans were slow to replace the barter system with Roman-minted money—slower than Jews in other regions, like the Judeans around Jerusalem, for example. Hillbillies from places like Nazareth didn't have much money and found themselves at a distinct disadvantage, even in religious matters. They were unable to buy animals to sacrifice when they journeyed to the Temple in Jerusalem. They had to drive their own sacrificial livestock down the River Jordan at great effort and expense. So Jesus didn't care much for money. "Render unto Caesar the things that are Caesar's"—money, that is—"and unto God the things that are God's"—namely your soul and your living (Matthew 22:21). He knew something about the special insidiousness of money. In replacing goods, it tends to become a god-thing, an idol to which all else bows. Having no value itself, it gives value to everything. It is meaningless unless it attaches to something you want, but since it attaches to everything, it becomes the very standard of value.

Since money can substitute for holdings in land, money has over time become more valuable than land. Most people would rather have half a million dollars than the equivalent value in real estate. The cash is more flexible. You can always buy some land and maybe have a little left over for landscaping or building.

Money is supposed to raise the quality of life, but does it really? Doesn't it require constant sacrifice in the quality of smell and taste and touch and hearing and sight? We endure ugly, smelly, tasteless situations in order to get money to take us out of the situations. Such work can destroy peace of mind and interfere with spiritual experience—by making you hold your breath, if not something worse.

Money has been known to undermine relationships. Reading a magazine in the doctor's office, I ran across a poll about what married couples argue about. Money is at the top of the list. But remember that money is a convenient symbol or substitute for just about everything else—thanks to its abstraction. Many domestic spats over money may really be about something else—kids, housecleaning, in-laws, sex, pets, work, vacation, the meaning of life—and money only becomes the symbol of other shortcomings we perceive in our mates. In this way, money destroys our sense of reality. It's a roadblock of abstraction that stops the flow of thinking about particulars.

The symbolic potential of money caught Sigmund Freud's attention when he began to analyze the dreams of the Viennese middle class at the turn of the twentieth century. One thing he saw was a persistent symbolic connection between money and feces. One patient dreamed of buried treasure in a rustic outhouse while she was receiving treatment for an intestinal disorder. In Freudian terms, the capitalist represents the highest achievements of the anal character, the most successful at withholding and depositing, denying the body for the sake of greater rewards, cultivating the discipline of saving and investing. Suppressing an aversion to smell to get money fits the model perfectly.

My mother was no Freudian, but she always said that nothing

was dirtier than money. "Never put a penny in your mouth," she used to say. "Think about all the people who might have touched it and where it might have been put before you got it." The admonition made my mind reel. Sailors and whores and hoboes and sinners of all kinds—people who never gave a thought to washing their hands!—they all could have put that penny I was tempted to pop in my mouth into the pockets of their nasty pants, or someplace worse. It could have lain on the floor of a slaughterhouse or fallen in a sewer. The concept of "filthy lucre" was more than just a cliché to my brought-up-Baptist mind. "Cleanliness is next to godliness," I learned, so if money is the filthiest thing there is, it must be pretty far from God.

If I think of the smell of money as a metaphor for the things a person must endure to live in a place that pays good dividends—the cost in spirit (breath) that compensates negatively for monetary gain—what is my own smell of money in the Brazos Valley of Texas, where I continue to live much of my life? I won't count the loss of natural beauty because I honestly believe that in every place, the earth offers some allure—at least until it is reduced to a defiled state by being abused. I would be hard-pressed to name a naturally ugly place. No, what stinks in my hometown, metaphorically, is not the landscape I see from my window but the noise I hear (and so I return to Thoreau with the connection of breathing and hearing).

I'm out before first light every morning for my daily walk, and already the sound of oversized pickup trucks competes with the first songs of cardinals, kingbirds, and sparrows. How could such a small city make so much noise? Mainly by housing fifty thousand students at the big university where I teach, many of them nursing a Texas-sized identity crisis that requires them to drive fuel-wasting, space-hogging, air-sucking trucks the size of harvesters back and forth to the library, bar, and grocery store. Back in the 1980s, during one of the now uncountable oil crises, the experts said that when gas costs a dollar and a half a gallon, people would switch to economy vehicles and the market would support research into alternative forms of transport. Gas costs twice that much now, and in Texas we're still waiting for the big change, though hybrids and small sedans can at least be seen among the truck traffic. Back in the nineties, my brother-in-law and I stood on a corner in San Antonio one evening and, in the midst of a big traffic snarl, could not count a single sedan. It was all trucks and minivans and SUVs of one kind or another.

Pickups get bigger every year. I hear their roar as I sit on my back porch and write in my notebook. The notebook is handmade of cotton paper. One of the fathers of the truck drivers in my neighborhood probably owns the land in West Texas where the cotton was grown. Later I will type the words into a computer and print them out on recycled paper, the original pulp of which was produced in some stinking mill in a place like Georgetown, South Carolina. I used to take my vacation near there every summer. The round-trip cost about three hundred dollars in gas alone. It would have cost four times that much for four of us (Jackie, me, Myrth, and a friend) to fly. Drive or fly, we would be using the expensive product of the oil refineries that make the air in places like Port Arthur and Pasadena into an olfactory offense.

Curiously, the word *olfactory* sounds close to the way Texans pronounce *oil factory*. They may be on to something. Oil factories—not only refineries but every petroleum-burning machine in our environment, including cars, trucks, trains, planes, gas-driven mowers and leaf blowers and WeedEaters, power plants, and all the others—may not have replaced the olfactory element of our experience, but they have certainly changed the way we smell—and see, hear, taste, and feel—the world around us.

We Americans enjoy stench-free driving only by displacing the smell. Most of the gases our cars emit—like carbon dioxide—don't stink in the nostrils the way that methane does, so they are all the more dangerous and insidious when they overload the atmosphere and overwork the trees, creating the conditions for global warming. I remember learning as a schoolchild that because the natural gas used for home heating and cooking has no smell, an odor must be added to the mix before it is marketed. By smelling it, we can escape danger during a gas leak. The refining process with gasoline works the other way around as far as I can tell. Its offensive smells and most immediate poisons are refined away. As a result, the air seems cleaner in the car-choked cities, but the CO_2 emissions will ultimately take their toll.

Just as people accustom themselves to the smell of money in refining towns, so the ear of the city dweller can reduce the sound of truck and airplane to background noise. But listen. On my back porch, the traffic noise is more persistent than the song of the mockingbird. The most territorial of local songbirds, the mockingbird takes a breath now and then. The traffic never does. It claims the air as its own. Its mighty exhalation challenges the stumpy trees of the post oak savannah that surrounds this place to take it all in, to convert it back to oxygen and make it fit for human consumption. The very thought is enough to send you running to the oxygen bar. But I just go inside.

❧ The problem with the allegory of the Great Inhalation is largely rhetorical. Language patterns such as allegory, metaphor, and analogy depend upon the reader accepting the identification between unlike terms that the author offers. The initial connection made by the joke about the smell of money—linking the cattle, oil, and paper/pulp industries—is believable enough. But the rest is risky. Will the etymological connection between breath and spirit still convince in an age in which science undervalues one side of the equation (spirit) and religion undervalues the other (breath, material life)? The entire allegory depends upon that connection. Otherwise, yoga is just exercise, and breathing remains a rather mundane, involuntary process that either we have or we don't. Bad smells are just an inconvenience. As one version of the old rock and roll song says, "They say the best things in life are free, / but you can tell it to the birds and the bees, / I want money (that's what I want)."

And so we come to the non-ending. As it turns out, the possibility that the allegory has failed doesn't destroy the power of the anecdote for me. The memory persists and with it the feeling that something important passed among me and Jackie and the waitress and the doomed cattle on the high plains of West Texas. So the question becomes, how do I convey the feeling of importance to others?

The alternative I find myself left with is to jettison the allegory and leave the fragment of the West Texas tale as an *image*—an act of the imagination that dwells upon a *presence,* something from the past that will not go away but remains present as a scene in the mind as real today as it was yesterday. It connects to other images at the level of particular, material life—to the paper mills, the chemical plants, the oil refineries, to the stories of our fathers and mothers—but resists the abstraction of metaphysical meaning and spiritual significance.

In rhetorical studies today, the word *image* usually implies something literally visual, like a painting or a magazine ad or a bit of film footage—the kind of thing discussed in Roland Barthes's classic essay "Rhetoric of the Image," or the concept of the "image event" in Kevin DeLuca's book *Image Politics: The New Rhetoric of Environmental Activism,* or in any popular treatment of celebrity or political image—the concept of *image as visual impression* that goes back at least to Richard Nixon's five o'clock shadow and shifty eyes in the first televised debate of a US presidential campaign, when the handsome and well-composed John F. Kennedy won the day. The studies in visual rhetoric, presidential rhetoric, and environmental rhetoric all favor the treatment of the image as an artifact of photography, print media, television, cinema, and now digital culture.

But this view cannot contain the smell of money, or any smell for that matter, or any touch or taste. The current concept of the image favors vision—the look, the gaze, the spectacle—and sometimes sound, thanks to audio-visual technology. Even ancient rhetorical concepts like *vividness* and *clarity* favor visual and sonic impressions.

The smell of money demands the *verbal image*—an idea that derives from literary modernism—not a visual but a mental image cast into language, and not limited to the sense of sight or sound but potentially embracing all the senses. It would not be called an image at all except perhaps for its relationship to *imag*ination, under its most austere definition: the making of impressions and memories in the mind.

Though its history parallels the history of photography, the verbal/mental image as theorized by the poet Ezra Pound and the literary critic I. A. Richards may well have arisen in competition with, as much as under the influence of, the photographic image. The image can be recognized by a series of formal features, in prose as in poetry, which my friend Chris Holcomb and I described in a recent book on prose style:

First, the image invokes multiple senses.

Second, the image orients a text to the body, summoning the physical experience of the audience to energize the reading experience.

Third, the image suggests, often without completing, a longer story. (Holcomb and Killingsworth 142)

The image might be merely a phrase, such as *the almost visible stink of the feedlot*. Or it might involve a list or catalog of related phrases, such as *the sulfurous stench of the Carolina paper mill, the airborne reek of the Gulf coast refinery, the gag-inspiring whiff of the West Texas feedlot*. Any element of the list could be expanded into a complete anecdote, the longest form of an image, such as the whole story of the man and woman's encounter with the smell of money. The expandability or compression of the image contributes to its rhetorical power. Energy resides in the author's restraint—the reluctance to tell all—and in the resulting stimulation of the reader's imagination.

In Pound's definition, "An 'Image' . . . presents an intellectual and emotional complex in an instant of time," producing "that sense of sudden liberation; that sense of freedom from time limits and space limits; that sense of sudden growth, which we experience in the presence of the greatest works of art." From his contemporary and fellow modernist, the Irish novelist James Joyce, Pound would have known the term *epiphany*, to which, in this definition, he relates the image as an overpowering presence that captures the moment and possesses the reader's imagination like a little verbal demon.

Pound is concerned primarily with authorship and artifact—the greatest works of verbal art, mainly poetry—but his definition also involves an effect of reception—the sense of liberation experienced by the audience—and thus it has strong implications for prose performance. In uttering the phrase "the smell of money," the pizza restaurant waitress transported Jackie and me out of the immediate context of the West Texas parking lot and feedlot and sent us on a mental tour of all the places across the southern United States, from the Atlantic Ocean to Rio Pecos, where the smell of money is always bad and always requires a physical and psychological adjustment to a downturn in the quality of life that livelihood makes necessary. We were not in the presence of artistic genius but rather in the spell of *genius loci,* the spirit of the place, channeled by the unwitting waitress, who was momentarily transformed by context and happenstance into a poet of the western plains. The effect was practically accidental, a collision in space and time of the right mix of experience and language, author and audience.

Such is the nature, and such the rhetorical risk, of imagery, according to I. A. Richards. The image, he says, is deeply tied to experience and in particular the experience of the senses. Rhetorical success depends upon a correspondence of the experience invoked in the text and the memory of the reader. The "smell of money" might strike the first-time hearer, maybe a tourist from France or New York, merely as the folk wit of the western United States. The tourist receives the phrase not as an image but only as a *metonym,* a figure of speech that substitutes something closely associated with West Texas cattle—money, that is—for the corralled cattle themselves, the actual source of the stench. The metonym is a pretty good one, a decent joke, but without the correspondence of experience and memory, it lacks the full power of the image. It falls short of producing what Richards calls *attitudes,* the "imaginal and incipient activities or tendencies to action" that arise from language (112). An attitude—literally a position of the body—precedes an action. To create or change an attitude is generally what we mean when we say we want to *persuade, sway,* or *move* a reader. Effective speech or writing prepares the mind for action. For Jackie and me, the phrase "smell of money" mobilizes irony and resentment. The metonym is not itself the image but rather an evacuation of the image. Money—the ultimate metonym, which can substitute for practically anything—erases the reek of cow terror and the resulting human, and humane, disgust.

This response suggests how the modernist concept of the image connects with cognitive science and animal studies as well as ethics and political ecology. First, imagist theory anticipates the ideas of Temple Grandin. Grandin believes that autistic people, like many nonhuman animals, think not in abstractions or in language but in pictures—a state of mind arrestingly foreshadowed by Pound, who advised the would-be poet, "Go in fear of abstractions." Also like Pound, Grandin uses language associated with vision—for him, *image;* for her, *thinking in pictures*—though minimal scrutiny reveals that, like the poet, she doesn't confine herself strictly to visual impressions. She's really talking about thinking in complex images that require the use of many senses, not just vision. In her own words, "Animals and people with autism . . . think by associating sensory-based memories such as smells, sounds, or visual images into categories" (201).

In narrating one of her many successful attempts in making animal-processing plants more attuned to animal welfare, Grandin writes, "Operating the controls in the machine shop enabled me to practice later via mental imagery. I had to visualize the actual controls on the chute and, in my imagination, watch my hands pushing the levers. I could feel in my mind how much force was needed to move the gates at different speeds" (25). Her experience is tactile as much as visual. The force she feels in her hands becomes, in her imagination, the force exerted upon the bodies of the animals. Like many animals, autistic people are supersensitive to pressure upon the body. A hug, Grandin explains, can be fearsome, not because the touch from a loving person is unwanted but because it produces sensory overload. With her gift of tactile sensitivity, she empathetically puts herself in the position of cattle in the chutes leading to slaughter and then redesigns this terrifying world to make the animals' last minutes of life less upsetting.

In this way, thinking in images suggests an ethics of care such as we find in Kathleen Dean Moore's thinking, notably her idea that "the most loving thing you can say to a person is 'Look.' And the most loving stance is not a close embrace, but two people standing side by side, looking out together on the world" (49). It's more than looking, though. We've got to account for touch and smell and taste as well as sound and sight if we are going to get a sense of presence that stays with us, that won't let us go. The people to whom we say "look" may remember a tug at the arm that goes with the pointing finger; they may remember the smells of damp soil and evergreens, the light stench of sweat or damp wool from hiking companions.

Smells, it is said, are tied more deeply to memories than any of the other senses. Brownies cooking in the kitchen can send you back to childhood faster and deeper than any old snapshot. In *A Natural History of the Senses,* Diane Ackerman says to live is to smell. You can cover your eyes to block out sights and plug your ears to muffle sound. But because to breathe is to smell, she says, there's no escaping olfactory sensations (unless one is suffering from chronic anosmia). You'll collapse or die if you hold your breath too long.

She's overlooking something important, though. Like the experts who predicted that people would buy smaller, more efficient cars when the price of gas got high enough, Ackerman underestimates the worker's and consumer's power to make mental adjustments, like the cartoon frog in Al Gore's movie *An Inconvenient Truth,* which boils to death without a complaining wiggle as the temperature in its laboratory bath gradually increases. If employers will pay us more money, we will buy expensive gas and endure offensive smells. We will buy water and air if we need to. The stink of the refinery, the feedlot, the paper mill becomes first the "smell of money"—a joke—and then it becomes nothing at all, something you don't even notice.

How would I conclude this coda on the power of the verbal image if I follow the guidance of Ezra Pound and Temple Grandin, to "go in fear of abstractions," and add an element about the need for caring and sensing in a world of numbness and dissociation? I would offer vivid images as foils for the smell of money. Something like this:

I'm driving Uncle Tunk to see the new Korean War Memorial in Washington, DC. He's telling me about the bad time in Korea, after his best friend (my father) died and he discovered all at once that young men are not immune to death.

"Do you know what a dead man smells like?" he asks me.

"No," I say, hands on the wheel, eyes on the road.

"Smells just like a dead cat or a dead rat." He pauses and lets that sink in. Then he goes on, "Do you know what a man smells like who's been burned to death by napalm?"

I stay quiet.

"He smells just like the skin of a duck or chicken does when you singe off the last feathers after you pluck it."

He doesn't say these things to shock me, but to communicate the depth of his realization. He wants me to understand mortality at the level of the senses, in my body. He wants the knowledge to sink in.

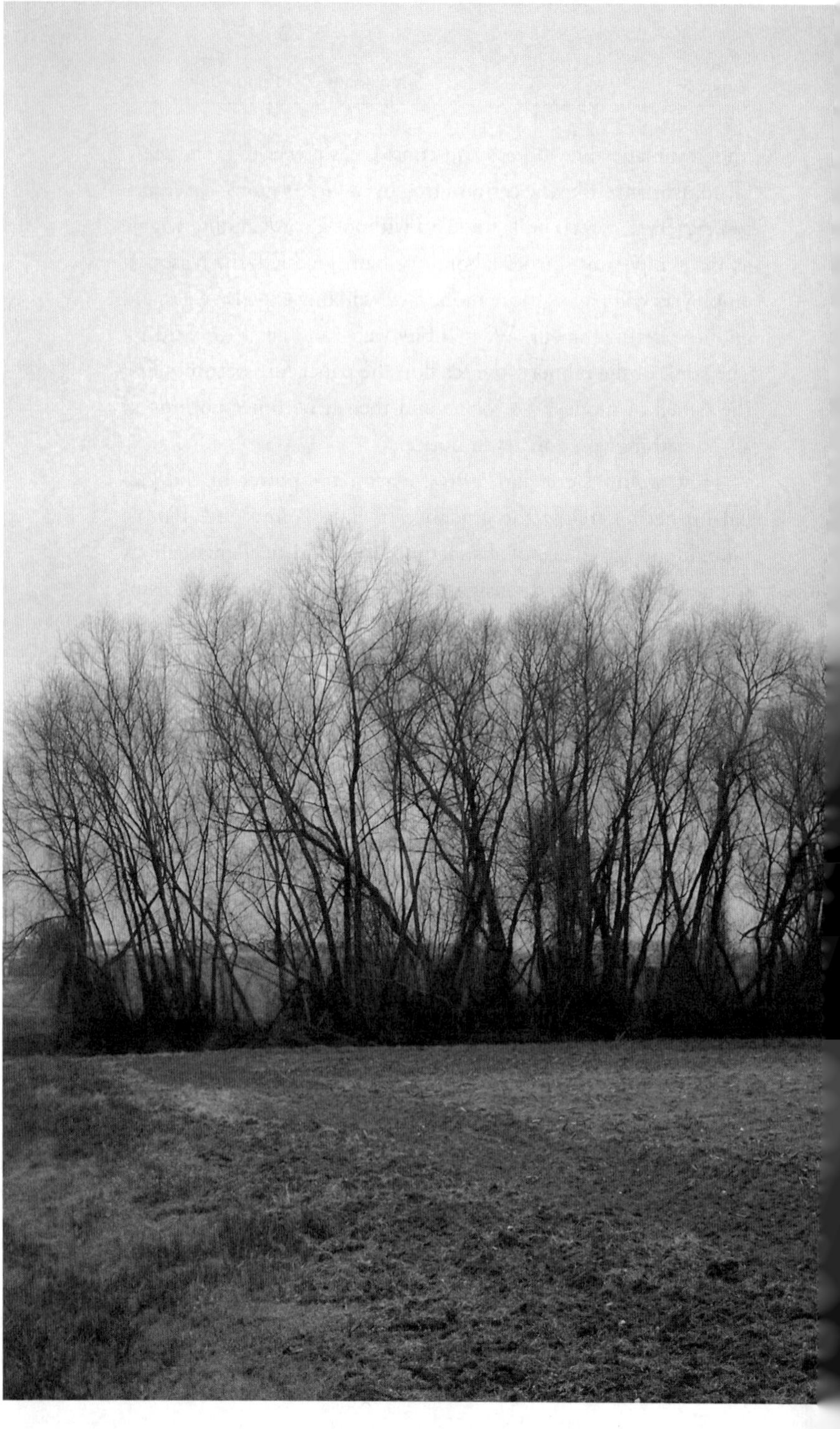

10 The Presence of Roadkill

> Pray to their spirits. Ask them to bless us:
>   our ancient sisters' trails
> the roads were laid across and kill them:
>   night-shining eyes
> The dead by the side of the road.
>
> Gary Snyder, "The Dead by the Side of the Road"

❧   *Roadkill* is often spelled as two words, but it is more and more frequently written as a compound, the space disappearing, the monosyllables creeping closer. Either *roadkill* is such an increasingly powerful and signifying presence that it deserves its own word, or it's such a disturbing and obscene by-product of our lives that we make a word for it—like *pornography* or *environmentalism*—so we can file it away and ignore it as best we can.

Even in its two-word form, it's relatively new to the language. Both the *Online Etymological Dictionary* and *Merriam-Webster Online* give 1972 as the date of its origin as a term meaning *an animal killed by vehicular traffic*. The same sources give an even more recent date, 1992, for its first figurative use to describe *any helpless victim*. The venerable *Oxford English Dictionary* cites usages going back to the 1940s, but only in scientific journals and reports (such as this citation from a 1943 issue of *Ecological Monographs:* "From the above table one can readily see that road kills are relatively unimportant to Hungarian partridge abundance in this area").

If we accept the 1970s as the time in which the word passed into common usage, the birth of *roadkill* as a linguistic concept coincides closely with the earliest appearance of the words *environ-*

mentalism and *environmentalist*, which (in their current meanings) the *OED* dates at 1970. The timing is not merely coincidental. The new terms appeared just after the first Earth Day in 1970. *Roadkill* joined the English vocabulary in the same year as the publication of Frances Moore Lappé's *Diet for a Small Planet*, which spoke eloquently of the desecration of life and the waste of resources in the feedlot system of meat production. The book motivated a good part of my generation to go vegetarian—an almost unthinkable shift in lifestyle for Americans, eccentric to the point of perturbing, before Lappé made it fashionable and politically interesting (though the concept itself was pretty old: the Hindus had practiced it for centuries; the poet Shelley wrote a polemic in favor of a vegetable diet in the early 1800s; Thoreau considered the option in *Walden*).

The new words and movements and books in the 1970s signaled a new awareness that something was happening to animals on an increasingly large scale, in feedlots and on highways. Other animals (humans, that is) were paying an inflating price for improvements in the quality of their lives, greater access to larger quantities of protein than ever before, higher levels of mobility (social and geographical), values realized in the federally funded interstate highway system, which was rendered fully operational in the early seventies, sending cars full of well-fed middle-class families to new jobs and new adventures and transporting livestock from feedlots and slaughterhouses to super-sizing fast-food outlets and mega-supermarkets in every town of any size at all.

As *roadkill* enters the picture—and the language—there appears a questioning eye, a cocked head, a barking voice, a forepaw scratching at the edge of human awareness. It wants you to know that what the people now known as *environmentalists* were saying is true. The sacrifice zone of human progress is widening.

The beloved dog or cat falls within the deadly circle with increasing frequency, joining the slowest and easiest to surprise at seventy miles per hour—the possum that runs in circles when spooked, the armadillo that jumps to startle a natural enemy, buying time to get away, only to meet its fate more squarely on the grill of an oncoming car or truck. The old riddle, "Why does the chicken cross the road?"—answer: "To get to the other side"—gets a new answer: "To show the possum how it's done." Armadillo roadkill is christened "possum on the half shell." Bad taste, cruel humor, or nervous laughter works hard to keep roadkill at bay, to distance *us* from *it* (or *I* from *it*, *ego* from *id*). But nothing can fully dispel the worry at the edge of human awareness that the next helpless victim may be the human race. The lesson of Rachel Carson's *Silent Spring*, a decade old in 1972 when *roadkill* entered the English language, was starting to sink in.

If we choose to consider the meaning of an animal's fate as a splatter on the highway, to accept roadkill as a mental and spiritual as well as a physical and linguistic presence, we join company with a surprising number of fine writers who have confronted the issue in prose and poetry. Among the best examples are

- William Stafford's ode on finding a roadkilled pregnant deer with a still living fawn inside ("Traveling through the Dark")
- Gary Snyder's "The Dead by the Side of the Road" (from the Pulitzer Prize–winning collection of poetry *Turtle Island*) with its poignant observation of how our roads cross well-worn animal trails—the ancient paths of our "sisters" in the wild world

- Barry Lopez's reverent essay "Apologia," which tells how the author extends his time on a long road trip to stop and pay homage to each roadkilled creature he sees by removing its body from the exposed position on the road or roadside. Further homage appears in the act of writing the essay and the description of the corpses encountered—an imprinting of memory that recovers the sacred from the desecrated.

In the poem "Cock Pheasant," my friend Lowell Mick White thinks of all the ways he has memorialized a bird that his car struck dead on the highway. First, he turns around and goes back: "I was sixty yards past the bird / by the time I stopped." Second, he records his feeling and confesses a criminal act. Finding the pheasant "warm and limp," he gathers it into his arms, "feeling guilty, not wanting to be seen." It's not only shameful to have killed the bird but illegal to collect it, because, as he tells us, it's "out of season." Third, he takes the bird home, cleans it, feeds the guts to the feral cats by his Dumpster, ages it three days in his refrigerator, cooks it "in a Dutch oven with leeks, / marsala, garlic, and mushrooms," and washes it down with a bottle of Argentine merlot. Having ingested the roadkill, he says, "The cock pheasant and I became one." Fourth, he saves the feathers in a plastic bag and later ties "soft-hackled wet flies with them, / with my iridescent covert feathers." Fifth, two years down the road, on a "drizzly / midday,"

> *north of Yellowstone, I*
> *caught a cutthroat trout on one of*
> *those flies, and released it.*

Sixth, having become one with the roadkilled bird and found a measure of atonement in sparing the life of the trout caught with the feathers of the bird he could not have spared, he writes the poem and publishes his memorial to the world.

The writing is like the objects crafted from the animals' skins described in Gary Snyder's poem—such as "a pouch for magic tools" made from the skin of a roadkilled ringtail—or, in Mick White's poem, the dinner made from the fresh kill and the flies tied later from pheasant feathers and used in catch-and-release fishing, the continued efforts of the poet to stay in communion with the wild—without and within—and not to look away when the modern world collides with it, to acknowledge the continuing presence of roadkill as a haunting force that possesses, obsesses, pursues the poet (and then the sympathetic reader). The writing keeps the memory and the image in circulation, refusing to accept the usual outlook on roadkill—disgust and neglect, or at best, unfortunate waste, the collateral damage of human progress.

During the time that *roadkill* was entering the language, in the late sixties and early seventies, soldiers in Vietnam had begun to use the word *waste* as a verb meaning *to kill*, as in "Charlie approached the village, and we wasted him." The ancient poets, from Sophocles to Shakespeare, taught that the waste of life was tragic, not a matter of habit or routine.

❧ Stafford wrote in the 1960s, Snyder in the 1970s. By the time Lopez produced his essay in the late 1990s and Mick White published "Cock Pheasant" in 2005, roadkill—both literal and figurative—was everywhere. The jokes proliferated—visual as well as verbal, such as the frequently reproduced postcard or poster showing an armadillo or possum painted over with a double yellow line on the highway, as if the road workers couldn't bother to pause for roadkill; or Gary Larson's cartoon of a spatula-wielding bird (bipedal like a human) approaching a splattered critter on a highway over the caption "Secret tools of the common crow." Now there are references in popular music—such as Greg Brown's metaphor about roadkill on the information highway in his song "Slant 6 Mind"—and bands that use roadkill in their names or song titles. There is a field guide to identifying crushed creatures—Roger Knutson's *Flattened Fauna*—no photographs included, only silhouettes of squashing patterns for commonly roadkilled animals.

The topic came to the fore for me as a nature writer about the same time Mick published his poem, when I was working with Gentry Steele, my colleague in anthropology, on the project that would become our book *Reflections of the Brazos Valley*. Any account of how we experienced the native fauna of our region would have been incomplete without our acknowledging that people living in suburban and rural Texas are most likely to encounter wild animals (other than birds) as corpses passed on the pavement. The Brazos Valley essay, as I conceived it, had to include reflections on roadkill, on how suburban development infringes on habitat, on the interchange of diurnal and nocturnal life, and on the simple shock of coming face to face with dead and dismembered animals on a daily basis.

As the photographer for the project, Gentry appreciated my coverage of the topic and, like me, found roadkill to be alternately disturbing and fascinating. He told me that years ago he came to be known as the "roadkill king" among his graduate students because he encouraged them to collect dead things for use in his archaeology labs and courses on animal anatomy. He would sometimes come home to find plastic bags of roadkill on his doorstep, gifts from his grad students (which reminded me of the offerings my cats used to leave for me—the head and forepaws of a young rabbit, a dead bird or mole or mouse in the food dish). Our editors and pre-publication reviewers likewise found the roadkill passages compelling if somewhat unusual for the genre in which we were working—the regional nature book, meant for the coffee table, in which the text loosely supports or augments the dominant attraction of the photographs. In this case, the roadkill segments definitely supplemented the photographs. No one ever suggested that Gentry add some photographs of animals sacrificed to the gods of human mobility.

Why not? Beyond the revulsion we might expect from the ordinary reader of coffee-table nature books—the yuck factor—we could have predicted a critically edgier and intellectually more rigorous, but no less offended, response from opponents of "eco-porn" among eco-critics if we had decided to portray the horrific dismemberment and bloody mess of roadkill in full-color, straight-on photography (which you can find on the web, along with the animal snuff films and the human porn). We would be appealing to the side of visual experience that caters to morbid curiosity (if not sadism) and the highway experience of rubber-necking at accident sites.

Of course, not all roadkill is disgusting. Occasionally you find a clean kill (loving pictures of which are also available on the web, also a kind of eco-porn). I recently collected a perfectly preserved great horned owl from the freezer of a friend who had picked it up off the side of the road. I took it to the Texas Cooperative Wildlife Collection for skinning and preservation. But could the photograph of such an object really embody the phenomenon of roadkill as it is experienced and depicted in literature—a smeary offense against nature, a wasteful by-product of mechanized civilization, the explosive confrontation of the animal body with overpowering technology, the intersecting of superhighways with the ancient pathways of deer, raccoon, possum, javelina, armadillo, coyote, rat, squirrel, tarantula, rattlesnake, and owl?

The question of why we can't photograph roadkill within the bounds of good taste is related to the question of whether we can even see roadkill for what it is. The best alternative I have to offer is a photograph that Jackie made during the formative time of the Brazos Valley book but not intended specifically for use in the project. The image represents the discarded remains of a small dog that we found on a river-access road leading under a bridge over the Brazos River near Marlin, Texas. Here is the text that resulted from the encounter and that actually made it into the book:

> The water and the wind seem to be the main animating forces on this winter day. I see wisps of dirty gray fiber fluttering in the breeze around the desiccated corpse of a skunk and stuck in stiff blades of winter grass—signs of the lingering cotton trade in these parts left by trucks carrying product to market. On the little road down to the river, we find the almost perfectly preserved skeleton of a small dog, dumped here dead no doubt, but flattened by subsequent traffic and picked clean by crows and other carrion-eaters. In an earlier stage of decay is a goat beneath the bridge. I've found animal remains on river access roads all over Texas. I guess the idea is to dump the dead things and hope the river will carry them someplace else—the afterlife maybe. (Steele and Killingsworth 22)

The photograph could have illustrated the slightly ironic prose with its transcendentalist undercurrent. But it could never stand for anything like a typical roadkill encounter—it's too clean and neat. Infrequently used, the road on which we found the corpse allowed it to rot in peace in the prevailingly dry air and be pecked clean by undisturbed vultures, crows, and fire ants. The larger carrion-feeders frequently become roadkill victims themselves on busier highways. The skeleton and bits of fur that remained of the dog were never scattered to the four winds by the rush of interstate traffic. They were never washed away or spirited off to landfills by a municipal cleaning crew. They were left to desiccate on the macadam of a one-lane back road, forming an image that reminded us first of a lab specimen and later, when viewed as a photographic text, of a cave painting or some other fetish of a hunting people who might have themselves picked the creature clean of meat and organs before contemplating and re-producing the formal beauty of its raw remains.

The more we looked at it, and with the distance of time, imagination, and representational technology (camera and computer), the less it seemed like roadkill. Rather, it became a reflection of how different species (*Homo sapiens* included) interact over time in a natural and predictable way. It tells us truths about who we are—and who we are not. But it does not comprehend animal death on the roadways.

※ People are diurnal creatures, and nature writers have long waxed eloquent on how the night constitutes an alternate world inhabited by creatures with organs and habits modified for nocturnal life. As we humans sleep or retreat with increasing predictability to the protective shells of our lives—rooms lit bright as the sun by electric light from energy made in the dark belly of the coal-fired power plant or nuclear reactor (or by the sun itself, channeled by day through solar panels and stored in black batteries for the time when darkness arrives)—the animals of the night come out to hunt, to forage, to propagate their kind. Some of them work exclusively after dark; others press the edges of nightfall and stay active in the long shadows of dusk and dawn.

One seemingly trivial invention of modern technology has proved maybe more fatal to the creatures of the night than any other—the automotive headlight. Paved roads, faster cars, and more powerful trucks are certainly the instruments of death itself, but the headlight extends the time of travel into the realm of night, confounding millennia of evolution programmed into the brains and nervous systems of the night animals. The program says, you don't have to worry about one large and particularly ferocious predator at night. That's when human beings sleep and take refuge from their own inbred fear of the dark. The headlight breaks the natural order and becomes the instrument of dismay. "Deer in the headlights" is the expression we use for the person caught completely unaware by the prospect of imminent danger. "He had that deer-in-the-headlights look when the professor asked the last question in his oral exam." Thanks largely to the headlight, animals I may never have seen—or never even knew that I shared habitat with, except through my reading or through chance encounters on rare forays into the night—have appeared in full light as fatalities on the highways and side streets of my world.

A friend invited me over to identify the corpse of a hawk she couldn't find in her bird book. She was surprised to find the specimen at the end of her long driveway that leads down to a paved county road. I drove out to take a look. One glance at the "furry" legs and a quick assessment of the size told me it was a barred owl. It must have met the vehicle head-on because its head was mangled. That's what caused my friend's confusion. The owl was likely hunting from the big oak by the driveway, waiting for mice to make a nocturnal venture onto the clean open space of the blacktop. The road's edge is useful to owls in this way—like shooting ducks on a pond—but ultimately it becomes perilous. Even in the country, bad timing means certain death in the sudden illumination of headlights. The owl must suffer momentary blindness before being quickly dispatched.

When I was in grad school in Tennessee, I rented a small house for a while, the third of four rentals lined up on a short lane off a remote country road. The birdwatching was good, but the neighbors were a little worrisome.

One day the guy living in the house closest to the main road got irritated by the yard dog in the second house. It barked too much. He got out his .44 pistol and shot the dog dead. No one heard the shot but me. I went out to check on things, and the neighbor—Lonnie was his name—was just returning the gun to a leather holster he was holding in his free hand. His wife looked on from the window, her hand over her mouth. "Shot the damn thing," he told me and went inside. The dog—a beagle mix of some kind—lay dead inside its little fenced enclosure. No one said anything to the sheriff. The dog's owner asked no questions. That's the kind of neighborhood it was (so don't talk to me about the peacefulness of rural life).

The neighbor in the fourth house on the lane, closest to the woods and next door to me, was a grad student in business, a French Canadian from Quebec City. One night he took out his trash and encountered a creature that scared the *sacré merde* out of him. He came around to my place to describe the thing. "Long snout, rows of *ugly* teeth, white and furry, red-eyed, naked tail—hissing like crazy, going to attack, for certain."

"A big rat?"

"No, no, much too big, enormous."

"Fox?"

"No, no, too ugly, too much hissing."

"Raccoon?"

"No little mask. I've seen the raccoon. Never saw this kind of thing."

Only on the edge of sleep that night did it occur to me that he had seen a possum. I started laughing. Poor guy, spooked by a possum. Guess they don't have them up north.

Next day, I revealed my insight. "Yes, of course, *opossum,*" he said (pronouncing the *o*). "That was it. I've seen the pictures. Very ugly."

A mildly perturbing thought crossed my mind at that point: I'd never seen a possum alive in the wild, only as roadkill. The number of roadkilled possums I'd seen must have convinced me of the creature's stupidity and harmlessness. Maybe I needed to rethink my judgment—of the Canadian and the possum.

I waited another two decades before I had my own encounter with a living specimen. One warm Texas night, the dog made her usual patrol of the yard before bedtime. Out of nowhere I heard her barking like mad and went out to discover that she had something trapped under the planked deck in the backyard. She wouldn't come out when I called her and whistled, so I went back inside and got a flashlight and my hiking stick. The barking went on unabated the whole time, and there was another sound just outside my range of comprehension. I got down and crawled under the deck far enough to shine the light and see what was up. The thought of a rabid coon or a rattlesnake crossed my mind. The dog was between me and the threatening thing. She kept up the barking but looked back at me as if to say, "Hey, I got it this far; now you kill it, man." I still couldn't see the thing, so I pushed a little closer and finally got the light directed onto it. It was a possum, baring its impressively pointed teeth and hissing ominously. That was the sound I'd been hearing, and this was the image that my former neighbor had faced by his trash can that night twenty years before. I finally got the whole picture.

I was working up the nerve to move closer, maybe threaten the dread marsupial with the stick and hold the dog at bay so it could escape. Then I heard a rattling sound coming from the direction of the back door. The barking ceased abruptly, and the dog unceremoniously departed the scene.

I heard Jackie calling and realized that she'd been standing at the door, shaking the pooch's food bowl. Food Provider prevailed while Great Hunter was left to face the beast alone. But in the absence of the canine threat, Dread Marsupial quit hissing and made a swift exit. I slid out from under the deck, got to my feet, and joined Jackie and Myrth to watch as the surprisingly agile gray-white fur ball used claws and prehensile tail to climb the low chain-link fence beyond the deck and drop over into the relative quiet of the local woods.

A month later, in an effort to catch a raccoon that had been laying claim to our attic by climbing up a pyracantha shrub (never mind the inch-long thorns) and clambering in through the wooden venting while we tried to sleep at night, we set a trap in the backyard. Our first catch was a possum, if not the same one, then its identical twin. We just turned it loose, and it never came back. Two cans of cat food later, we got the coon. It had to be relocated to keep it from coming back.

So by the time I reached my early forties, I'd seen only two living possums, though I'd hiked and camped in their woods and shared habitat with them most of that time. I would estimate that I'd seen at least a hundred of them dead on the road during the same interval. In March 2012, I killed one myself. That's how I found out about its poorly adapted behavior in the headlights. I was driving on a dark two-lane state road at night when I saw it up ahead in the center of my lane, crossing toward the shoulder. Another car was approaching from the other direction, so there was no question of swerving to avoid it. Jackie and I were both urging it to hurry along. I slowed down as much as I could in the closing distance without skidding. It looked up and, with its beady red eyes, seemed to catch sight of the headlights bearing down. But instead of hurrying off the road, it began to turn in circles. The thud was, as they say, sickening.

Possums aren't the only animals I know better as roadkill than as living creatures. I mentioned owls. There's also the armadillo. I'd seen dozens of roadkilled specimens before I saw my first living example. On a hike at dusk by the Huntsville State Park camping ground in the piney woods of East Texas, Jackie, Myrth, and I were startled by an armadillo performing its jumping act when we happened too close to the place where it was hiding or foraging in the shrubs. We stood there stunned—the very effect that evolution must have intended—while it scampered away. I caught its retreat briefly in the beam of the flashlight.

My neighborhood in College Station seems to attract them. You can see them digging around in the conveniently soft flower beds and hedgerows, grubbing for their favorite insects at dusk and dawn. You can hear them snuffling outside the window in the wee hours of the morning, the same times you might hear the eerie descending whistle of the screech owl.

During a very dry season at Canyon of the Eagles State Park, Jackie and I saw several armadillos extending their foraging hours into broad day. The sunlight revealed what we'd never seen in the dingy roadkilled specimens or the chance sighting in dusky half-light—how pink they are and covered with bristly hairs. They are nearly blind, so we were able to get very close before they heard us and scuttered off.

I'd seen maybe a dozen roadkilled javelina, mostly on I-10 in West Texas where they lie among the scores of deer run down every night in that district (and where, my students tell me, no one drives a new truck without first installing a special protective grill), before I saw small herds of the piglike beasts grazing beside the roads and foot trails at Big Bend National Park and walking boldly in the middle of the paved roads of Bentsen–Rio Grande Valley State Park, now closed to automotive traffic.

I was waiting for my car at a Texas car wash one day when a young woman came in, clearly upset, and asked the guy at the register if the stubborn remains of a roadkilled deer could be removed from the underside of her sedan. "That'll cost you extra, ma'am." (Mind you, no one in Texas dares suggest that roadkilling is hurting the deer population. Rather, it exposes their serious overpopulation and the loss of predators other than humans in the region.)

I've never seen a badger in the wild, but in New Mexico I saw a roadkill. I've seen more muskrats, beaver, and nutria dead on the side of the road than swimming in the ponds and rivers I've lived near all my life. My friends saw a roadkilled river otter, rare to the point of extinction in our region.

On walks and bike rides in Tennessee and Texas, I've seen roadkilled rat snakes (black and gray), rattlesnakes, garter snakes, glass snakes, ribbon snakes, ring-necked snakes, water snakes (banded and diamond-backed), cottonmouths, copperheads, hognose snakes, and bull snakes—all of which I've also seen alive in the wild. Corn snakes, milk snakes, green snakes, and king snakes I've never seen roadkilled, only alive. And there's the one species I've seen only as roadkill: in the middle of a two-lane county road near Bastrop, Texas, Jackie and I got off our bikes to stare in wonder at the remains of a coral snake, unwound like a lost necklace glistening red, black, and yellow on the road. Jackie made a picture of it.

I've never met that deadly little beauty in its living state, before or since. Jackie took inspiration from the sight and made a necklace with stones of the right color in the right sequence. My friend Brian Shaw bought it and wears it nearly every day.

We sometimes brake for roadkill. Turn the car around and go back. You never know what you'll see. It's a mixed blessing for the curious but concerned naturalist. You have to wonder how much roadkill a place can stand. The vultures (turkey and black), crows, ravens, coyotes, and cleaning crews stay busy where we live.

In Texas, it's illegal to collect fresh roadkill for food, skins, or any useful purpose—no matter the season. It seems a waste, but the game wardens tell us that the law is meant to keep the unsporting among us from hunting with their vehicles or otherwise covering up poaching by crying "Roadkill!" Recently, some counties have been experimenting with programs that officially "harvest" the roadkill every night and distribute good cuts of venison and pork (from feral hogs, which like deer are grossly overpopulated in our state) to the local food banks. It may seem insensitive—Let them eat roadkill!—but the truth is that the qualified poor who gain access to this windfall protein may actually be getting healthier meat than the kind that people who can afford supermarket prices are buying everyday—feedlotted, factory-farmed, fatty, and chemically enhanced. I cannot get to the bottom of the ironies that pile up around the heaps of roadkill in my world.

I only ever saw a gray fox once in the wild, a streak of silver and russet fur, dashing along a path near the Tsankawi ruins in northern New Mexico, a descendant of the foxes that the Anasazi, the ancient ones who made the cliff dwellings in that place, saw running the game trails as they watched from their perches for elk and bison and deer and turkey coming up the narrow valley, before the bees that now make honey in those same cliffs came from Europe with my ancestors and then went feral, to the delight of the local bears. I saw the fox in the 1980s. Driving to work some twenty years later with the increasing traffic from my suburban neighborhood that edges the Texas countryside—heading north with the cars going to the university from the spate of new housing south of my place—I saw a roadkilled gray fox—fresh, it seemed, and perfectly preserved. As the traffic rolled slowly by, I got a good look. It was laid out with the head pointed toward the oncoming traffic, toward me, the eyes open and not yet harvested by the crows. The fur was so beautiful that I thought of harvesting it myself. I knew these many witnesses in their cars and pickups wouldn't rat me out to the authorities, a gray-bearded man jumping out of his car to collect roadkill, so long as I didn't further delay their progress through the traffic snarl. They would dismiss me as a biologist or a fool, or simply ignore me the same way they ignore the roadkill. I guess it was the eyes of the fox that kept me in my car.

❧ Even bringing up roadkill in polite conversation is an affront to good manners and good taste. A friend and fellow scholar once told me at a meeting on environmental literature that it seems like a Texas or Southern topic—code for the kind of thing not to be mentioned at national meetings, as suspicious as a Southern accent. He was trying to save me from embarrassment, but he helped me in ways he had not yet imagined. The comment tipped me off that roadkill is perhaps our best example of sacrifice zoning. It's not an exclusively Southern phenomenon. I've seen roadkill all over the country, in urban as well as rural settings. I've seen it in the National Parks. But like the South—and like other sacrifice zones in the nation, the Indian country of the Southwest given over to coal and uranium mining and the desert lands impounded for military purposes—roadkill needs to be rendered invisible. It needs to be denied, dismissed, eliminated as a significant presence in our lives.

In a summer job I had in 1974 with the Knoxville Community Development Corporation (the old Housing Authority), one of the tasks of my work crew was to keep the streets in the neighborhoods of our district clear of dead cats, dogs, rats, raccoons, possums, and squirrels. We had big flat shovels, like snow shovels, to use in the work. It was nasty duty, habitually assigned to the least favored members of the team—usually not me, both because I had befriended the assistant foreman and because, as a recently minted college graduate, I could be trusted with the chain saw (in the weird logic of the management).

This one time, though, the assistant foreman got on the wrong side of the foreman, who decided to get at him by sending him out to remove a large roadkilled collie from the middle of one of our streets. I was riding in the assistant foreman's truck that day, so he and I got the assignment. "Too funky!" he kept saying as we slipped the shovels under either end of the big dog, bloated with the heat, and lifted it together into the truck bed. We put damp bandannas over our faces to try to decrease the stench that reached our nostrils, but to little avail. The smell was implanted in my olfactory center for days afterward. We took the dead dog to the landfill and shoveled it out of the truck bed as quickly as we could. We cursed the foreman all the way back to the job site.

So I know firsthand the work that goes into rendering roadkill invisible to the citizens of even the poorest neighborhoods. My crew worked in federally funded housing projects in east Knoxville. We cleared abandoned lots and maintained them until the new seventies-era, single-family dwellings could be constructed and populated. In the heat and moisture of the Tennessee summer, we fought back the weeds, we destroyed rat and raccoon habitat, and we kept the streets free of disease-bearing, funky, flattened fauna. Most of us earned minimum wage for the work. My friend the assistant foreman confided to me that he paid out 90 percent of his salary in bills at the first of the month—rent, utilities, car payment, grocery tab—and by the end of the month supplemented his salary by hunting for money dropped in the parking lots of big hotels. The Hyatt Regency was his most productive territory. I got into the habit of checking the streets myself. We were living in the shadows of what had become invisible to our fellow citizens. Like rats and roaches, we got our livelihood from the detritus of urban life. The surplus cash, the unwanted weeds, the roadkill put food on our table.

※ In the spring semester of 2012, my students in a course on environmental writing hated it when I asked them to write about roadkill. I assigned the poems by Stafford and Snyder, the essay by Lopez. I read them a few of the pertinent anecdotes from *Reflections of the Brazos Valley*. I lectured on the fragmentation of habitat, the increase in vehicular traffic, rampant urbanization. We told the jokes, recalled the posters with the yellow-lined armadillos in the middle of the road, sang the songs like "Dead Skunk in the Middle of the Road (Stinking to High Heaven)" by Loudon Wainwright III (the only really big hit for this accomplished songwriter). But the assignment was a bust.

In their papers, some confessed that they could not bring themselves to think hard about the topic; it was just "too gross." Others repeated what they'd heard or read in class, but without much effort to join the conversation or "own" the topic. Others actively resisted, saying they couldn't find the passion to worry about squashed rodents when so many human problems existed in this world (two of these papers were authored by students who had written movingly about their church-sponsored mission work among the poor in foreign countries, their Christian sympathy unmoved by dead animals on local roads). The most personal papers channeled the topic into stories about the death of beloved pets on streets near their childhood homes. In each of these three papers, the focus shifted to the emotional trauma of the young child faced with the reality of death for the first time; in each case the pain lifted when a new pet arrived.

It was the last assignment of the course, and that may explain the lack of energy and engagement (especially among the several graduating seniors). I didn't have time to talk over the failure of the assignment with the students. But after some reflection on my own, it occurred to me that the missing element in my teaching on the topic was the concept of sacrifice zoning and willed invisibility, how we muster all of our resources in civil institutions (like the Knoxville Community Development Corporation or the local waste management office or the animal control bureau) along with language, manners, and personal psychology, in the effort to avoid confronting the presence of roadkill.

Roadkill constitutes a bloody mark on the record of progress, an accusation against the ethics of our daily activity as mobile human beings. It demands denial, a turning of the head, the refusal to see what lies (and dies) before us—the image too close to our own deaths—the bloody insides exposed that should be contained by fur and skin—the creature fitted by evolution for the night-time woods and fields left dead on the pavement of our daylit lives. The horror, the pity, the waste, the disgust are all too much to bear. In forcing my students to look, I had (like the poet Mick White) become one with roadkill itself, the presence that offends and earns the stiffest resistance.

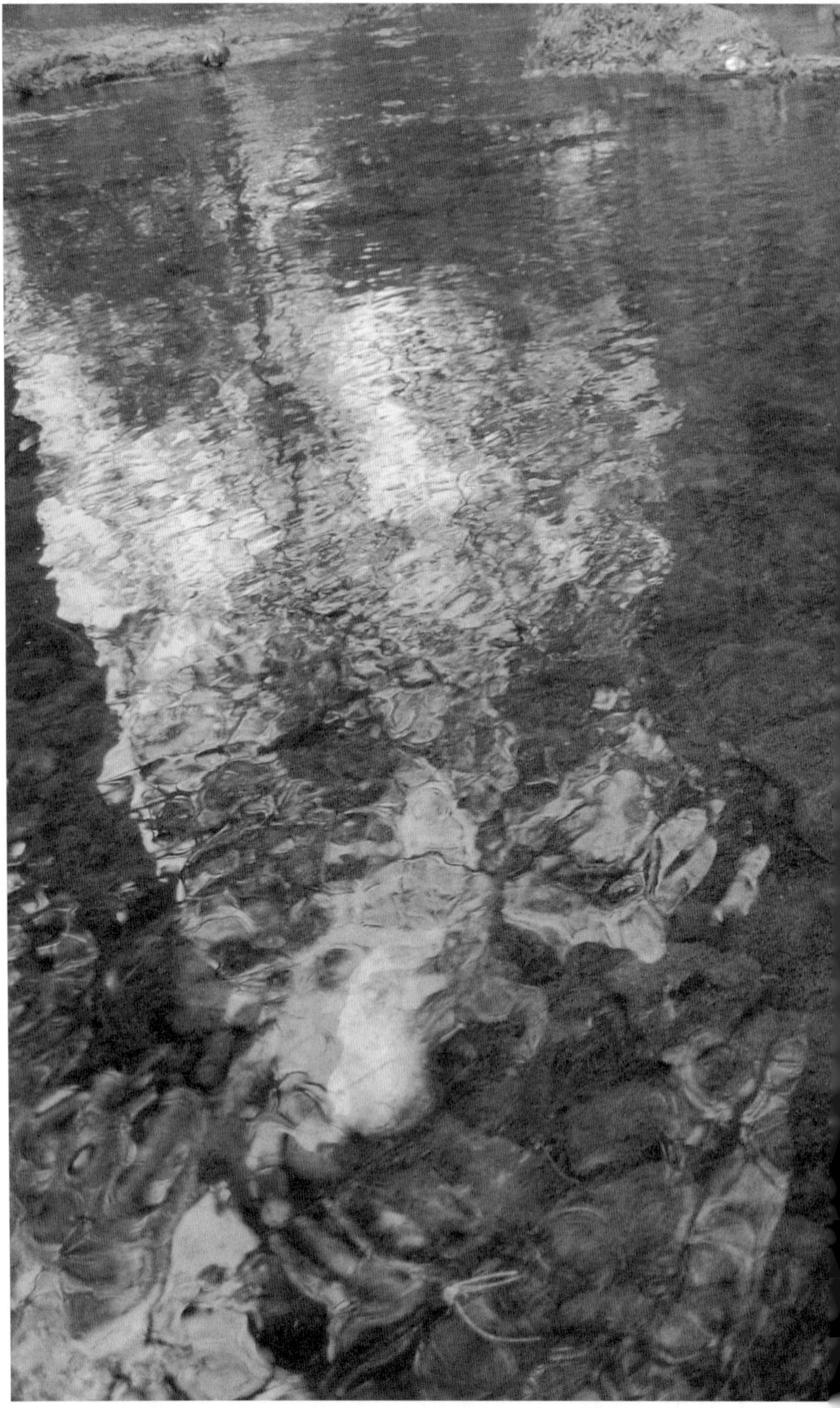

Reprise. World's End
Seeing and Sustenance

"You're writing about the end of the world?" my mom
   asked as I rubbed her hands. "That's what you're work-
   ing on now?"
"Kind of," I said, eyes still scanning the foam-waved
   rollers, seeing them gone.
"I don't like thinking about that sort of thing," she said.
   "Do you really think it's going to happen?"
"What?"
"The end of the world."
"It's always happening."
She frowned at me, a face of many words, most
   saying, *Don't get smart with me.*
Craig Childs, *Apocalyptic Planet*

Every culture, every generation, every person occupies a world. They receive the world at birth, and they remake it in life. It ends when they die, and it doesn't just end for them, but for everybody and everything connected with them. You can call this world a world*view,* if you like, but it's more than a way of *seeing* the world, more than a perspective. Every culture, every generation, every person engages physically and ecologically with the world. They don't only watch it or play lightly over its surface. They dig deep and change the very nature of the world. And the version of nature with which they've cocreated their world, to some extent, dies with them—either because, like their bodies and their belongings, it doesn't work anymore, or because it loses some of its connections and meaning in their absence. The meaning begins to fade long before the person dies or the generation passes. Like their bodies, the world they've made begins to lose its power. Just as they resist their own death, they resist the loss of meaning and power in their world well before they begin to die.

When I announced I was going to be a vegetarian, as a twenty-five-year-old adult in the mid-1970s after reading Frances Moore Lappé's *Diet for a Small Planet,* I was not prepared for the reaction I got from my mother. She took my decision as a personal affront. She didn't merely disagree; she was insulted, defensive, angry beyond any reason I could grasp. I didn't see at the time that I had become an agent of destruction—a world-unmaking force, an apocalyptic character in her life story. I was forecasting and causing her to face her own death.

She was a Depression baby who came of age during World War II. During her youth, only wealthy folks could get good meat on a daily basis. Later, during the war, people on the home front were asked to sacrifice their own protein needs as part of the rationing, the total mobilization of the American people in the war effort. In the economic expansion of the postwar years, the increasingly prosperous and socially mobile members of her generation could give their children what had been denied them. So we became the best-fed nation in the world, at least as far as access to a variety of groceries and total availability of protein was concerned. The factory farms and feedlots churned out supermarket shelves full of canned goods, white bread, frozen produce, and choice cuts of fine meats. Children grew taller and heavier—*healthier* by the standards of undernourishment that had prevailed in the thirties and forties, when "skinny" was never a compliment. Now the nation was thriving, right?

Maybe not. In the sixties and seventies—when the leaders of the emerging environmental movement first caught the attention of young adults who fancied themselves intellectuals and social critics, like me—Lappé and other prophets were saying that unforeseen consequences with agricultural and industrial systems, including the energy-intensive methods of meat production, loomed on the near horizon, problems with personal and political implications. (And, by the way, the personal *is* political, the feminists of that day were telling us.) Eating meat had become a political problem because, as Lappé argued, grain enough to feed the world was fed to livestock in the US system: as the nation reached the pinnacle of world power, its citizens ate higher on the food chain than anyone else on earth; our cattle ate better than poor people in many countries. And the problem had a personal side as well: too much of a good thing was leading to habits of consumption that, by my daughter's generation, would make us the fattest nation in the world.

My mother—caught between the receding history of Depression hunger and the emerging history of the Obesity Epidemic—became bipolar about food. She was always a slender woman herself, but watching the world grow fat around her, she stayed on the case of her children, especially her daughters, to stay trim and fit, to "watch their weight" and "count their calories," to diet (and take diet pills if necessary), even as she continued to bring the sugary desserts and marbled meats to the table, the foods whose preparation and delivery were essential to her self-concept as a lady, a *Southern* lady, a successful wife and mother. As much as by gardening, sewing, and decorating, she made her world by baking, stewing, and roasting—not to mention shopping. My generation continued to live and expand the contradiction. Among other addictions, we grew prone to eating disorders and experiments with alternative diets like my vegetarianism, rejecting in body and mind, or at least questioning and worrying over, many of the signs of wealth that our parents had worked to give us—symbols of a world that died with my mother on that day in January 1999, on the brink of the millennium, the classic date for the passing of worlds in the apocalyptic narratives that have thrived in both the religious and secular milieu of the three generations that straddle my own world.

❧ Although we somehow survived the Cold War with its threat of Mutual Assured Destruction, the apocalyptic visions of those days also survived the passing of my mother's generation and even enjoyed a revival. We look to science to assure us that, though the world will surely end—and has more or less ended in ages of fire and ice in the deep past (witnessed by the great extinctions in the paleontological record, the advancing and receding glaciers and deserts in the geological record)—the end is decidedly *not* near by the ordinary way of measuring time but way off somewhere in a future that you have to be a geologist or an astronomer even to comprehend. We look to theology to give us an alternative to apocalyptic angst and anger, to provide a gentler, more loving image of God's ways to humankind and a humane attitude of stewardship toward the rest of life on earth. But the appeal of catastrophic stories about the end of the world reaches beyond scientific proof and religious faith; it is also rooted in phenomenal, emotional, existential, and psychological reality—even a deeply felt desire: all too often, the apocalypse amounts to a glimpse of your own terrifying death projected onto someone else's world.

The vision also speaks to our place in history. It calls to mind the awareness of death and destruction and power (or powerlessness) that characterizes a generation defined by war, like mine. I was born into the Cold War, my father killed in one of its hot moments; I came of age during the Vietnam era and am growing old in the days after 9/11. Nature itself seems to mimic politics in such a world, characterized by aggression, competition, and endangerment—open coercion and stylized threats, one species fighting to retain its superior status while others sink into extinction at an alarming rate. *Homo sapiens* becomes the counterpart in nature of a superpower in the political world. Nature writing—when it does not work to defend or justify the aggression, the violence, the competition of the reigning world, in the manner of the big-budget nature films, with their penchant for tales of predation and survival—is alternately escapist and resistant. It becomes either an act of retreat that seeks a place of peace and refuge in the face of so much death and danger or an act of resistance that imposes an alternate vision on a violent world.

Or the recourse to nature becomes a form of therapy, undergirded by concerns about the inclination to obesity, addiction, and anxiety in current American culture. For a short time, my daughter worked for an organization that featured "wilderness therapy" for troubled girls in their teens. Their parents, full of hope and desperation, sent these adolescents to the woods in search of the little girls that had somehow been lost along the way. As a Texas Master Naturalist, I worked with a Junior Naturalist program for several summers (after I passed my background check to prove that I was less likely to compound the troubles of the children with some perversion of my own). It was designed to get kids out of the house and away from electronic stimulation and introduce them to the kind of natural history that I learned in science camp those many years ago. The training I received in preparation for the program included a workshop called "Project

Wild," which showed us games we could use to teach ecological concepts like habitat fragmentation and carrying capacity. We were urged to read the best-selling book *Last Child in the Woods*, by Richard Louv, as a foundation for our work. Its stated purpose was to "save" the next generation from "nature-deficit disorder." Therapy of this kind is not just for kids either. There's plenty of reading designed to show adults the way back to nature and good health, such as the psychologist James Swan's *Nature as Teacher and Healer: How to Reawaken Your Connection with Nature* and David Abram's *Becoming Animal* (favorably reviewed and blurbed on Amazon.com by Richard Louv).

I hope I won't seem too dismissive if I say that I worry about the therapeutic trend in current nature writing and education programs. I share many values with Louv, Swan, and Abram. I applaud their commitment to mental health and their concern about the place of the child who's lost touch with nature and the adult who's lost touch with the child (or the animal) inside. I believe in the power of nature to heal and restore balance in people's lives.

But what does it say about us as a people that we must be lured out of our comfortable dwellings and our "comfort zones" with a view of nature as therapy or medicine? To me, it says that we are definitely keeping one foot in the door even as we step outside. For all my appreciation of psychotherapy, which has helped me numerous times along the way, and for psychotherapists, one of whom I count among my best friends, I cannot shake the impression that the aim of the business is always adjustment to social norms (as opposed to personal transformation or liberation, for example). The most honest assessment of counseling I ever heard came from my brother-in-law, who told me that, as an army chaplain, he could not afford in his talks with soldiers to take up the high ethical questions about the rightness or wrongness, the justice or injustice of war; that was not his business. His business (and the main source of his own post-traumatic stress disorder) was helping the soldiers find the resources and attitudes they needed to get back to the battlefield in good enough shape to do their part in destroying the enemy.

So the irony that strikes me in thinking of nature as therapy is that it becomes a matter of going outside to get well enough to come back inside and do the kind of work that may be rendering the outside unlivable. If the work itself does not sustain us, no amount of temporary escape will sustain us either.

By contrast, the epiphanies on my morning walks or drives in the country—the scent of dirt that brings the full grief of a mother's death, the whiff of smoke that makes the wildfires of Texas suddenly real, the sight of a hawk or heron or rising moon that obliterates self-enclosure in the mind—suggest an experience that may begin with one foot still indoors, like the therapeutic approach, but that ends with the self dragged out of hiding and exposed to a different world. It brings relief and a feeling of wholeness, for sure, but it also raises questions about what's going on in that indoor life. You re-engage with an attitude.

꽃 As for gaming in nature in programs like "Project Wild," I'm struck with a similar irony: doesn't it amount to taming the play of children to teach them the value of wildness? Isn't it more about our own lack of imagination, our poverty of stories and images, than about getting the kids involved? When I work with kids, I've had more success with old-school methods, like storytelling and splashing in the creek. I find they have plenty imagination of their own; they just need permission to use it.

I sat with a group of fifth graders in a semicircle on the floor around my chair, as if we were having a campfire talk. Their teacher had contacted me through the Texas Master Naturalist program and invited me to speak during Endangered Species Week (we seem to reserve a week for just about everything, even endangered species). I passed around a jar of Houston toads preserved in formaldehyde and let the children come close and touch a skinned sample of an Attwater's prairie chicken and a black-footed ferret that I'd borrowed from the Texas Cooperative Wildlife Collection. One bright lad, stroking the fur of the ferret, asked if the animals were real and, if so, why had we killed them since they were endangered. I told him these had probably been roadkills that some naturalist collected on a drive in the country.

He looked at the ferret and said, "No wonder it's so flat."

"No," I said, as the teacher muffled a chuckle, "it's flat because they have to remove its internal organs to preserve it this way." I showed him the stitches in the belly. "What you see here is just its skin and fur."

"Oh," he said. "Ewww."

The best part came when I showed them a painting that I'd taken off the wall in my house and dragged along to the classroom. My dad had given it to me after he retired from medical practice. It had hung in his office for years. It depicts an old pathway leading down through sand dunes and sea oats to an open beach. Weathered old boards are placed in the path—I know their purpose—to keep sandburs from sticking in your bare feet when you walk to the beach—I know it because, as my dad knew, the picture is exactly like the path leading from the old rental house to the beach at Hilton Head.

I ask the students to take an imaginary walk with me down to the beach. I lead them down the path, through the hot, loose sand near the dunes, out onto the pavementlike expanse of the golden strand, the sound of the waves breaking and the smell of saltwater in the light breeze, until we come to the story of finding the dead loggerhead turtle on the beach and then the story of seeing the live one laying eggs at night and dragging herself back to the water in the moonlight. I show them a big sea turtle shell I had brought along from the wildlife collection. They gather closer to touch its leathery top, its bone-white underside.

Without any prompting, they tell their own stories, about going to Galveston and Corpus Christi and Florida, of seeing dolphins and crabs and gulls, of camping with their parents in woods and seeing bears, of going to grandma's farm and finding a snake, of finding a snake in the creek behind the community center. When the class time is over, the teacher has to shoo them out of the room because they're still standing around telling me their stories while I try to tie a little lesson in natural history to each episode.

Later, when I explain the "method" I use to my fellow Master Naturalists in training sessions, it doesn't sound like much. I hear objections like "kids these days are bored by stories; they need films and games and activities, they are 'active learners.'"

I'm no good at these trainings. What I want to say in response, but restrain myself as I yield the floor to the Project Wild specialist, is this: if it's action you want, let them go with my friend, the biologist Dwight Bohlmeyer, down to the Little Brazos River with his nets and scopes and collection jars. Let them pull monsters and curiosities out of the water and off the bank, let them get wet and muddy, even lie down in the water and let the stream pour over them, let Dwight explain what they find and show how it fits into the ecosystem of this place, and let them go home with stories to tell. Let them come to the open house at the lab the week before and feed minnows to the water snakes and snapping turtles, let them look at the fuzzy antennae of moths under the scope, let big green grasshoppers walk on their arms, let them find the camouflaged creatures in the chunks of sargasso weed that Dwight collected at Galveston and put into the saltwater aquarium just for them (it's better than "Where's Waldo?"). Let them learn about adaptation and predation with the animals and plants of their home region. Let their parents and grandparents stand by, amazed that these odd and ugly things can absorb the kids' attention so fully, so completely, and let the adults also go home with stories to tell and the prospect of seeing with new eyes a different world on their morning walks.

❧ I sit in the sunshine coming in the tall window of the adobe house on the mesa west of Taos, and in the ancient tradition of wintertime, I tell ancestor stories. I tell my daughter and her new husband about her maternal grandfather who lived off the grid the same way they do. I tell her about her paternal grandfather who died in Korea. And I tell her my own story of growing up as a middle-class boy in the Cold War era.

She tells me of her summer patrols in the high Sierra, where she sees the ptarmigan and snowshoe hare on the glaciated granite near the alpine lakes, where she walks the trail named for John Muir, who was still alive when her great-grandparents were born. She tells me she got a letter from her great aunt, my mother's youngest sister, who was amused at hearing that a young couple lives in a house with no running water or indoor plumbing and with the limited electricity that a single solar panel can provide. The aunt wrote, "We lived 'off the grid' till 1947!"

When it warms up outside, we walk down to the Rio Grande Gorge and watch the river flow. A hooded merganser floats by on living water. A bald eagle rises from a sandy bank and flies up the rocky mesa.

Acknowledgments

I am grateful for help from many quarters in writing this book, above all to my wife and frequent coauthor Jackie Palmer, who was my chief companion and sounding board during the process of writing, and to our daughter, Myrth Killingsworth, also a writer and naturalist, who was the first reader of the draft manuscripts. Myrth has always been my teacher, even as a young child, but this time, her mature comments and criticisms were valuable in a new and joyous way. My distinguished editor Shannon Davies at Texas A&M University Press provided guidance and encouragement throughout the process and helped me steer a middle course between academic discourse and general-audience nature writing. No one could have been luckier in finding such an editor and friend. I also owe a debt of gratitude to Charles Backus, the director of Texas A&M University Press; Mary Lenn Dixon, the long-time editor-in-chief; and associate editor Patricia Clabaugh. For her beautiful design and photography, I am grateful to Mary Ann Jacob. The Texas A&M University students in my graduate seminar on nature writing and my undergraduate course on environmental rhetoric endured a number of trial versions of these chapters as lectures and informal readings and also provided the inspiration for some of my commentaries and stories. A trial version of some of the stories repeated here first appeared in my essay "Birdwatcher," published in *ISLE* under the editorship of Scott Slovic, to whom I owe a debt of thanks for his encouragement and help on many occasions and for his untiring service to the study and practice of nature writing. Pieces of the chapters were given as lectures at my own and other universities. I would like to thank the organizers of these events who invited me and covered the costs of some of my work: Ben Crouch at Texas A&M University, Daneen Wardrop at Western Michigan University, Matthias Schubnell and Emily Clark at Incarnate Word University, Diana Ashe at the University of North Carolina at Wilmington, Betsy Verhoeven at Susquehanna University, and Carolyn Miller at North Carolina State. Friends and colleagues who read my work and made valuable suggestions include Larry Oliver, Chris Holcomb, Betsy Verhoeven, Jimmy Guignard, Bill Haddock, Sarah Hart, Lisa D'Amico, Leigh Bernacchi, Michael Beilfuss, and Scott Sanders. I am especially grateful to my dean, José Luis Bermúdez, and department head Nancy Warren at Texas A&M for supporting the research leave that allowed me to complete work on the manuscript. Finally, I am continuously thankful for the loving family who got me started in this work and taught me so much along the way: my mother and father, Dolores P. and Lewis E. Jones Jr.; my sisters, Belle and Kathy; and my brother, Lewis.

Bibliography

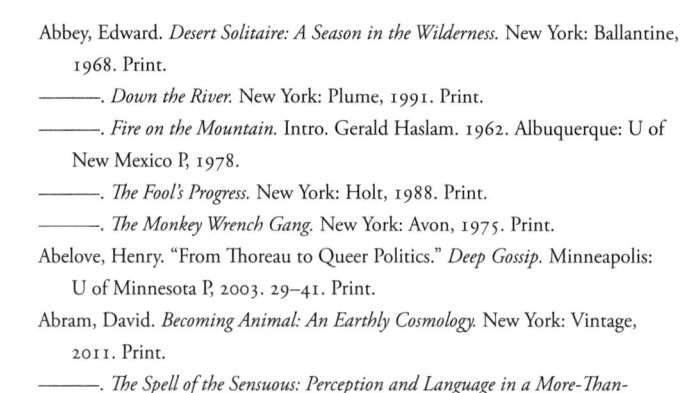

Abbey, Edward. *Desert Solitaire: A Season in the Wilderness.* New York: Ballantine, 1968. Print.
———. *Down the River.* New York: Plume, 1991. Print.
———. *Fire on the Mountain.* Intro. Gerald Haslam. 1962. Albuquerque: U of New Mexico P, 1978.
———. *The Fool's Progress.* New York: Holt, 1988. Print.
———. *The Monkey Wrench Gang.* New York: Avon, 1975. Print.
Abelove, Henry. "From Thoreau to Queer Politics." *Deep Gossip.* Minneapolis: U of Minnesota P, 2003. 29–41. Print.
Abram, David. *Becoming Animal: An Earthly Cosmology.* New York: Vintage, 2011. Print.
———. *The Spell of the Sensuous: Perception and Language in a More-Than-Human World.* New York: Vintage, 1997. Print.
Ackerman, Diane. *A Natural History of the Senses.* New York: Vintage, 1991. Print.
Adamson, Joni. *American Indian Literature, Environmental Justice, and Ecocriticism: The Middle Place.* Tucson: U of Arizona P, 2001. Print.
Angus, Ian, and Simon Butler. *Too Many People?: Population, Immigration, and the Environmental Crisis.* Chicago: Haymarket, 2011. Print.
Aristotle. *On Rhetoric: A Theory of Civil Discourse.* Trans. and ed. George A. Kennedy. New York: Oxford UP, 1991. Print.
———. *The Rhetoric and Poetics of Aristotle.* Intro. Edward P. J. Corbett. New York: Modern Library, 1984. Print.
Armbruster, Karla. "Into the Wild: An Ecofeminist Perspective on the Human Control of Canine Sexuality and Reproduction." *Ecofeminism and Rhetoric: Critical Perspectives on Sex, Technology, and Discourse.* Ed. Douglas A. Vakoch. New York: Berghahn, 2011. 39–64. Print.
Armstrong, Karen. *The Bible: A Biography.* New York: Grove, 2007. Print.
Asimov, Isaac. "The Eureka Phenomenon." *The Left Hand of the Electron.* New York: Dell, 1972. 185–98. Print.
Awiakta, Marilou. *Abiding Appalachia: Where Mountain and Atom Meet.* Memphis: St. Luke's, 1990. Print.

———. *Selu: Seeking the Corn-Mother's Wisdom.* Golden: Fulcrum, 1994. Print.
Badiou, Alain. *Ethics: An Essay on the Understanding of Evil.* Trans. Peter Hallward. London and New York: Verso, 2001. Print.
Barnhill, David Landis, ed. *At Home on the Earth: Becoming Native to Our Place; A Multicultural Anthology.* Berkeley: U of California P, 1999. Print.
Bass, Rick. *The Sky, the Stars, and the Wilderness.* New York: Houghton, 1997. Print.
———. *Why I Came West: A Memoir.* New York: Houghton, 2008. Print.
Becker, Ernest. *The Denial of Death.* New York: Free Press, 1973. Print.
Beja, Morris. *Epiphany in the Modern Novel.* Seattle: U of Washington P, 1971. Print.
Bercovitch, Sacvan. *The American Jeremiad.* Madison: U of Wisconsin P, 1978. Print.
Bergland, Renée L. *The National Uncanny: Indian Ghosts and American Subjects.* Hanover: UP of New England, 2000. Print.
Berman, Morris. *The Reenchantment of the World.* Ithaca: Cornell UP, 1981. Print.
Berry, Wendell. *The Unsettling of America: Culture and Agriculture.* San Francisco: Sierra Club Books, 1977. Print.
Beston, Henry. Excerpts from *The Outermost House.* Finch and Elder 366–75.
Bookchin, Murray. *The Ecology of Freedom: The Emergence and Dissolution of Hierarchy.* Palo Alto: Chelsea, 1982.
Breen, Steve. "They once inhabited a vast swath of North America but their numbers have been greatly reduced." Editorial cartoon. *San Diego Union-Tribune* 29 Sept. 2011.
Brokaw, Tom. *The Greatest Generation.* New York: Random, 2001. Print.
Brown, Bill. "Thing Theory." *Critical Inquiry* 28.1 (autumn 2001): 1–22. Print.
Brown, Brian Edward. "Sequoyah vs. Tennessee Valley Authority: The Tellico Dam and the Submersion of the Cherokee Sacred Homeland." *Religion, Law, and the Land: Native Americans and the Judicial Interpretations of the Sacred Land.* Westport: Greenwood, 1999. 9–38. Print.
Brown, Lester R. *Building a Sustainable Society.* New York: Norton, 1981. Print.
Brugge, Doug, Jamie L. deLemos, and Cat Bul. "The Sequoyah Corporation Fuels Release and the Church Rock Spill: Unpublicized Nuclear Releases in American Indian Communities." *American Journal of Public Health* 97.9 (2007): 1595–1600. Print.
Buell, Lawrence. *The Environmental Imagination: Thoreau, Nature Writing, and the Formation of American Culture.* Cambridge: Harvard UP, 1995. Print.

Bullard, Robert. *Dumping in Dixie: Race, Class and Environmental Quality.* Boulder: Westview, 1990. Print.

———, ed. *Confronting Environmental Racism: Voices from the Grassroots.* Boston: South End, 1993. Print.

"Bury My Heart in the Tellico Valley." *Americans before Columbus* 8.1 (1 Dec. 1979): 1, 8. Print.

Carson, Rachel. *The Sea around Us.* New York: Oxford UP, 1951. Print.

———. *Silent Spring.* New York: Fawcett Crest, 1962. Print.

———. *Under the Sea-Wind.* Intro. Linda Lear. 1941. New York: Penguin, 2007. Print.

Childs, Craig. *Apocalyptic Planet: Field Guide to the Everending Earth.* New York: Pantheon, 2012. Print.

"Churchrock, the Tragedy of Another Three-Mile Island." *Americans before Columbus* 8.1 (1 Dec. 1979): 1–2. Print.

Commoner, Barry. *The Closing Circle: Nature, Man, and Technology.* New York: Random, 1971. Print.

———. *Making Peace with the Planet.* New York: Pantheon, 1990. Print.

———. *Science and Survival.* New York: Viking, 1967. Print.

Cox, Robert. "Nature's 'Crisis Disciplines': Does Environmental Communication Have an Ethical Duty?" *Environmental Communication* 1.1 (2007): 5–20.

D'Amico, Lisa. "Art Suitable for Framing: The Big-Budget Nature Film and the Myth of 'Untouched' Spaces." Rhetoric Society of America. Philadelphia, PA, 25–28 May 2012. Conference presentation.

———. "Ecopornography and the Commodification of Extinction: The Rhetoric of the Big-Budget Nature Film." Diss. Texas A&M University, 2013.

Davis, Mike. *Ecology of Fear: Los Angeles and the Imagination of Disaster.* New York: Vintage, 1999. Print.

———. *Planet of Slums.* New York: Verso, 2007.

deBuys, William. *Enchantment and Exploitation: The Life and Hard Times of a New Mexico Mountain Range.* Albuquerque: U of New Mexico P, 1985.

Deloria, Vine, Jr. *God Is Red: A Native View of Religion.* 2nd ed. Golden: Fulcrum, 1992. Print.

DeLuca, Kevin Michael. *Image Politics: The New Rhetoric of Environmental Activism.* New York: Guilford, 1999.

Dempsey, Luke. *A Supremely Bad Idea: Three Mad Birders and Their Quest to See It All.* New York: Bloomsbury, 2008. Print.

Department of Homeland Security. "Universal Adversary Dynamic Threat Assessment, Ecoterrorism: Environmental and Animal-Rights Militants in the United States." 7 May 2008. http://www.humanewatch.org/images/uploads_DHS_ecoterrorism_threat_assessment.pdf.

Dickinson, Emily. *Complete Poems*. Ed. Thomas H. Johnson. Boston: Little, Brown, 1960. Print.

Dillard, Annie. "Living like Weasels." *Fifty Great Essays*. Ed. Robert DiYanni. 2nd ed. New York: Penguin, 2005. 94–99. Print.

———. *Pilgrim at Tinker Creek*. In *Three by Annie Dillard*. New York: Harper, 1990. 1–260. Print.

Dobrin, Sidney I., and Sean Morey, ed. *Ecosee: Image, Rhetoric, Nature*. Albany: State U of New York P, 2009. Print.

Douglas, Ann. *The Feminization of American Culture*. New York: Knopf, 1977. Print.

Dunlap, Thomas R. *Faith in Nature: Environmentalism as Religious Quest*. Seattle: U of Washington P, 2004. Print.

Edwards, Andres R. *The Sustainability Revolution: Portrait of a Paradigm Shift*. Gabriola Island: New Society, 2005. Print.

Ehrlich, Paul R. *The Population Bomb*. 1968. San Francisco: Sierra Club, 1969. Print.

Eichstaedt, Peter H. *If You Poison Us: Uranium and Native Americans*. Santa Fe: Red Crane, 1994. Print.

Eiseley, Loren. *The Immense Journey*. New York: Time, 1962. Print.

Elkins, James. *The Object Stares Back: On the Nature of Seeing*. New York: Harvest, 1996. Print.

Emerson, Ralph Waldo. *Essays and Lectures*. Washington, DC: Library of America, 1983. Print.

———. Introduction. *Walden and Other Writings*. Thoreau xi–xxxi.

Erikson, Erik H. *Life History and the Historical Moment*. New York: Norton, 1975. Print.

Faulkner, William. "Nobel Prize Acceptance Speech." 10 Dec. 1950. http://www.nobelprize.org/nobel_prizes/literature/laureates/1949/faulkner-speech.html.

Federal Bureau of Investigation. "Putting Intel to Work Against ELF and ALF Terrorists." Washington, DC: Federal Bureau of Investigation, 2008. http://www.fbi.gov/news/stories/2008/june/ecoterror_063008.

Finch, Robert, and John Elder, eds. *Nature Writing: The Tradition in English*. 2nd ed. New York: Norton, 2002. Print.

Freud, Sigmund. *Totem and Taboo: Some Points of Agreement between the Mental

Lives of Savages and Neurotics. Trans. James Strachey. Intro. Peter Gay. New York: Norton, 1989. Print.

Frost, James. "Modernism and the New Picturesque." *Technical Communication, Deliberative Rhetoric, and Environmental Discourse.* Ed. Nancy W. Coppola and Bill Karis. Stamford: Ablex, 2000. 113–38. Print.

Fuller, Thomas. "Myanmar Backs Down, Suspending Dam Project." *New York Times* 30 Sept. 2011. http://www.nytimes.com/2011/10/01/world/asia/myanmar.

Gadgill, Madhav, and Ramachandra Guha. *Ecology and Equality: The Use and Abuse of Nature in Contemporary India.* New York: Routledge, 1995.

Gallagher, Tim. *Falcon Fever: A Falconer in the Twenty-First Century.* Boston: Houghton, 2008. Print.

Gannon, Thomas C. *Skylark Meets Meadowlark: Reimagining the Bird in British Romantic and Contemporary Native American Literature.* Lincoln: U of Nebraska P, 2009. Print.

Garrard, Greg. *Ecocriticism.* London: Routledge, 2004. Print.

Gibson, James William. *A Reenchanted World: The Quest for a New Kinship with Nature.* New York: Holt, 2009. Print.

Goodstein, Eban S. *Economics and the Environment.* 3rd ed. New York: Wiley, 2002. Print.

Gottlieb, Robert. *Environmentalism Unbound: Exploring New Pathways for Change.* Cambridge: MIT P, 2001. Print.

Grandin, Temple, and Catherine Johnson. *Animals in Translation: Using the Mysteries of Autism to Decode Animal Behavior.* New York: Harcourt, 2005. Print.

Graves, John. *Goodbye to a River: A Narrative.* New York: Vintage, 1960. Print.

Guha, Ramachandra. *Environmentalism: A Global History.* New York: Longman, 2000. Print.

———. *The Unquiet Woods: Ecological Change and Peasant Resistance in the Himalaya.* 1989. Berkeley: U of California P, 1990. Print.

Gumbrecht, Hans Ulrich. *Production of Presence: What Meaning Cannot Convey.* Stanford: Stanford UP, 2004. Print.

Guthrie, Arlo. "Great Grand Coulee Dam." http://www.youtube.com/watch?v=-h73mS3Co3k. N.d. Video of musical performance, with commentary.

Guthrie, Woody. "Grand Coulee Dam." http://www.woodyguthrie.org/Lyrics/Grand_Coulee_Dam.htm.

Hamilton, Clive. *Requiem for a Species: Why We Resist the Truth about Climate Change.* New York: Earthscan, 2010. Print.

Hardin, Garrett. "The Tragedy of the Commons." *The Environmental Handbook*. Ed. Garrett De Bell. New York: Ballantine, 1980. 31–50. Print.

Hays, Samuel P. *Beauty, Health, and Permanence: Environmental Politics in the United States: 1955–1985*. Cambridge: Cambridge UP, 1987. Print.

Heidegger, Martin. "The Question Concerning Technology." *Basic Writings*. Ed. D. F. Krell. New York: Harper, 1977. 283–317. Print.

Heise, Ursula K. *Sense of Place, Sense of Planet: The Environmental Imagination of the Global*. New York: Oxford UP, 2008. Print.

Hitt, Christopher. "Toward an Ecological Sublime." *New Literary History* 30.3 (1999): 603–23. Print.

Holcomb, Chris, and M. Jimmie Killingsworth. *Performing Prose: The Study and Practice of Style in Composition*. Carbondale: Southern Illinois UP, 2010. Print.

Johnson, Sandra Humble. *The Space Between: Literary Epiphany in the Work of Annie Dillard*. Kent: Kent State UP, 1992.

Justice, Daniel Heath. *Our Fire Survives the Storm: A Cherokee Literary History*. Minneapolis: U of Minnesota P, 2006. Print.

Kerridge, Richard, and Neil Samuells, eds. *Writing the Environment: Ecocriticism and Literature*. London: Zed, 1998. Print.

Killingsworth, M. Jimmie. "Birdwatcher." *ISLE* 16 (2009): 591–603. Print.

———. *Walt Whitman and the Earth: A Study in Ecopoetics*. Iowa City: U of Iowa P, 2005. Print.

Killingsworth, M. Jimmie, and Jacqueline S. Palmer. "The Discourse of Environmentalist 'Hysteria.'" *Quarterly Journal of Speech* 81 (1995): 1–19.

———. "Ecopolitics and the Literature of the Borderlands: The Frontiers of Environmental Justice in Latina and Native American Writing." Kerridge and Samuells 196–207.

———. *Ecospeak: Rhetoric and Environmental Politics in America*. Carbondale: Southern Illinois UP, 1992. Print.

———. "Millennial Ecology: The Apocalyptic Narrative from *Silent Spring* to *Global Warming*." *Green Culture: Environmental Rhetoric in Contemporary America*. Ed. Carl G. Herndl and Stuart C. Brown. Madison: U of Wisconsin P, 1996. 21–45. Print.

———. "*Silent Spring* and Science Fiction: An Essay in the History and Rhetoric of Narrative." *"And No Birds Sing": The Rhetoric of Rachel Carson*. Ed. Craig Waddell. Carbondale: Southern Illinois UP, 2000. 174–204. Print.

Knutson, Roger M. *Flattened Fauna: A Field Guide to Common Animals of Roads, Streets, and Highways*. Berkeley: Ten Speed Press, 1987. Print.

Kosek, Jake. *Understories: The Political Life of Forests in Northern New Mexico.* Durham: Duke UP, 2006. Print.

Krech, Shepard, III. *The Ecological Indian: Myth and History.* New York: Norton, 1999. Print.

Kuletz, Valerie L. *The Tainted Desert: Environmental and Social Ruin in the American West.* New York: Routledge, 1998. Print.

LaDuke, Winona. *All Our Relations: Native Struggles for Land and Life.* Cambridge: South End, 1999. Print.

Langbaum, Robert. "The Epiphanic Mode in Wordsworth and Modern Literature." *New Literary History* 14 (1983): 335–58. Print.

Lappé, Anna. *Diet for a Hot Planet: The Climate Crisis at the End of Your Fork and What You Can Do about It.* New York: Bloomsbury USA, 2011. Print.

Lappé, Frances Moore. *Diet for a Small Planet.* 20th anniversary ed. New York: Ballantine, 1991.

———. *Eco-Mind: Changing the Way We Think, to Create the World We Want.* New York: Nation Books, 2011. Print.

Larsen, Amy. "'I Was Ready for a Mending': Rhetorics of Trauma and Recovery in Doug Peacock's *Grizzly Years* and *Walking It Off.*" *Rhetoric Review* 30.4 (2011): 406–22. Print.

Lear, Linda. *Rachel Carson: Witness for Nature.* 1997. Boston: Mariner, 2009. Print.

Le Guin, Ursula K. *The Left Hand of Darkness.* 1969. New York: Ace, 2000. Print.

Lehman, David, and John Brehm, eds. *Oxford Book of American Poetry.* New York: Oxford UP, 2006. Print.

Leopold, Aldo. *Sand County Almanac, and Sketches Here and There.* New York: Oxford UP, 1989. Print.

Lindsey, Hal, with C. C. Carlson. *The Late Great Planet Earth.* 1970. New York: Bantam, 1973. Print.

Lopez, Barry. "Apologia." *Literature and the Environment: A Reader on Nature and Culture.* Ed. Lorraine Anderson, Scott Slovic, and John P. O'Grady. New York: Longman, 1999. 75–79. Print.

Louv, Richard. *Last Child in the Woods: Saving Our Children from Nature-Deficit Disorder.* Expanded ed. New York: Algonquin, 2008. Print.

Luhmann, Niklas. *Ecological Communication.* Trans. John Bednarz Jr. Chicago: U of Chicago P, 1989. Print.

Lynas, Mark. *The God Species: Saving the Planet in the Age of Humans.* Washington, DC: National Geographic, 2011. Print.

Manes, Christopher. "Nature and Silence." *The Ecocriticism Reader: Landmarks in Literary Ecology.* Ed. Cheryll Glotfelty and Harold Fromm. Athens: U of Georgia P, 1996. 15–29. Print.

Martinez-Alier, Joan. *The Environmentalism of the Poor: A Study of Ecological Conflicts and Valuation.* Cheltenham and Northhampton: Edward Elgar, 2002. Print.

Matthiessen, Peter. "How to Kill a Valley." *New York Review of Books* 7 Feb. 1980: 31–36. Print.

———. *Indian Country.* 1979. New York: Penguin, 1984. Print.

Maturana, Humberto R., and Francisco J. Varela. *The Tree of Knowledge: The Biological Roots of Human Understanding.* Rev. ed. Boston: Shambhala, 1998. Print.

McGinn, Bernard. *The Foundations of Mysticism: Origins to the Fifth Century.* New York: Crossroad, 1991. Print.

McKibben, Bill. *Eaarth: Making a Life on a Tough New Planet.* New York: St. Martin's Griffin, 2011. Print.

———. *The End of Nature.* 1989. New York: Random House, 2006. Print.

———. *Enough: Staying Human in an Engineered Age.* New York: Holt, 2003. Print.

———, ed. *American Earth: Environmental Writing since Thoreau.* Intro. Al Gore. New York: Library of America, 2008.

McMurry, Andrew. *Environmental Renaissance: Emerson, Thoreau, and the Systems of Nature.* Athens: U of Georgia P, 2003. Print.

McNeil, Lynda. "The Nine Mile Canyon Coalition: Rhetorical Landscapes, Responsible Public Land Use." *Rhetoric, Literacies, and Narratives of Sustainability.* Ed. Peter N. Goggin. New York: Routledge, 2009. Print.

McPhee, John. *Encounters with the Archdruid.* New York: Farrar, 1971. Print.

Miller, F. DeWolfe. *Christopher Pearse Cranch and His Caricatures of New England Transcendentalism.* Cambridge: Harvard UP, 1952. Print.

Mitchell, Joni. "Big Yellow Taxi." McKibben, *American Earth* 490–91. Print.

Mogen, David. *Honyocker Dreams: Montana Memories.* Lincoln: U of Nebraska P, 2011. Print.

Moore, Kathleen Dean. *The Pine Island Paradox.* Minneapolis: Milkweed, 2004. Print.

Morton, Timothy. *The Ecological Thought.* Cambridge: Harvard UP, 2010. Print.

Murchison, Kenneth M. *The Snail Darter Case: TVA versus the Endangered Species Act.* Lawrence: UP of Kansas, 2007. Print.

Nathan, Leonard. *Diary of a Left-Handed Birdwatcher.* St. Paul: Graywolf Press, 1996.
Nelson, Richard. *The Island Within.* New York: Vintage, 1991. Print.
———. *Make Prayers to the Raven: A Koyukon View of the Northern Forest.* Chicago: U of Chicago P, 1983. Print.
Nichols, Ashton. *The Poetics of Epiphany: Nineteenth-Century Origins of the Modern Literary Moment.* Tuscaloosa: U of Alabama P, 1987.
Nixon, Rob. *Slow Violence and the Environmentalism of the Poor.* Cambridge: Harvard UP, 2011. Print.
Nordhaus, Ted, and Michael Shellenberger. *Break Through: Why We Can't Leave Saving the Planet to Environmentalists.* Boston: Houghton Mifflin, 2007. Print.
———. *The Death of Environmentalism.* 2004. http://www.thebreakthrough.org/PDF/Death_of_Environmentalism.pdf.
Norgaard, Kari Marie. *Living in Denial: Climate Change, Emotions, and Everyday Life.* Cambridge: MIT Press, 2011. Print.
Norton, Brian G. *Sustainability: A Philosophy of Adaptive Ecosystem Management.* Chicago: U of Chicago P, 2005. Print.
Oelschlaeger, Max. *The Idea of Wilderness: From Prehistory to the Age of Ecology.* New Haven: Yale UP, 1993. Print.
Olson, Sigurd. "Northern Lights." Finch and Elder 432–35.
Owen, David. *Green Metropolis: Why Living Smaller, Living Closer, and Driving Less Are the Keys to Sustainability.* New York: Riverhead, 2009. Print.
Palmer, Laura. "Throwing a Monkey-Wrench into the Works: Including Radicals in the Teaching of Technical/Environmental Writing." *Proceedings of the 2011 IEEE International Professional Communication Conference.* 17–19 Oct. 2011, University of Cincinnati. IEEE Catalog Number: CFP11IPC-CDR.
Pasternak, Judy. *Yellow Dirt: An American Story of a Poisoned Land and a People Betrayed.* New York: Free Press, 2010. Print.
Peacock, Doug. *Grizzly Years.* New York: Holt, 1990. Print.
Peterson, Tarla Rai. *Sharing the Earth: The Rhetoric of Sustainable Development.* Columbia: U of South Carolina P, 1997. Print.
Phillips, Dana. *The Truth of Ecology: Nature, Culture, and Literature in America.* New York: Oxford UP, 2003. Print.
Plater, Zygmunt. "Reflected in a River: Agency Accountability and the TVA Tellico Dam Case." *Tennessee Law Review* 49.4 (1982): 747–87. Print.
Plumwood, Val. *Feminism and the Mastery of Nature.* London: Routledge, 1993. Print.

Pope, Alexander. *An Essay on Man.* 1733–34. http://www.theotherpages.org/poems/pope-i.html.

"Post-Apocalyptic Movies." Internet Movie Database. http://www.imdb.com/list/2WCgJcXeSEQ/?start=1&view=detail&sort=listorian:asc.

Pound, Ezra. "'A Retrospect' and 'A Few Don'ts' (1918)." Chicago: Poetry Foundation, 2010. http://www.poetryfoundation.org/learning/poetics-essay/237886.

Richards, I. A. *Principles of Literary Criticism.* New York: Harcourt, 1926. Print.

Richardson, Robert D., Jr. *Henry Thoreau: A Life of the Mind.* Berkeley: U of California P, 1986. Print.

Robinson, William Paul. "Uranium Production and Its Effects on Navajo Communities along the Rio Puerco in Western New Mexico." *The Proceedings of the Michigan Conference on Race and the Incidence of Environmental Hazards.* Ed. Bunyan Bryant and Paul Mohai. Ann Arbor: University of Michigan School of Natural Resources, 1990. 175–86. Print.

Rome, Adam. "Earth Day in South Carolina." Message to the author. 28 July 2012. Email.

———. *The Genius of Earth Day: How a 1970 Teach-In Unexpectedly Made the First Green Generation.* New York: Hill and Wang, 2013. Print.

Roy, Arundhati. "The Greater Common Good." *Friends of the Narmada Website.* April 1999. 16 pp. http://www.narmada.org/gcg/gcg.html.

Rozelle, Lee. *Ecosublime: Environmental Awe and Terror from New World to Oddworld.* Tuscaloosa: U of Alabama P, 2006. Print.

Sale, Kirkpatrick. *The Green Revolution: The American Environmental Movement 1962–1992.* New York: Hill and Wang, 1993. Print.

———. *Rebels against the Future: The Luddites and Their War on the Industrial Revolution.* New York: Basic, 1996. Print.

Schueler, Donald G. "Southern Exposure." *Sierra* 77.6 (1992): 42. *Academic Search Complete.* EBSCO. Web.

Schlyer, Krista. *Continental Divide: Wildlife, People, and the Border Wall.* College Station: Texas A&M UP, 2012. Print.

Siebert, Charles. *The Wauchula Woods Accord: Toward a New Understanding of Animals.* New York: Scribner, 2009. Print.

Silko, Leslie Marmon. *Ceremony.* New York: Viking, 1977. Print.

———. "Landscape, History, and the Pueblo Imagination." Barnhill 30–50.

———. "The Man to Send Rain Clouds." http://dwc.hct.ac.ae/fnd/engread/readingcomp-rainclouds-read.htm.

———. *The Turquoise Ledge: A Memoir.* New York: Viking, 2010. Print.

Snyder, Gary. "The Dead by the Side of the Road." *Turtle Island.* New York: New Directions, 1974. 7–8. Print.

———. *A Place in Space: Ethics, Aesthetics, and Watersheds.* Washington, DC: Counterpoint, 1995. Print.

SRIC (Southwest Research and Information Center). "Church Rock Uranium Mill Tailings Spill and Uranium Legacy Remembrance and Action Day." SRIC Information Sheet. 7 Dec. 2009. Print.

Stafford, William. "Traveling through the Dark." *Literature and the Environment: A Reader on Nature and Culture.* Ed. Lorraine Anderson, Scott Slovic, and John P. O'Grady. New York: Longman, 1999. 79–80. Print.

Stambor, Howard. "Manifest Destiny and American Indian Religious Freedom: Sequoyah, Badoni, and the Drowned Gods." *Native Americans and the Law: Contemporary and Historical Perspectives on American Indian Rights, Freedoms, and Sovereignty.* New York: Garland, 1996. 193–223. Print.

Steele, D. Gentry, and M. Jimmie Killingsworth. *Reflections of the Brazos Valley.* College Station: Texas A&M UP, 2007. Print.

Stephenson, Neal. *Reamde.* New York: Morrow, 2011. Print.

Stiglitz, Joseph. *The Price of Inequality: How Today's Divided Society Endangers Our Future.* New York: Norton, 2012. Print.

Strayed, Cheryl. *Wild: From Lost to Found on the Pacific Crest Trail.* New York: Knopf, 2012. Print.

Sullivan, Robert. *The Thoreau You Don't Know: What the Prophet of Environmentalism Really Meant.* New York: Harper Collins, 2009. Print.

Swan, James A. *Nature as Teacher and Healer: How to Reawaken Your Connection with Nature.* Rev. ed. 1992. Lincoln: iUniverse Authors Guild Backinprint.com, 2000. Print.

Tapahonso, Luci. *Seasonal Woman.* Illus. R. C. Gorman. Santa Fe: Tooth of Time, 1982. Print.

Thoreau, Henry David. *The Journal 1837–1861.* Ed. Damion Searls. New York: New York Review of Books, 2009. Print.

———. *The Maine Woods.* New York: Book of the Month, 1996. Print.

———. *Walden and Other Writings.* New York: Modern Library, 2000. Print.

———. "Walking." *Walden and Other Writings* 625–63.

Tyler, Ron. *The Big Bend: A History of the Last Texas Frontier.* 1975. College Station: Texas A&M UP, 1996. Print.

Vergano, Dan. "What, Me Worry? Scientists Explain Why the End of the World Will NOT Arrive in 2012." *USA Today Weekend* 7–9 Dec. 2012. 8–9, 12.

Vizenor, Gerald, ed. *Survivance: Narratives of Native Presence.* Lincoln: U of Nebraska P, 2008. Print.

Waddell, Craig, ed. *"And No Birds Sing": The Rhetoric of Rachel Carson.* Carbondale: Southern Illinois UP, 2000. Print.

Walls, Laura Dassow. *Seeing New Worlds: Henry David Thoreau and Nineteenth-Century Natural Science.* Madison: U of Wisconsin P, 1995. Print.

———. "Walden as Feminist Manifesto." *Interdisciplinary Studies in Literature and Environment* 1.1 (1993): 137–44. Print.

Wheeler, William Bruce, and Michael J. McDonald. *TVA and the Tellico Dam 1936–1979.* Knoxville: U of Tennessee P, 1986. Print.

White, Lowell Mick. "Cock Pheasant." *2River View* 9.2 (winter 2005). http://www.2river.org/2RView/9_2/poems/white01.htm.

Whitman, Walt. *Complete Poetry and Collected Prose.* New York: Library of America, 1982. Print.

Wildcat, Daniel R. *Red Alert! Saving the Planet with Indigenous Knowledge.* Golden: Fulcrum, 2009.

Williams, Terry Tempest. *Refuge: An Unnatural History of Family and Place.* New York: Vintage, 1991. Print.

———. *When Women Were Birds: Fifty-Four Variations on Voice.* New York: Farrar, 2012. Print.

Wolfe, Cary. *Animal Rites: American Culture, the Discourse of Species, and Posthumanist Theory.* Chicago: U of Chicago P, 2003. Print.

———. *Critical Environments: Postmodern Theory and the Pragmatics of the Outside.* Minneapolis: U of Minnesota P, 1998. Print.

Wolfe, Cary, ed. *Zoontologies: The Question of the Animal.* Minneapolis: U of Minnesota P, 2003. Print.

Woods, Gioia. "Sci-Animism: American Poetry and Science." *ISLE* 15.2 (2008): 199–210. Print.

Worster, Donald. *A Passion for Nature: The Life of John Muir.* New York: Oxford, 2008. Print.

Zerubavel, Eviatar. *The Elephant in the Room: Silence and Denial in Everyday Life.* New York: Oxford UP, 2006. Print.

Index

Abbey, Edward, 54, 62–63, 219
Abram, David, 248, 290
Ackerman, Diane, 260–61
Adamson, Jodi, 117
Agassiz, Louis, 171
Albright, Madeleine, 26–27
Alcoholics Anonymous, 91
alcohol problem, 87, 91
allegory. *See* smells
All the Pretty Horses (McCarthy), 163
American Dream argument, 166–67
American Indian Literature, Environmental Justice, and Ecocriticism (Adamson), 117
The American Jeremiad (Bercovitch), 52
Americans before Columbus, 65–66
ancestor stories, 294
Angus, Ian, 187–88
An Inconvenient Truth, 163–64
Apocalypse of John (Revelation), 146–48
apocalyptic moments: about mother's death, 3, 209–10; with vegetarian announcement, 286–88
apocalyptic narratives: as anxiety relief, 176–78; appeal persistence, 288–89; cultural resurgence, 162–67; distinction problem, 178–79; environmentalism, 142–43, 148, 160–61, 174–76; film portrayals, 162–64; in nature writing, 3–4; pro-development, 137–38, 144; religious writings, 167–69; as resentment narrative, 159–60; in science, 171–73; as search for the new, 169–70; survivor themes, 169, 176; about 2011 weather, 159
Apocalyptic Planet (Childs), 178–79, 285
"Apologia" (Lopez), 266
Arab Spring, 167
Aristotle, 177
armadillos, 276
Armageddon. *See* apocalyptic narratives
Armstrong, Karen, 147–48
Asian cranes, 30–31
Asia trip, author's, 24–33
Asimov, Isaac, 228
atomic bomb, 90
attitude and language, 258
autism, 259–60
automobiles, 252–53, 254. *See also* road kill
Awiakta, Marilou, 53–55, 65

Baker, Howard, 48, 51
Bandelier National Monument, 118
Barthes, Roland, 255
Bass, Rick, 4, 8

Beale, Walter, 192
beauty dilemma, 99
Becker, Ernest, 1
Becoming Animal (Abram), 290
Begay, Fred, 112
Bell, Mrs., 13–14
Benally, UNC Resources v., 67
Bercovitch, Sacvan, 52
Bethe, Hans, 119
Bible, 2, 7, 133, 168, 250
Bible study class, 145–47
The Big Year, 231
bike rider, Water Canyon Park, 72, 73–74
bird moments: Asia trip, 30–31; Bosque Preserve, 77–78, 80–83, 118; childhood/youth, 14–16, 17–21, 211; ditch bank, 85, 87–89; in father-son film, 231; highway detour, 91; Knoxville area, 79; morning walks/runs, 213–14, 232–33, 237–38; at Old Hickory Lake, 62; at San Jacinto Monument, 212–13; swamp tour, 216–17; Water Canyon hikes, 74
Black, Jack, 231
Blood Meridian (McCarthy), 163
Bohlmeyer, Dwight, 293–94
Bookchin, Murray, 117
Bosque del Apache National Wildlife Preserve, 77–83, 118
Brave New World (Huxley), 205
Break Through (Nordhaus and Shellenberger), 160
breathing, 240–41, 243–45, 246–48, 249–50
Brecht, Bertolt, 177–78

Bridgers, Ben, 50
Brown, Greg, 268
Brown, Lester, 184, 186
Buddha Land, South Korea, 31–32
Building a Sustainable Society (Brown), 184
bumper sticker, 35–36
"Bury My Heart in the Tellico Valley," 65
Bush, George H. W., 140
Bush, George W., 55, 165
Butler, Simon, 187–88

Campbell, John W., Jr., 205
Camp Socareda, 59–60
Caprock canyon country, 152
Carson, Rachel, 142–45, 148, 191–92, 195–97, 201–206, 248
Carter, Jimmy, 48–49
Cash, Johnny, 62
catchment areas, 124–25
catharsis, 177–78
Catholicism, 113–15
catstrophicism perspective, evolution, 171–73
Ceremony (Silko), 117
Chaco Canyon, 118
Charleston, South Carolina, 12, 108
Charlie the parrot, 86
Cherokee people: Awiakta's writings, 53–55, 65, 112; Church Rock connection, 67–68; Tellico Dam controversy, 48–56, 65–66, 127
Chew, Joe, 71
childhood/youth, author's: bird moments, 14–16, 17–21, 211; at Camp Socareda, 59–60;

with grandparents, 1–2, 7, 12, 107–108; hunting experiences, 16–20, 30; reading and writing, 11, 12–15, 220. *See also* mother, author's
Children of Men, 162
children's programs, nature-based, 289–90, 291–94
Childs, Craig, 178–79, 194, 285
China trip, author's, 24–26
Chota homeland, Tellico Dam controversy, 48–53, 65–66
Church Rock catastrophe, 66–67, 68, 120–25, 129. *See also* uranium mining
civil rights movement, 39–40, 160
climate change, 148–49, 163–64, 179, 188–89, 194
Clinton, Bill, 26
Close Encounters of the Third Kind, 231
Cobb, Ron, 36–37
"Cock Pheasant" (White), 266–67
Cold War context: apocalyptic visions, 164, 176, 288–89; Carson's critics, 201–202; childhood writing, 13; and Christian-oriented millenialism, 145–47; Church Rock catastrophe, 66–67, 68, 120–25, 129; environmentalism's rhetoric, 161; Korean War, 11–12, 13, 27–28, 41; in Korea visit, 29; millennial ecology, 144–45; New Criticism movement, 225–26; and sacrifice zoning, 130–31; science fiction film, 202–203; Vietnam War, 38–41, 43–44, 267; White Sands Missile Range, 54, 90, 118

college years, author's, 23, 35–36, 43–48
commodification of nature, 193
Commoner, Barry, 43
Company-Faculty Forum, 133–38, 148–50
conservationism, 37, 140
cottonmouth myth, 61
coyotes, 74, 80, 85, 236–39
Cranch, Christopher Pearse
cranes, 30–31, 80, 81–82
creationism, 171
Cronkite, Walter, 127
cuckoo, yellow-billed, 79

Dad. *See* stepfather, author's
D'Amico, Lisa, 193
dam projects, 60–63. *See also* Tellico Dam controversy
Darwinism, theoretical shifts, 171–72
Davis, Mike, 172–73, 174
dawn moments. *See* morning walks/runs
The Dawn of the Dead, 163
The Day after Tomorrow, 162
The Day after Trinity, 119
"The Dead by the Side of the Road" (Snyder), 263, 265, 267
death: of fathers, 11, 38, 41; of grandparents, 107–108; of individual worlds, 285–86; of mothers, 2–8, 291; Oppenheimer's statement, 90; retreat from, 288–89. *See also* apocalyptic narratives; roadkill
The Death of Environmentalism (Nordhaus and Shellenberger), 141–42, 160

Deep Ecology, 117
defensiveness, state of. *See* denial-distraction-defensiveness
déjà vu moment, 68–70. *See also* Church Rock catastrophe; Socorro return
Deliverance (Dickey), 61
Deloria, Vine, Jr., 112
Dempsey, Luke, 209
denial-distraction-defensiveness: about land relationship, 91–92, 96–99; apocalyptic narratives, 177–78; cultural prevalence, 188–89, 191–92; in déjà vu moment, 68–70; with hero stories and rhetoric, 204–207; pioneer image, 101–102; in professional ambitions, 99, 115; with social issue avoidance, 116–17. *See also* sacrifice zoning
The Denial of Death (Becker), 1
Dennehy, Brian, 231
desecrated land, 126
Desert Solitaire (Abbey), 219
Diary of a Left-Handed Birdwatcher (Nathan), 209
Dick, Philip K., 202, 204
Dickey, James, 61
Dickinson, Emily, 157
Dickson, Bruce, 126–27
Diet for a Small Planet (Lappé), 264
Dillard, Annie, 219
dioxin pollution, 126
dispensational theology, 139–40, 146–47
distraction, state of. *See* denial-distraction-defensiveness

ditch bank, Socorro's, 83–89
dogs: co-evolution of, 238–39; and coyotes, 237, 238, 239; hunting trips, 18–19; pets, 76, 85; roadkill, 273, 274
dolphins, 230, 232
"Do Not Go Gentle into That Good Night" (Thomas), 157
downstream phenomenon, 125–26. *See also* sacrifice zoning
Down the River (Abbey), 63
dream, sunrise, 210
drought, Texas, 157–58, 186
DuLuca, Kevin, 256
Dune (Herbert), 205
Dunn, Winfield, 128
Dylan, Bob, 199

Earth Day, 36–37, 38, 42–43
earthquake, Japanese, 149, 166
eco-epiphany. *See* epiphany
ecology: in Carson's *Sea Around Us,* 195–96; defining, 35–36; Earth Day significance, 36–37, 38, 42–43; millennial-oriented, 144–45; social-oriented, 116–17, 150–54; symbol for, 36–37
Ecology of Fear (Davis), 172–73
economics: as change and awareness obstacle, 186–89; development project promises, 47–48; externalizing of nature, 141–42; financial crisis, 185; as sustainability component, 151, 186–87
eco-porn, 269
Ecospeak (Killingsworth and Palmer), 55, 135, 140, 142–43

eco-spirituality, 116–17, 247–48
ecosystem people, 123–26, 186
eco-terrorist label, 9, 131
ego-negation, 217–18, 229–30
Ehrlich, Paul, 144
Eiseley, Loren, 228–29
Ely, Linda, 53
Emerson, Ralph Waldo, 217–19, 226
Endangered Species Act, 46, 48
The End of Nature (McKibben), 144
energy efficiency, costs, 186–87
Energy Use and Development forum, 133–38, 148–50
engagement problem. *See* denial-distraction-defensiveness; escape perspective
environmentalism: apocalyptic narratives, 142–43, 148, 160–61; change challenge, 187; cultural emergence, 36–38, 42–43; identification reluctance, 115, 148–51; individual behavior impact, 181–88; as more than Ideology, 63; negativity arguments, 5–6, 174–76, 187; oppositional rhetoric, 134–36, 139–42; as resistance movement, 131; and roadkill linguistics, 263–64; spirituality connection, 116–17, 247–48. *See also* sustainability ideal
Environmentalism of the Poor (Martinez-Alier), 185
Environmental Protection Agency, 37
epiphany: about mother's death, 3, 209–10; as affirmation, 210–14; during autumn rain, 232–33; cultural popularization, 224–25; 227; in Eisley's story, 228–30; in nature writing, 3–4; New Criticism movement, 225–27; as re-engagement, 291; as restoration, 214–16; sharing urge, 218–24, 230–32; sister's, 222–24, 227–28; with verbal image, 257; wildness element, 216–18
Erikson, Erik, 103–105
escape perspective: in eco-spirituality, 116–17; with hero stories, 204–207; Hilton Head vacations, 20–23; refuge and retreat compared, 69–70, 197; in science fiction and fantasy, 199–203; in sentimentality *vs.* romanticism, 198–99. *See also* denial-distraction-defensiveness
ethics component, in sustainability, 151
"The Eureka Phenomenon" (Asimov), 228
evolution, 171–73, 238–39, 240–41
Ezzell, Patricia, 127

"A Fable for Tomorrow" (Carson), 143–44, 203–204
family theme, in apocalyptic narratives, 169, 176
fantasy, 192, 199–201, 206
father, author's: in childhood writing, 13; death, 11–12, 27, 33, 41; medals, 106, 109; photograph of, 108–109. *See also* stepfather, author's
Faulkner, William, 225–26
feedlot smells, 241
financial crisis (2008), 166–67, 185

Finney, Jack, 202
Fire on the Mountain (Abbey), 54
fishing, 21, 62
Flattened Fauna (Knutson), 268
flood control system, Socorro, 84
food resources, 184, 186, 286–88
Foreman, Dave, 150–51
foxes, 278–79
freedom, 154
Freeman, David, 55
Freud, Sigmund, 251
fundamentalist quality, pro-development rhetoric, 137–40. *See also* spirituality and religion

gallinule, purple, 216–17
genres, literary, 192, 199–205
Glen Canyon Dam, 62–63
global warming, 148–49, 163–64, 179, 188–89, 194
Global Warming (Schneider), 144
Goliath George, 50–51
Goodbye to a River (Graves), 157, 219
Gore, Al, 163–64
Gorman, R. C., 113
gothic tradition, science fiction's uses, 204
gradualist perspective, evolution, 171–73
Grandin, Temple, 238–39, 259–60
grandparents, author's, 1–2, 7, 12, 107–108
Graves, John, 157, 219
great blue heron, 211
"The Great Inhalation," rhetorical limitations, 254–55. *See also* smells
green capital approach, 142

Green Metropolis (Owen), 5–6, 181–82
Greenpeace, 150
Greenville, South Carolina: childhood, 12, 13, 14, 16; death of neighbor, 61–62; father's medals, 106–107; and Kent State shootings, 40; photograph incident, 108–109; stepfather's later life, 16, 223–24
Gulf Oil, 133–35

Hamlet (Shakespeare), 177
Hardin, Garrett, 154
Harrison, Gary, 68
hawks, 74, 213–14
headlights and night creatures, 271–73, 275–76
hellfire rhetoric, 137–38
Herbert, Frank, 205
Hereford feedlot, 241
heron, great blue, 211
hero stories, 204–207
high school years, author's, 38–42
Hilton Head Island, 20–23, 47, 78, 211, 231–32
Hitt, Christopher, 218
hognose snake incident, 222
Holcomb, Chris, 256–57
"How to Kill a Valley" (Matthiessen), 49–53
hunting experiences, childhood, 16–20, 30
Hurricane Katrina, 166
Huxley, Aldous, 205

identity processes, 103–105, 115, 150–51

ignorance/neglect problem, 125–26, 128. *See also* denial-distraction-defensiveness
"I Heard a Fly Buzz When I Died" (Dickinson), 157
illusion, as form of escape, 199
Image Politics (DuLuca), 256
imagery, verbal, 255–61
imagination, 291–94
The Immense Journey (Eiseley), 228–29
Indian Country (Matthiessen), 49–53, 66–67
individual behavior, environmental impact, 181–88
individualism theme, in apocalyptic narrative, 169
ingenuity theme, in apocalyptic narrative, 169
In the Spirit of Crazy Horse (Matthiessen), 66
Invasion of the Body Snatchers (Finney), 202–203
invisibility, willed. *See* sacrifice zoning
Isaiah, Book of, 133
island biogeography, 196–97
issue coverage. *See* media coverage

Jackson, Wes, 126–27
javelina, 276–77
Jenkins, Jerry B., 167–68
jeremiad-oriented rhetoric, 52–53. *See also* apocalyptic narratives
Jesus Movement, 146–47, 168
jogging, ditch bank, 85–87
Johnson, Sandra Humble, 219
Jones, Belle: caretaking of father, 88, 223; childhood, 12, 18, 104, 202; epiphany of, 222–25, 227–28
Jones, Bob, Jr., 12, 40
Jones, Kathy (later Langston), 12, 22, 109, 223
Jones, Lewis. *See* stepfather, author's
Joyce, James, 226–28
Junior Naturalist program, 289–90

kangaroo rat incident, 221–22
Katrina, Hurricane, 166
Kennedy, John F., 40, 143
Kent State, 40
Killingsworth, Myrth, 24, 27, 83, 152–53, 154, 294
Kim Dae Jung, 26–27
Kim Jon Il, 26–27
King, Martin Luther, Jr., 160
Klamath River, 57
Knoxville, Tennessee: bird sightings, 79, 83; college experiences, 41, 45–46; grandmother's funeral, 107–108; move from, 96, 105–106; summer roadkill job, 280–81; TVA visit, 127; yoga class, 246; Zombie Walk, 55–56. *See also* Tellico Dam controversy
Knoxville Journal, 41, 128
Knutson, Roger, 268
Korean War, 11–12, 13, 27–28, 41
Korea trip, author's, 24–31
Krajicek, John, 128
Kuletz, Valerie L., 101, 118, 122, 124
Kunstler, James Howard, 169
Kyung Ju, South Korea, 31–32

lake recreation, 58–63
Land Institute, 126–27
Langmuir Lab, 71, 77
Langston, Kathy Jones, 12, 22, 109, 223
language and rhetoric: for attitude change, 258; and environmentalism's emergence, 161, 263–64; fundamentalist quality, 137–40; limitations for smell descriptions, 254–55; millennial theme, 142–44, 148; for opposition to environmentalism, 5–6, 134–36, 139–42; with totalizing terms, 134–39, 145; for verbal images, 255–61
Lappé, Frances Moore, 264, 287
Larson, Gary, 267–68
Last Child in the Woods (Louv), 290
The Late Great Planet Earth (Lindsey), 146, 159
Lear, Linda, 191, 195
Least Heat-Moon, William, 126
Left Behind (LeHaye and Jenkins), 147, 167–68
The Left Hand of Darkness (Le Guin), 199
Le Guin, Ursula K., 199
LeHaye, Tim, 167–68
Leopold, Aldo, 97–98
liberalism crisis, 138–40
Life History and the Historical Moment (Erikson), 103–105
lightning bugs, 1
lily-of-the valley, 2
Lindsey, Hal, 146, 159
Little Tennessee River, 46–47. *See also* Tellico Dam controversy

living water, 59
Lonesome Dove (McMurty), 61
"look" moments, 230–32, 260. *See also* epiphany
Lopez, Barry, 266
Los Alamos National Lab, 118–19
"Lost Eloheh Land" (Matthiessen), 49–53
Louv, Richard, 290
"Love Sick Blues" (Williams), 238
lupus, mother's, 22, 24, 107, 244
Lyell, Charles, 171, 173

MagCorp, 187–88
The Maine Woods (Thoreau), 216
Majors, Ted, 35
mallard story, 17–18
The Man Who Killed the Deer (Waters), 116–17
Mao Zedong, 24
Martinez-Alier, Joan, 185
Marx, Karl, 102
The Matrix, 69
matrix question, 69–70, 102–103
Matthew, Gospel of, 2
Matthiessen, Peter, 49–53, 65, 66–67, 123
McCarthy, Cormac, 163, 177
McKibben, Bill, 144, 192
McKinney, Rita, 35
McMurty, Larry, 61
McPhee, John, 194
medals, father's, 106, 109
media coverage: as alienation factor, 128; and historical neglect, 122–23; language rigidity, 135; nuclear industry events, 67, 121–22, 123,

129; Tellico Dam controversy, 49–50, 54, 65–66, 127–28
Melehes, Nick, 13–14
melodrama, 192, 198–201, 203–207
memory, 87–88
Memphis Greens, 150, 151
Methodist Church, Bible study class, 145–47
metonym *vs.* image, 258–59
military activity: attitudes about, 130; desert lands occupation, 54, 90, 118; pollution production, 188. *See also* Korean War; Vietnam War
millennial rhetoric, 142–44, 148
Miller, Carolyn R., 192
Miller, F. DeWolfe, 45, 72, 217
modernism context, science fiction, 201–202
money, smells connection, 241–43, 245, 249–53
Monsanto Corporation, 144, 205
moon rise, 212
Moore, Kathleen Dean, 9, 230–31, 232, 260
morning walks/runs: bird moments, 213–14, 232–33, 237–38; coyotes and dogs, 238–39; on ditch bank, 83–89; dolphin watching experience, 231–32; epiphany potential, 214–15, 291; and mourning for mother, 2–3; and nature-based therapy, 291, 294; sounds during, 237, 252; sunrise dream, 210; and wildfire smoke, 158, 209–10
mother, author's: daughter's epiphany about, 224; death of, 2–3, 7–8; illness, 22, 24, 244; on money, 251–52; photograph incident, 108–109; proto-epiphanies from, 220–22; religious beliefs, 6–7; and vegetarianism, 286–88. *See also* father, author's
mothers' role, nature writing, 3–6, 8
Mountain States Legal Foundation, 136–38
"mouse" in kitchen, 221–22
Moyers, Bill, 139
Mustang Drive, Socorro, 84–86, 89, 95–96
mysticism, 116–17, 229–30. *See also* spirituality and religion
myth and ideology, 102

NAMES program, 105–106, 109–11
Nathan, Leonard, 209, 210
National Environmental Policy Act, 37
National Geographic, 122–23
National Indian Youth Council, 65
Native American Graves Protection and Repatriation Act, 66
Native Americans in Mining and Engineering Science (NAMES), 105–106, 109–11
natural history. *See* nature writing
A Natural History of the Senses (Ackerman), 260–61
nature-deficit disorder, 290
nature writing: childhood, 14–15; as communion invitation, 9; human element, 192–94; morning routine, 83–84, 86; role of mothers' deaths, 3–6, 8. *See also specific authors, e.g.,* Carson, Rachel; Moore, Kathleen Dean; Thoreau, Henry David

Navajo people, 66–68, 112–13, 118, 130
negativity arguments, environmentalism's tone, 5–6, 174–76, 187
neglect/ignorance problem, 125–26, 128. *See also* denial-distraction-defensiveness
Nelson, Gaylord, 38
neoclassical sustainability, 180–81
New Criticism movement, 225–27
New Mexico Tech: journey to, 92–96; Langmuir Lab relationship, 71; Los Alamos connection, 119; writing classes, 105–106, 109–11, 115
New Naturalist's Wager, 179
News-Sentinel, 128
New York City, 181–83
New York Review of Books, 49
nighthawks, 82–83
night walking, 239–40. *See also* twilight settings, epiphanies
9/11 impact, 165–66
1984 (Orwell), 135, 205
Nixon, Richard M., 37
Nixon, Rob, 123–24
noise, 252–54
Nordhaus, Ted, 141–42, 159–60, 173
North Korea, 26–27
Norton, Brian, 154
nuclear industry, 54–56, 66–68, 118–23, 149, 166

Old Hickory Lake, 62
On the Beach, 176
"On Willow Creek" (Bass), 4
opossums, 273–75

Oppenheimer, Robert, 90
Oregon, 12–20, 30, 80, 83, 220–22
Orwell, George, 135, 205
osprey, 21
Owen, David, 5–6, 181–84
owls: in birding film, 231; east of Corona, 91; roadkill victims, 269, 272–73; Thoreau's night walks, 240; Water Canyon hiking, 74, 75
oxygen bars, 249–50

Palmer, Jackie: Asia trip, 24, 27; authorship, 117–18, 135, 140, 160–61; childhood, 242, 245–46; environmentalist activities, 150; meeting of, 247; opossum anecdote, 275; parenthood and the outdoors, 152–53; parrot of, 86; photograph framing, 109; retirement, 235–36; snake incidents, 222, 277–78; vacations, 24; Water Canyon hikes, 76
paper mill smells, 241–42
parenthood and social ecology, 152–54
parents. *See* father, author's; mother, author's; stepfather, author's
parrot, Jackie's, 86
Pascal's Wager, 179
Pasternak, Judy, 120, 122, 123, 124
Pawley's Island, 24, 211–12
personal worlds, always-ending, 285–86
Peru, industrial pollution, 187–88
pesticides, 143–44. *See also Silent Spring* (Carson)
Peterson, Tarla Rai, 126–27, 150

petroleum, 253–54
pheasants, 20, 30
Pilgrim at Tinker Creek (Dillard), 219
The Pine Island Paradox (Moore), 230–31
pioneering myth, 101–103
Planet Earth, 193
Plater, Zygmunt, 55
Platte River, Eisley's epiphany, 229–30
Poetics (Aristotle), 177
pollution, industrial, 187–88
Pond, Ezra, 257–58
The Population Bomb (Ehrlich), 144
positive stepson identity, 104–105
possums, 273–75
PrairyErth (Least Heat-Moon), 126
pro-development position, language rigidity, 134–36
Project Wild, 289–90
Pueblo incident, 29
punctuated equilibrium theory, 172
purgative experience, apocalyptic narrative, 176–78
purple gallinule, 216–17

quail, 82, 87, 237–38
Quammen, David, 194
quiet times: childhood hunting, 17; Taos morning walks, 237; Tennessee hiking, 45–46; Water Canyon hike, 74, 75, 76. *See also* noise

raccoons, 275
reading and writing: childhood experiences, 11, 12–15, 220; joke about, 182; as nature barriers, 248–49. *See also* nature writing

Reagan, Ronald (and administration), 138–39
Real Bird, Henry, 238
Reamde (Stephenson), 225
Reflections of the Brazos Valley (Steele and Killingsworth), 268–70
refuge and retreat, escape compared, 69–70, 197
Refuge (Williams), 4–5
religion. *See* spirituality and religion
Renco Group, 187–88
Rennert, Ira, 187
Reno, Phil, 112
resource omnivores, 124, 186–87
Revelation, Book of, 146–48
rhetoric. *See* language and rhetoric
Richards, I. A., 258
Rio Puerco, 67, 120, 124–25
roadkill: abundance of, 276–79; in Brazos Valley project, 268–69; humor themes, 265, 267–68; legislation about, 278; linguistic significance, 263–65; literary treatments, 265–67; in music, 268; night creatures, 271–73, 275–76; photographic portrayals, 268–71; as sacrifice zone, 279–81; writing assignment failure, 281–82
The Road (McCarthy), 163, 177
Robinson, Paul, 124
Rocky Mountain National Park, 153
romanticism, 197–99, 200–201
Rome, Adam, 42
roseate spoonbills, 212–13

sacrifice zoning: Church Rock catastrophe, 66–67, 120–25, 129;

sacrifice zoning (*cont.*)
concept origins, 130–31; desert lands occupation, 54, 90, 118; petroleum consumption, 254; with professional ambitions, 99; roadkill, 264–65, 279–82. *See also* Tellico Dam controversy
San Augustin Plains, 118
Sanctuary Movement, 114–15
Sand County Almanac (Leopold), 97–98
sandhill cranes, 80, 81
Sangre de Cristos, 92
San Jacinto Monument, 212
Santa Fe visit, 92–95
sassafras smell, 2
scaled quail, 237–38
Schneider, Stephen, 144
Schueler, Donald G., 101
science fiction, 199–205
SCRU Party, 43
The Sea Around Us (Carson), 191, 192, 195–97
Seasonal Woman (Tapahonso), 113
sea turtles, 211–12, 293
Selu (Awiakta), 53–55, 65
sensory experiences: and brain evolution, 238–39, 240–41; and breathing, 247; childhood, 2; and mourning for mother, 2–3; night walking, 239–40; verbal images, 259–60. *See also* epiphany; smells
sentimentality, 197–98
September 11 attacks, 165–66
Sequoyah, Ammoneta, 53
Sequoyah, Lloyd, 51, 53
Sequoyah Plant, 55

sex talk, parish school, 115
Shakespeare, William, 177
Shaw, Brian, 278
Sheldon, Alice Bradley, 204
Shellenberger, Michael, 141–42, 159–60, 173
Shelley, Percy Bysshe, 264
Shuey, Chris, 122, 127, 129–30
siblings. *See* Jones *entries*
silence. *See* quiet times
Silent Autumn, 144
Silent Spring (Carson), 142–43, 191–92, 201–204, 205–206, 248
Silko, Leslie Marmon, 117
Silkwood, Karen, 122
Silva Mind Control, 246
sixties turmoil, 38–41, 43–44, 267
The Sky, the Stars, the Wilderness (Bass), 4, 8
"Slant 6 Mind" (Brown), 268
slow violence phenomenon, 123–25
smells: and breathing, 243–45, 247; childhood, 2; as danger signals, 243; of death, 261; language limitations, 254–55; money connection, 241–43, 245, 249–53; and mourning for mother, 2–3; from petroleum consumption, 253–54; smoke from wildfire, 158–59, 185, 209–10; verbal imagery for, 255–61
snail darters, 46–47, 48
snakes, 222, 277–78
snow geese, 80
Snyder, Gary, 263, 265, 267
social ecology, 116–17, 150–54
Socorro return: Bosque Preserve visit,

77–83; ditch bank visit, 83–89; highway detour, 90–91; purpose, 71; Water Canyon hike, 71–77
solitude, 219
"Song of Myself" (Whitman), 235
"Song of the Rolling Earth" (Whitman), 11
sounds, night, 240. *See also* noise; quiet times
"Southern Exposure" (Schueler), 101
South Korea, 26–33
Southwest Research and Information Center (SRIC), 122, 127, 129
sparrow-hawk interaction, 213–14
The Spell of the Sensuous (Abram), 248
Spielberg, Steven, 231
spirituality and religion: and breathing, 243–47; Catholicism period, 113–15; childhood/youth, 6–7, 39; in Christian-oriented millenialism, 145–47, 167–70; cultural yearning for, 244–46; dispensational theology, 139–40, 146–47; environmentalism connection, 247–48; in millennial ecology, 144–45; mother's role, 6–7; of New Critics, 226–27; and social issue avoidance, 116–17
spiritus, 244–46
spoonbill, roseate, 212–13
SRIC (Southwest Research and Information Center), 122, 127, 129
Stafford, William, 265
Steele, Gentry, 268
stepfather, author's: childhood presence, 12, 15–21, 220; Hilton Head house, 21–23; illness/death, 88, 222–24; Korea trip, 24–33; sky watching anecdote, 16. *See also* father, author's
Stephenson, Neal, 225
stepson identity, 103–105
storytelling approach, 291–94
Strayed, Cheryl, 5, 8
Student Committee for a Radical Union, 43
sublime places, 216
summer of 2011, weather, 157–59
sunrise moments, 210
A Supremely Bad Idea (Dempsey), 209
survivalist taxi driver, 134
sustainability ideal: as contradiction masking, 180–81, 185–89; and dam projects, 57; expectations of, 161–62; and family, 152–55; for political compromise, 140; three E's of, 151; urbanization problem, 181–85
swamp tour, Louisiana, 216–17

The Tainted Desert (Kuletz), 101, 118
Taos residence, 236
Tao Te Ching, 215
Tapahonso, Luci, 113
Tate, Allen, 226
Tellico Dam controversy: Cherokee interests, 48–56, 65–66, 127; Church Rock connection, 67–68; media coverage, 49–50, 54, 65–66, 127–28; opposition themes, 46–48; realizations about, 56–59
Tennessee Valley Authority. *See* Tellico Dam controversy

terror experience, in Santa Fe, 93–94, 102
Texas Master Naturalists, 193–94, 289–90, 292–93
therapy, nature-based, 289–91
thinking in images, 259–60
Thomas, Dylan, 157
Thompson, Paul, 126–27
Thoreau, Henry David, 191, 216, 239–41, 264
three Ds. *See* denial-distraction-defensiveness
Three Mile Island, 67, 121–22
Time magazine, 139
Too Many People? (Angus and Butler), 187–88
totalizing terms, defined, 145. *See also* language and rhetoric
tourism and colonialism, 102
transparent eyeball, Emerson's, 217–18
"Traveling through the Dark" (Stafford), 265
Tropical Storm Lee, 158–59
tsunami, Japanese, 149, 166
turkeys, wild, 83
turtles, sea, 211–12, 293
TVA. *See* Tellico Dam controversy
twilight settings, epiphanies, 211–13, 214–15

UNC Resources v. Benally, 67
Under the Sea Wind (Carson), 195
uniformitarianism theory, 173–74
United Nuclear Corporation, 67–68
University of New Mexico, 68, 112, 115, 168
uranium mining, 66–68, 118, 119–23, 130. *See also* Church Rock catastrophe
urbanization problem, sustainability ideal, 181–85
US 380, traffic stop, 89–91
USA Today Weekend, 175

vegetarianism announcement, 286–88
verbal images, 255–61
Vietnam War, 38–41, 43–44, 267
visual rhetoric, 255–61

Walden (Thoreau), 191
Ware Shoals, South Carolina, 1–2, 7, 12, 107–108
waste, linguistic change, 267
Waste Isolation Pilot Plant (WIPP), 119
Water Canyon Park, 71–77
water resources: Church Rock catastrophe, 66–67, 120–25, 129; commercialization, 184, 249, 261; downstream phenomenon, 125–26; green capitalization approach, 142; local knowledge test, 128; sustainability problem, 89, 186, 236
Waters, Frank, 116–17
water skiing, 58
Watt, James, 136–40, 206
weather, 2011 summer, 157–59
Weil, Andrew, 175
Wheeler, Bruce, 49, 56
When Women Were Birds (Williams), 5, 35
White, Mick, 266–67

White Sands Missile Range, 54, 90, 118
Whitman, Walt, 11, 23, 24, 62, 235
Whitman's Poetry of the Body (Killingsworth), 115
whooping cranes, 81–82
wilderness therapy, 289–91
wildfire, 158–59, 185, 209–10
wildlife moments: Bosque Preserve, 80–81; childhood, 220–21; morning times, 85, 87, 232–33, 236–39; sharing urge, 220–24, 230–32; Water Canyon hikes, 74, 75–76. *See also* bird moments; roadkill
Wild (Strayed), 5
Williams, Hank, 238
Williams, Terry Tempest, 4–5, 8, 35
wolf sighting, 220–21
woodpecker, pileated, 21
Wordsworth, William, 226–27
World Book Encyclopedia, 14, 15
World Made by Hand (Kunstler), 169
worlds, always-ending, 285–86
World's End, 162
writing. *See* nature writing; reading and writing

Y2K bug, 165
yellow-billed cuckoo, 79
Yellow Dirt (Pasternak), 120, 123
yoga, 244–48, 255

zombies, 55–56, 169, 176, 204, 263

A WARDLAW BOOK

Inspired by the initiative of Chester Kerr, former head of Yale University Press, and supported by dozens of friends and colleagues, the Wardlaw Book designation honors Frank H. Wardlaw, the first director of Texas A&M University Press, and perpetuates association of his name with a select group of titles appropriate to his reputation as a man of letters, distinguished publisher, and founder of three university presses: South Carolina, Texas, and Texas A&M.

WITHDRAWN